The Book of Micah

The Book of Micah

Introduction and Commentary

William McKane

St Mary's College
St Andrews

T&T CLARK
EDINBURGH

T&T CLARK LTD
59 GEORGE STREET
EDINBURGH EH2 2LQ
SCOTLAND

First published 1998

ISBN 0 567 08615 1

British Library Cataloguing-in-Publication Data
A catalogue record for this book is available from the British Library

Typeset by Fakenham Photosetting Limited, Fakenham, Norfolk
Printed and bound by Bookcraft Ltd, Avon

CONTENTS

PREFACE

References to commentaries, books and articles are given briefly in the body of the text and the full details are supplied by the Bibliography. The foundations of the commentary are the Hebrew Bible, the Ancient Versions and the Jewish mediaeval commentators. The building has been completed with the help of the critical scholarship of more recent times and I owe a particular debt to Stade and Wolff, since the structure of the book of Micah, which was outlined by Stade and enriched by Wolff, is the one I have adopted.

I am indebted to the Revd. John Job who has read the second proofs. He has contributed to the accuracy of the English translation from Hebrew and his expertise in Greek and Latin has been of great value in respect of the Septuagint and Vulgate.

BIBLIOGRAPHY

COMMENTARIES ON MICAH
(IN CHRONOLOGICAL ORDER)

Rashi, Kimchi and Ibn Ezra from מקראות גדולות.

Hitzig, F. *Die zwölf kleinen Propheten.* ĶeH (Leipzig, 1881).

Ryssel, V. *Untersuchungen über die Textgestalt und die Echtheit des Buches Micha* (1887).

Wellhausen, J. *Skizzen und Vorarbeiten 5. Die kleinen Propheten übersetz mit Noten* (Berlin, 1892).

Marti, K. *Das Dodekapropheton.* KHC 13 (Tübingen, 1904).

von Orelli, C. *Die zwölf kleinen Propheten.* Kurzgefasster Kommentar zu den heiligen Schriften Alten und Neuen Testaments (München, 1908³).

Smith, J. M. P. *A Critical and Exegetical Commentary on Micah.* ICC (Edinburgh, 1912).

Schmidt, H. *Die grossen Propheten übersetz und erklärt.* Die Schriften des Alten Testaments (Göttingen, 1915).

Wade, G. H. *The Books of the Prophets Micah, Obadiah, Joel and Jonah.* The Westminster Commentary (1925).

Weiser, A. *Die Propheten Hosea, Joel, Amos, Obadiah, Joel and Jonah.* ATD (Göttingen, 1956²).

Robinson, Th. H. *Die Zwölf Kleinen Propheten. Hosea bis Micha.* HAT (Tübingen, 1964³).

Rudolph, W. *Micha, Nahum, Habakuk, Zephanjah.* KAT (Gütersloh, 1975).

van der Woude, A. S. *Micha: Die Prediking van het Oude Testament* (Nijkerk, 1976).

Mays, J. L. *Micah: A Commentary* (London and Philadelphia, 1976).

Wolff, H. W. *Dodekapropheton 4, Micha.* BKAT (Neukirchen-Vluyn, 1982).

Hillers, D. R. *A Commentary on the Book of the Prophet Micah.* Hermeneia: A Critical and Historical Commentary on the Bible (Philadelphia, 1984).

OTHER WORKS

Aistleitner, J. *Wörterbuch der Ugaritischen Sprache.* Berichte über die Verhandlungen der sächsischen Akademie der Wissenschaften zu Leipzig 106, 3 (Berlin, 1967).

Alcalay, R. *The Complete Hebrew–English Dictionary* (Jerusalem, 1963).

Alt, A. 'Micah 2.1–5, ΤΗΣ ΑΝΑΔΑΣΜΟΣ in Juda'. *Interpretationes ad Vetus Testamentum pertinentes Sigmundo Mowinckel septuagenario missae* (Oslo, 1955) = *KS* iii 373–381 (München, 1959).

Barthélemy, D. and Milik, J. T. *Discoveries in the Judaean Desert i, Qumran Cave 1* (Oxford, 1955).

Barthélemy, D. *Las Devanciers d'Aquila VTS* 10 (Leiden, 1963).

Bartke, H. 'Die Latifundien in Juda während der zweiten Hälfte des achten Jahrhunderts v. chr'. *Hommages à André Dupont Sommer* (Paris, 1971), 244–250.

Bartlett, J. R. 'The Use of the Word ראש as a Title in the Old Testament', *VT* 19 (1969), 1–10.

Beyerlin, W. *Die Kulttradition Israels in der Verkündigung des Propheten Micha*, FRLANT N.F. 54 (1939).

Brin, G. 'Micha 2.12–13: a textual and ideological study', *ZAW* 101 (1989), 118–124.

Brockelmann, C. אל ידי, *ZAW* 26 (1906), 29–32.

Brockington, L. H. *The Hebrew Text of the Old Testament: The Readings adopted by the Translators of the New English Bible* (Oxford, 1973).

Brown, F., Driver, S. R. and Briggs, C. A. *A Hebrew and English Lexicon of the Old Testament* (Oxford, 1907; 1966 reprint).

Brown, J. P. 'The Mediterranean Vocabulary of the Vine', *VT* 19 (1969), 146–170.

Budde, K. 'Die Rätsel von Micha 1', *ZAW* 37 (1917–18), 77–108.

Burrows, M., Trever, J. C. and Brownlee, W. H., *The Dead Sea Scrolls of St. Mark's Monastery: the Isaiah Manuscripts and the Habbakuk Commentary* (New Haven, 1950).

Cannawurf, E. 'The Authenticity of Micah iv 1–4', *VT* 13 (1963), 26–33.

Carmignac, J. 'Précisions apportées au vocabulaire de L'Hébreu biblique par la guerre des Fils de Lumière contre les Fils de Ténèbres', *VT* 5 (1955, 345–365).

Cathcart, K. J. 'Micah 2 and Nahum 3.16–17'. *Current Issues in Linguistic Theory* (Philadelphia, 1988), 195.

Cowley, A. E. *Gesenius' Hebrew Grammar* (Oxford, 1910^2).

Donner, H. *Israel unter den Völkern*, *VTS* 11 (Leiden, 1964).

Driver, G. R. 'Suggestions and Objections', *ZAW* N.F. 14 (1937), 168–171.

Driver, G. R. 'Linguistic and Textual Problems: Micah', *JTS* 39 (1938), 264–268.

Driver, G. R. *Canaanite Myths and Legends*. Old Testament Studies no. 3 (Edinburgh, 1956); 2nd edition by J. C. L. Gibson (Edinburgh, 1978).

Driver, G. R. 'Hebrew Notes on Prophets and Proverbs', *JTS* 41 (1940), 162–175.

Driver, G. R. 'Abbreviations in the Massoretic Text', *Textus* 1 (1960), 114–131.

Driver, G. R. *JSS* 10 (1965), 114. A review of M. Dahood, *Proverbs and Northwest Semitic Philology.*

Duhm, B. 'Anmerkungen zu den zwölf Propheten: III Buch Micha', *ZAW* 31 (1911), 81–93.

Ehrlich, A. B. *Randglossen zur Hebräischen Bibel: Textkritisches, Sprachliches und Sachliches*, i (Hildesheim, 1908), v (1912).

Ehrman, A. 'A Note on שׁי in Mic. 6.14', *JNES* 18 (1959), 156.

Eissfeldt, O. 'Ein Psalm aus Nord-Israel', *KS* 4 (1968), 63–72.

Elliger, K. *Liber XII Prophetarum.* Biblica Hebräica Stuttgartensia (Stuttgart, 1970).

Fisher, L. R. 'The Temple Quarter', *JSS* 8 (1963), 34–41.

Fitzmeyer, J. A. 'lᵉ as a preposition and a particle in Micah 5.1(2)', *CBQ* 18 (1956), 10–13.

Fritz, V. 'Das Wort gegen Samaria. Mic 1.2–7', *ZAW* 86 (1974), 316–331.

Gaster, T. H. 'Notes on the Minor Prophets', *JTS* 38 (1937), 163–165.

Gaster, T. H. *The Scriptures of the Dead Sea Sect* (London, 1957).

Gordon, R. P. 'Micah vii 19 and Akkadian kabāsu', *VT* 28 (1978), 355.

Graetz, H. *Emendationes in plerosque Sacrae Scripturae Veteris Testamenti libros* (Breslau, 1893).

Gunkel, H. 'Der Micha-Schluss. Zur Einführung in die literaturgeschichtliche Arbeit am Alten Testament', *ZS* 2 (1924), 145–178.

Hammershaimb, E. 'Einige Hauptdenken in der Schrift des Propheten Micha', *Studia Theologica* 15 (1961), 11–34.

Hyatt, J. P. 'On the Meaning and Origin of Micah 6.8', *Anglican Theological Review* 34 (1952), 232–239.

Jastrow, M. *A Dictionary of the Targumim and the Midrashic Literature* (New York, Berlin, London, 1926).

Jepson, A. 'Kleine Beiträge zum Zwölf prophetenbuch', *ZAW* 56 (1938), 85–100.

Köhler, L. 'Archäologisches', *ZAW* N.F. 5 (1928), 213–226.

Köhler, L. and Baumgartner, W. *Hebräisches und Aramäisches Lexikon zum Alten Testament.* 3rd edition by W. Baumgartner, B. Hartmann and E. Y. Kutscher (Leiden, 1967–1990).

Lescow, Th. 'Das Geburtsmotiv in der Messianischen Weissagungen bei Jesaja und Micha', *ZAW* 79 (1967), 172–207.

Lescow, Th. 'Redaktionsgeschichte Analyse von Micha 1–5', *ZAW* 84 (1972), 182–212.

Levi, I. *The Hebrew Text of the Book of Ecclesiasticus* (Leiden, 1969).

Lohse, E. *Die Texte aus Qumran Hebräisch und Deutsch* (München, 1964).

McKane, W. *Proverbs: A New Approach* (London, 1970).

McKane, W. *A Critical and Exegetical Commentary on Jeremiah*, ICC (Edinburgh, i, 1986; ii, 1996).

McKane, W. 'Micah 1.1–7', *ZAW* 107 (1995), 420–434.

McKane, W. 'Micah 2.12–13', *JNSL* 21 (1995), 83–91.

McKane, W. 'Micah 2.1–5: Text and Commentary', *JSS* 42 (1997), 7–22.

Meek, T. J. 'Some Emendations in the Old Testament', *JBL* 48 (1929), 162–168.

Mendicki, N. 'Die Sammlung und der neue Exodus in Micha 2.12–13', Kairos 23 (1981), 96–99.

Mendicki, N. 'Die Sammlung der Zerstreuten in Mic 4.6–7', *BZ* N.F. 27 (1983), 218–221.

Mowinckel, S. 'The Spirit and the Word in the Pre-exilic Prophets', *JBL* 53 (1934), 199–227.

Neubauer, A. (ed.) Abū'l Walid Marwān ibn Janāh, *The Book of Hebrew Roots* (Oxford, 1875).

Nicholson, E. W. 'Blood-Spattered Altars?', *VT* 27 (1977), 113–116.

Noth, M. *Überlieferungs-Geschichtliche Studien. Die Sammelnden und Bearbeitenden Geschichtswerke im Alten Testament* (Tübingen, 1957²).

Pixley, G. V. 'Micah—a Revolutionary', *The Bible and the Politics of Exegesis*, ed. D. Jobling (Cleveland, 1991), 53–60.

Pope, M. 'The Word שחת in Job 9.31', *JBL* 83 (1964), 269–278.

Pritchard, J. B. (ed.), *Ancient Near Eastern Texts relating to the Old Testament* (Princeton, 1955²).

Reviv, H. 'The Structure of Society', *The Age of the Monarchies: Culture and Society* (Jerusalem, 1979), 125–146.

Schleusner, J. *Novus Thesaurus philologico-criticus sive Lexicon in LXX*, i–iii (London, 1829).

Smith, W. R. *Lectures on the Religion of the Semites: The Fundamental Institutions* (London, 1927), Reprint 1969.

Soggin, A. 'Die prophetische Gedanke über den heiligen Krieg als Gericht gegen Israel', *VT* 10 (1960), 79–83.

Sperber, A. *The Bible in Aramaic: The Latter Prophets according to the Targum Jonathan*, iii (Leiden, 1962).

Stade, B. 'Bemerkungen über das Buch Micha', *ZAW* 1 (1881), 161–172.

Stade, B. 'Weitere Bemerkungen zu Micha 4 and 5', *ZAW* 3 (1883), 1–16.

Stade, B. 'Micha 2.4', *ZAW* 6 (1886), 122–123.

Stoebe, H. B. 'Und demütig sein vor deinem Gott', Wort und Dienst 6 (1959), 180–194.

Sutcliffe, E. F. 'A gloss in Jeremiah vii. 4', *VT* 5 (1955), 315–316.

Swete, H. B. *The Old Testament in Greek according to the Septuagint*, iii (Cambridge, 1907).

Torczyner, H. 'Dunkle Bibelstellen', *BZAW* 41 (1925), 274–280.

van der Westhuizen, J. P. 'The term *'tnan* in Micah', *OTSWA* 6 (1973), 54–61.

van der Woude, A. S. 'Micah in dispute with the pseudo-prophets', *VT* 19 (1969), 244–250.

von Soden, W. *Akkadische Handwörterbuch*, i–iii (Wiesbaden, 1965–1981).

Watson, W. G. 'Allusion, Irony and Word-Play in Micah 1.7', *Biblica* 65 (1984), 103–105.

Wernberg-Møller, P. 'Two Notes', *VT* 8 (1958), 305–308.

Wiklander, B. 'The Context and Meaning of NHR in Jeremiah 51.44', *SEA* 43 (1978), 60–64.

Wildberger, H. *Jesaja* i–xii. BKAT (Neukirchen-Vluyn, 1972).

Wildberger, H. 'Die Völkerwallfahrt zum Zion', *VT* 7 (1957), 62–81.

Willis, J. T. 'Some Suggestions on the Interpretation of Micah 1–2', *VT* 18 (1968), 372–379.

Willis, J. T. 'On the Text of Micah 2.1aα–b', *Biblica* 48 (1967), 534–541.

Willis, J. T. 'Micah 2.6–8 and the "People of God" in Micah', *BZ* 14 (1970), 72–87.

Willis, J. T. 'A Note on ואשר in Micah 3.1', *ZAW* 80 (1968), 50–54.

Wolff, H. W. 'Micah the Moreshite. The Prophet and his Background'. *Essays in Honor of Samuel Terrien* (Missoula, 1978,, 77–84. = *Mit Micha Reden* (1978), 30–40.

Ziegler, J. 'Beiträge zum griechischen Dodekapropheton', *Nachrichten von der Akademie der Wissenschaften in Göttingen* (Göttingen, 1943), 345–412.

Ziegler, J. *Duodecim Prophetae*. Septuaginta Vetus Testamentum Graecum Auctoritate Societatis Litterarum Gottingensis editum, XIII (1943, Göttingen; 1967²).

ABBREVIATIONS

Aq	Aquila
ATD	Das Alte Testament Deutsch
BDB	Brown F., Driver S. R. and Briggs C. A.
BKAT	Biblischer Kommentar. Altes Testament
BHS	Biblia Hebraica
BZ	Biblische Zeitschrift
BZAW	*Beihefte zur Zeitschrift für die alttestamentliche Wissenschaft*
CBQ	*Catholic Biblical Quarterly*
CML	*Canaanite Myths and Legends*
FRLANT	Forschungen zur Religion und Literatur des Alten und Neuen Testaments
GK	Gesenius–Kautzch
HAT	Handbuch zum Alten Testament
ICC	International Critical Commentary
JBL	*Journal of Biblical Literature*
JNES	*Journal of Near Eastern Studies*
JNSL	*Journal of North-West Semitic Languages*
JSS	*Journal of Semitic Studies*
JTS	*Journal of Theological Studies*
KAT	Kommentar zum Alten Testament
KB³	Köhler–Baumgartner, third edition
KeH	Kurzgefasstes exegetisches Handbuch zum Alten Testament
KHC	Kurzer Hand-commentar zum Alten Testament
KS	*Kleine Schriften*
MT	Massoretic Text
OTSWA	*Oude Testamentiese Werkgemeenskap van Suid Afrika*
Pesh.	Peshitta
SEA	*Svensk Exegetisk Årsbok*
Symm	Symmachus
Targ.	Targum
Theod	Theodotion
VT	*Vetus Testamentum*
VTS	*Supplements to Vetus Testamentum*
Vulg.	Vulgate
ZAW	*Zeitschrift für die alttestamentliche Wissenschaft*
ZS	*Zeitschrift für Semitistik und verwndte Gebiete*

INTRODUCTION

ADDITIONS IN THE EXTANT TEXT OF
MICAH 1–7

The additions which are discussed by Wolff (xxvii–xxxvi) differ in kind
and scope. They may consist of an elaboration of a single verse or they
may have the function of intertwining the contents of chapters 1–3
with those of chapters 4–5 and so improving the relatedness and
coherence of chapters 1–7. They may also, according to Wolff, have a
more sophisticated redactional intention and may be devices for
plotting a path along which Micah 1–7 progresses. This is done by
indicating a connection between an earlier verse and one that comes
later. By this deliberate redactional ploy a beginning and an ending are
identified, a turning which has gone full circle, and a scheme is thereby
imposed on the book of Micah.

Chapter 1
Wolff finds traces of a Deuteronomistic commentary at 1.1, 5, 7a and
13b. In none of these cases do the additions have architectonic
significance. They are not designed to give shape to the book of Micah
as a whole, only to provide an elaboration for individual verses. The
older form of the superscription ('The word of Micah from Moresheth
which he discerned concerning Samaria and Judah') was supplemented
so as to make it conform to the normative Deuteronomistic formula,
the additions being the information that it was the word of Yahweh
which Micah spoke and that he was active in the reigns of Jotham, Ahaz
and Hezekiah.

   The commentary which Wolff detects at vv. 5, 7a and 13b is
similarly limited in scope. In v. 7a the prediction that Samaria will be
reduced to a ruin (v. 6) is concentrated on her cultic installations
(figures, images, idols) which will be smashed to pieces. In v. 13b the
additional opinion expressed is that the fixation of Judah with military
equipment, with horses and chariots, was the daughter of Zion's capital
sin. The comment on v. 5 is less parasitic. It identifies בית ישראל (v. 5a)

with Judah and it equates the transgression of the northern kingdom (יעקב) with Samaria and the 'high places' of Judah with Jerusalem.. The topic is the fateful influence of Samaria on Jerusalem (cf. v. 9) and it links the destiny of the two cities (cf. 6.16) with special reference to apostasy and idolatry.

The theophany in vv. 3–4 is described by Wolff as the work of the Deuteronomistic school (xxviii). It is their editing of Micah 1–7 to adapt it for liturgical use. It is a kind of *introit* to the reading of the book of Micah in public worship (see further under *Sitz im Leben*). Verse 2, though it is apparently connected with v. 3 (כי) is said by Wolff (xxviii) to be an expansion of an entirely different kind from the others. It is an address to foreign nations, to a worldwide audience, made by Yahweh from 'his holy temple' and it is coupled with a demand for attention. The content of Yahweh's address is not given, but the reason for the confrontation is stated, not altogether clearly. בכם לעד can be rendered either 'as a witness among you' or 'as a witness against you'. The connection of v. 2 with v. 3 (despite כי) is, however defective, because the theophany is designed to introduce words addressed to Samaria and Judah and the superscription indicates a similar audience. Wolff (p. 8) prefers 'as a witness among you' and this translation weakens the redactional link which he discerns between 1.2 and 5.14. He does not hold that 1.2 and 5.14 are opening and closing redactional brackets, only that 5.14 (לא שמעו) is a deliberate redactional conclusion which picks up שמעו (1.2). With the translation 'as a witness against you' a case could be made out for opening (1.2) and closing (5.14) redactional brackets: a threat issued in 1.2 against the גוים becomes a prediction of judgement in 5.14; Yahweh will respond with anger to their heedlessness.

It should be remarked that none of the other references to foreign nations in chapters 4–5 repeat the universalism of 4.1–3 and predict that they they will embrace Yahwism. 4.5 is uncompromisingly particularistic, 1.2 may have a hostile intent and 5.8, 14 certainly have. Yahweh is to wreak vengeance on the nations; they are identified as his enemies (5.8) and they will be destroyed. Israel in the midst of the Gentile world, a dangerous situation, will be dominant (5.6–7) and, in another *scenario*, when a coalition of nations is massed against Jerusalem, Yahweh commands the defenders to rise up and crush their enemies (4.11–13).

Chapters 2 and 3

In this chapter Wolff (xxviii; 37–40) discerns Deuteronomistic commentary which has a wider function than that of supplementing or elaborating individual verses and which is designed to transfer the historical background of the eighth century BC to the period around 587 B.C. when Judah and Jerusalem faced the threat posed by Nebuchadrezzar. The effect of these interpolations (vv, 2, 3a, 4a, 4b, 5; 3. 4b) is to extend the scope of Micah's polemic and to emphasise the imminence of the judgement which Yahweh will inflict. Micah had addressed his indictments and threats to the leaders and rulers of the Judaean and Jerusalem communities, but now what is predicted as Yahweh's judgement is a national disaster, the fall of Judah and Jerusalem to foreign invaders. כי עת רעה היא (v. 3b) and ביום ההוא (v. 4a) indicate that the disaster is near and על המשפחה הזאת (v. 3a) that it will involve the entire community. In v. 4 (חלק ... לשובב) and v. 5 the lament is no longer made by the notables who have added field to field but by all the people.

Wolff's account of these adjustments in chapter 2 assumes that Deuteronomist commentators were active in Jerusalem redirecting the eighth century B.C. proclamation of Micah to the situation of peril in which Judah and Jerusalem stood around the year 587. That the Deuteronomists were located in Palestine and not among the Babylonian exiles is held by Noth (1957, 110 n. 1) and, to this extent, Wolff has his support.

Verses 12–13, which presuppose the existence of the diaspora, cannot be assigned to Micah of Moresheth and the reference which is solitary in chapters 1–3, is obviously out of context and anticipates the contributions of the *Heil* prophets in chapter 4–5. Verse 12 is an oracular promise to assemble the whole house of Jacob and to gather together the remnant of Israel. They will be like sheep in a fold, like a flock at pasture. This certainly envisages that the muster will be a preparation for their return to Jerusalem and it may be even an explicit part of the promise. How v. 13 integrates with v. 12 is obscure. The exiles follow their leader and break out of a prison and Yahweh leads their march home. The reason for the appearance of vv. 12–13 at the end of chapter 2 is not clear, but it may have something to do with an intention to interlace the contents of chapters 1–3 with those of chapters 4–5 and so to improve the appearance of wholeness in Micah 1–7.

At 3.8a את רוח יהוה is a later addition which overloads the line and is grammatically suspect. The presence of את (Wellhausen, 138) and the absence of ו (Wolff, 138) accentuates the impression that it disturbs the triad (כח ;משפט ;גבורה) which is joined by the copula. The intention of the glossator is to remove any misconception that Micah is affirming confidence in his own power and moral sense and to link the claims which he makes to his possession of the spirit of Yahweh. This intention to vest the prophet's authority in Yahweh makes the expansion similar to the deuteronomistic elaboration of the superscription in 1.1 which Wolff (above, p. 1) has identified, where 'word of Micah' is replaced by 'word of Yahweh'.

Chapters 4 and 5

עד רחוק (v. 3) is a minus in Isa. 2.4 and it overloads the line. Its function, according to Wolff (84) is to enhance the universalism of vv. 1–3, its world-wide scope, and so its sense is 'to the ends of the earth' not 'into the distant future'.

Verse 5 is an addition (Wolff, 86) and is a liturgical confession by the Jerusalem community (Wolff, 94). It is less than a riposte to vv. 1–3 (Wolff), a throwing of cold water on the ideal future which they portray, as I have suggested, and is more of a separation of the state of affairs as they are at the present from those predicted in vv. 1–3. Prophetic vision notwithstanding the community must adhere to the confession of faith that Yahweh is Israel's God and that the גוים worship their own gods. Hence, in the sphere of the public liturgy, vv. 1–3 do not require that a new form of affirmation should be substituted for the old one and Israel's particularism is not to be influenced by a prophetic descrying of universal homage to Yahweh and Jerusalem and the advent of world peace. It does not seem far wrong to describe this as a rejoinder to vv. 1–3, but Wolff's account has a bearing on his view (xxxii) that the transmission of the book of Micah, its enlargement on the basis of chapters 1–3, took place in Jerusalem, in the context of public worship, at assemblies whose function was to lament the fall of Jerusalem, though in connection with which prophets of hope were also heard.

The intention of v. 7b (Wolff, 86) is to connect the prediction of vv. 1–4 in which Israel is not mentioned, with the promises made to the lame and the scattered among the exiles that they will be gathered together by Yahweh (vv. 6–7a). Verse 7b adds to this the specification of a destination: a return to Jerusalem where Yahweh will be king over them for all time coming. This is part of Wolff's case (90) that vv. 1–8 is a unit which asks the question, 'What will the end of Jerusalem be?' and that v. 7b provides an answer to this question which, unlike vv. 1–4, is aimed to awaken the interest of the diaspora (86).

Wolff (82f.) sets out vv. 1–8 as a unit (of which vv. 4a, 5, 7b and 8 are secondary items), but there is a logical inconsistency between this procedure and his affirmation that v. 8 is not continuous with vv. 1–7 and is to be associated with the verses which follow at 4.9–5.5, especially 5.3. Nor is Wolff's view that 4.1–7 is a unity to be accepted. His argument that 'What will the end of Jerusalem be?' informs both vv. 1–4 and vv. 6–7 is less impressive than the separation between vv. 1–4, the homage offered to Yahweh and Zion by the Gentile world followed by world peace, and the gathering together of the diaspora (vv. 6–7a), two themes which are far removed from each other. Finally v. 8 is perhaps a deliberate correction, a substitution of Davidic kingship in Jerusalem for the kingship of Yahweh proclaimed in v. 7b and Wolff (86) remarks on this tension.

5.2 is an addition (Wolff, 101, 106, 117f.) generated by the delay in the fulfilment of the Messianic promise in v. 1. The reason for the delay is stated and, with an allusion to Isa. 7.14, a time-limit is set to the final period of subjection: the Messiah will come when a woman who is now pregnant brings forth a child.

Wolff also holds (xxx, 126, 133f.) that 5.8, 13, 14 are redactional insertions, but his argument falls to the ground if v. 8 is taken as a promise rather than a prayer and if his emendation of v. 13 is not accepted. According to Wolff vv. 8, 13, 14 are a redactional response (xxx) to the non-fulfilment of the promise that Israel will be dominant over the גוים (vv. 6–7) and vv. 13 and 14 are the answer of Yahweh to the prayer of v. 8. If v. 8 is a promise ('Your hand will be lifted up over your foes and all your enemies will be cut off') and, if the series of 'I shall cut off/pull up' verses is vv. 9–13 rather than vv. 9–12, Wolff's reasoning is undermined. Verse 14 is then a fragment reinforcing v. 8 ('I shall wreak vengeance with hot anger on the nations which disobey me').

Chapters 6 and 7
According to Wolff (xxxii, 139f.) 6.1 is a post-exilic redactional link which continues the polemic against foreign nations in 5.14 and is not

part of the legal process set out in vv. 2–5 which contains Yahweh's dispute (ריב) with Israel.

The other redactional additions which he identifies in chapter 6 are of different kinds and consist of elaborations of the Hebrew text which he supposes were made in the course of the sixth century B.C. For the most part these are small (vv. 9aβ, 10aβ, 12b, 14aβ, 14bβ), v. 16 being the most extensive. Verse 9aβ has the appearance of a marginal comment to the effect that when Yahweh speaks he had better be heard and תושיה is an item of wisdom vocabulary ('It brings success to fear your name'). It is triggered by the opening words of the verse קול יהוה לעיר יקרא. אצרות רשע 'ill-gotten wealth' is the contribution of someone who felt the need to supplement the list of crimes, perhaps with chapters 1–3 in mind and Micah's concentration on the sins of the wealthy in high places. 'And have deceitful tongues in their mouth' (v. 12b) is redundant after 'and its inhabitants utter lies' and looks like the contribution of a reader who wanted to dot every *i* and cross every *t*. It is a case of over-kill.

Verses 14aβ, 14bβ and 16 can be taken together in so far as Wolff is persuaded of their secondary character because they disturb the pattern of vv. 14–15. One respect in which they do this is by not maintaining the direct address (2nd person singular) of vv. 14–15 and another is that they break into the 'futility' theme. Thus וישחך בקרבך (14aβ) features the 3rd person verb and ואשר תפלט לחרב אתן (v. 14bβ) and v. 16 do not display the 'futility' pattern. Verse 14aβ is an explication of 'You will eat but not feel well fed', namely, 'You will suffer from constipation' and 'those whom you save I shall give to the sword' is an elaboration of 'You will remove from danger but not save', as if to say 'even if you remove them to safe place that safety will not be enduring'. Wolff's argument is stronger for vv. 14aβ, 14bβ than it is for v. 16.

Wolff (175) identifies פקדתך rather than מצפיך as the secondary element in v. 4. It interprets יום מצפיך: the day which the seers (prophets) predicted was a day of judgement.

Wolff (xxxiii–xxxiv) holds that the decision to locate 7.1–6, and especially 7.7, before the three psalms (7.8–20) which conclude the book was the deliberate plan of a post-exilic redactor Chapter 7.7 is perhaps a secondary riposte to the pessimism of vv. 2–6 rather than a constituent of vv. 2–7 in which case the redactional deliberateness discerned by Wolff is unfounded.

THE PREMISS

My premiss is that only Micah 1–3 (except 2.12–13) is to be assigned to the eighth century prophet Micah, that the book of Micah bridges the centuries and that its history spans the pre-exilic, the exilic and the post-exilic periods. The point of my departure is therefore that of Stade (1881, 161–172; 1883, 1–16; 1884, 291–297) and more recently, that of Wolff (1982, xxvii–xxxvi) and I shall not complicate the introduction by engaging with the opinions of those who assign the book, for the most part, to the eighth century B.C. and to the prophet Micah (Rudolph, 1975, especially pp. 136–140; Hillers, 1984), since I have already done this in the body of the commentary. My conclusion with respect to the book of Micah is similar to that at which I arrived concerning the book of Jeremiah (1986; 1996), that the proclamation of Micah in the eighth century B.C. has generated prophecy of different kinds in the succeeding centuries. These new prophets had different reasons for revering the name of Micah and for claiming the authority of that prophet.

Some discerned in the fall of Jerusalem and the exile the fulfilment of Micah's prediction of doom, but sensed that this could not be a final destination, the last chapter of Yahweh's dealings with Israel. If progress were to be made beyond this doom-laden impasse, the Jerusalem community (in which these prophets operated) must be fuelled with hope, promised redemption and descry a goal. New prophets of a different kind, and with other concerns, were impressed with the similarities between the present and the past, between the community lambasted by Micah in the eighth century B.C. and the sins of their community. What they lament is however a different state of affairs, not the ruthless oppression of the peasantry, the gross misuse of power and wealth by the leaders of the community, but a universal and alarming deterioration of order in their society, the crumbling of its foundations and the disintegration of its basic institutions.

The prophets of weal (the *Heil* prophets) encourage hope and without hope the life of a community cannot go on. They predict that Yahweh will bestow on Israel a glorious future and they are exposed to the risk of unreal optimism. The more pessimistic realists among the new prophets concentrate on the present state of society and describe, perhaps exaggerate, its ills. They prize the absence of self-deception and the rigour of their own scrutiny. They pursue integrity and truth tirelessly and are the sworn enemies of cant, shallowness and pretence in religion and morality. As they survey their community they are unpersuaded that, despite the fall of Jerusalem and the exile, it has absorbed the polemic delivered by Micah in the eighth century B.C. and they offer a revised version.

OUTLINE OF THE BOOK OF MICAH

The English translation which is assumed in this outline is the one given in the body of the commentary, where the emendations of the Hebrew text adopted are indicated.

Chapter 1

'I shall make Samaria a heap of ruins' (if these are Micah's words) are a prediction of the fall of Samaria and establish that Micah was active as a prophet before 722 B.C. Samaria's material splendour will be reduced to a ruin and her idolatrous cultic ornaments, which were financed by the proceeds of harlotry, will be broken in pieces. Micah discerns that Judah is now in danger and that Jerusalem is threatened by the Assyrians and he envisages how they will ravage the settlements of the Shephelah, including Moresheth from which he comes. He summons Judah and Jerusalem to mourning as if exile were already an accomplished fact.

There is a question whether Micah himself engaged in mourning rites (v. 8) and commanded the people of Judah to carry them out (v. 16) or whether this imagery is to be interpreted more freely and, in this connection, Wolff (27f.) concludes that v. 8 is an indication that Micah reinforced his message with symbolic action. He appeared barefoot and naked; he howled and moaned as mourners would in order to impress his hearers with the earnestness and urgency of his proclamation. Neither v. 8 nor v. 16 should be pressed so far as this and the imagery should not be interpreted so stringently. The language of mourning rites is used to convey Micah's acute prescience of deadly danger and approaching disaster, the coming death of Judah, and it is with this foreknowledge that he invites the people of Judah to shave their heads.

Chapter 2

Those who plan evil and evil-doing in their beds covet fields (cf. Isa. 5.8) and desire homesteads. What precisely is involved in taking fields by force, seizing houses and violating private property? It is not robbery with violence in the sense that naked force is used to expropriate land and to effect evictions from property, that possessions are seized at the point of the sword. It is ruthless and inhumane application of financial pressures and economic power in order to force small farmers from their land and to introduce farming on a larger scale. It is the destruction of a way of life, the loss of a social asset, a scale of values, and the abandonment of a source of family focus and commmunal solidarity. It is a process which Yahweh roundly condemns and for which he threatens punishment, 'I am planning evil for this people'.

A feature of the chapter is the unreasonable light in which the dispossessors (vv. 1–2) and the comfortable prophets (vv. 6–7)are made to appear. The dispossessors lament (v. 4) with an impudent incon-sistency that they have been deprived of the fields from which they drove the former owners by the exercise of a crude, inhumane financial pressure. Wearing the cap of *Heil* prophets they take exception to the litany of doom and retort 'Disaster will not overtake us'. Their claim that they have piety on their side ('Does Yahweh not deal benevolently with the upright?') comes too late in the day and Micah makes the riposte that they are the enemy of Yahweh's people and that their record condemns them, dismissing them with a final 'Rise and go' (vv. 8–10). He concludes with a withering observation: the prophet whom they would receive with open arms does not have the marks of a true prophet. If 'a man of wind' were to promise them a perpetual feast, uninterrupted plenty, they would welcome his prophecy with enthu-siastic applause (v. 11) The appeal to piety and the expectation that Yahweh will come to their rescue is a comical, and yet jarring illogicality, given the facts of the case. It illustrates the depth of their bondage and the extent of their crookedness, that they are the prisoners of illusion and the prey of self-deception. They have lost the faculty of distinguishing between falsehood and truth.

Chapter 3

There is a further reference in this chapter (v. 4) to a false religious expectation, a superficial nod to piety, which carries no conviction in view of the unspeakably coarse and calculated cruelty which has decimated the community. Those in high places who were responsible for its well-being and who had the power to do good have abused that power and done evil. When they catch 'religion' and wear the mask of piety, they summon the help of Yahweh, but he will not answer them.

The target of the prophet's harsh criticism in this chapter are the leaders and rulers of Judah (vv. 1, 9), especially those who hold sway in Jerusalem (v. 10), the new breed of officials who exercised authority under the king in the king's city, and the threat which he unleashes is aimed at that city and its temple (v. 12). The charge of corruption and deviousness is not laid so much against judges presiding over law-courts as it is against those who govern corruptly, 'who abhor what is right and make crooked what is straight' (v. 9), whose decisions are influenced by bribes (v. 11). This cancer has spread to religious leaders, to priests and prophets in contexts where bribery would not be expected to wield an influence and where its presence is obscene: priests give rulings for a fee and prophets prophesy for money. The theme of false prophecy is thus an element of the chapter. The prospect of financial reward influences the kind of oracle which a prophet utters and the capitulation to this incentive makes for comfortable and sham predictions: 'Is not Yahweh in our midst? Disaster will not overtake us' (v. 11). These prophets 'who predict prosperity for a bite of food' and adversity for those who dis-appoint their hopes for reward lead Yahweh's people astray (v. 5). Darkness will envelop them by night and by day and, when their vision perishes, they will be disconcerted and confounded (vv. 6–7). Micah, on the other hand, is convinced of the rightness of his proclamation of doom and this unwavering conviction is the source of his vigour and power.

How is the violent imagery in vv. 2–3 to be treated? There is no doubt that it adds up to the hating of good and the loving of evil (v. 2), but it certainly does not describe cannibalistic behaviour, not even extreme physical abuse or torture. The leaders do not cut their victims into pieces for the pot and relish the prospect of the meal which they are to make of them. Yet the imagery has a function and what it signifies when it is translated is 'their behaviour is as grotesque and inhuman as that of cannibals'. They have treated their own community with the same callous disregard as a cannibal would show in preparing a victim for the pot. The equanimity with which they have perpetrated so much suffering and ruin is staggering and their insensitivity is colossal.

Chapter 4

This chapter is a picture show. There is a variety of pictures and it moves swiftly from one slide to another. It begins with a depiction of a pilgrimage of the Gentile world to the Jerusalem temple and their embracing of Yahwism. This will be a prelude to universal peace, associated with Yahweh's rule over all nations and his government of them (vv. 1–3). This paradisal prospect does not bewitch everyone and it is countered by a secondary riposte which protests that Yahweh is Israel's God and will remain so. This vision of the future is not supported by the shape of the present. The nations worship their own gods and the gap beteen Yahwism and them is unbridgeable (v. 5). Universalism is replaced by unyielding particularism.

The scene shifts and we encounter a prediction that Yahweh will gather together the exiles, those who have become lame and have lagged behind, those who have become separated from the main body and are worn out. He will bring them back to Jerusalem and make a mighty nation of them (vv. 6–7). This expectation that the diaspora would return to Jerusalem was high towards the end of the exilic period and we notice here a difference of opinion whether Yahweh will be the king of the new community (v. 7b) or whether 'the dominion of the daughter of Jerusalem' (Davidic kingship and the splendour of the capital city?) will be restored (v. 8).

The historical background to vv. 9–10 is ostensibly the fall of Jerusalem in 587. This is certainly the impression which is created, but the account of the events is unconvincing. It is hard to believe that a population which had just suffered a disastrous defeat and were on the edge of exile could have been addressed with so complete a lack of sensitivity as they are in vv. 9–10, as if they were making a song about a small matter ('What have you to shout about?'). Or that orders to evacuate Jerusalem and prepare for the march into exile could have been issued in the same breath as the promise that Yahweh would rescue them from Babylon. They were so completely overwhelmed with grief at the fall of Jerusalem and so unspeakably weary at the prospect of deportation that they could not have looked beyond the sad consequences of defeat to absorb the promise of deliverance. Their mood did not accord with the reception of good news. Hence whatever be the precise date of vv. 9–10 it is later, perhaps much later, than 587.

The magnitude of the change of scene in vv. 11–13 is striking.

Mighty nations are now massed against Jerusalem and are titillated with the thought of its possession. 'But they do not know Yahweh's plans, nor do they discern what he has in mind, for he has gathered them as sheaves to the threshing-floor' (v. 12). Here the reality of warfare is entirely forsaken and the generalship with which this powerful coalition has to reckon is that of Yahweh. The defeat of the mighty nations by the daughter of Zion is a miracle wrought by Yahweh (v. 13) and cannot be accounted for by weight of armour. This emphasis on military victory recalls the oracles against foreign nations in the book of Jeremiah, where the note of triumphalism is sounded and joy at the prospect of Israel's standing on the neck of the Gentile world is uncontained.

Verse 14 is a fragment, but the setting which is envisaged for it is perhaps that of vv. 9–10 rather than vv. 11–13. The siege is laid against Jerusalem by Nebuchadrezzar and 'striking the ruler of Israel on the cheek' is a metaphor for the debunking of Zedekiah's royalty which is described in Jer. 39.4–7. The lot of those besieged is desperate and they are instructed to signal this by engaging in a mourning rite, 'Keep gashing yourself.'

Chapter 5

According to 4.7 Yahweh is to exercise kingship and at 4.8 an earthly king is to have his seat in Jerusalem, presumably a Davidic king. According to 5.1 a Messiah is to arise in Bethlehem, a David *redivivus* who will rule over Israel, shepherd them in Yahweh's strength and reflect Yahweh's majesty. His dominion will extend to the ends of the earth, the threat posed to Israel by the Gentile world will be removed and their safety will be assured. Here the nations are regarded as potential enemies whom the all-powerful Messiah will subdue (cf. 4.11–13).

5.2 is a secondary *apologia* triggered by the delay in the fulfilment of the prediction made in v. 1—an explanation of the delay. With an allusion to the woman who will give birth to Immanuel (Isa. 7.14) it is explained that the Messianic age will dawn when a woman who is (now) pregnant bears a child. At that time Israel will no longer suffer the dominion of its enemies, the exiles will return and the integrity of the community will be restored. The intention of the *apologia* is to declare that the prediction of v. 1 will soon be fulfilled and it is ineffective if a time-limit is not fixed for its fulfilment. It is an idle apology if it promises no more than that in the unspecified future a woman will become pregnant and bear a child and that this will be the sign of the breaking in of the Messianic age.

Verses 4 and 5 are incompatible with this Messianic hope and with reliance on the transformation which the Messiah's reign will bring. For hope that the Messiah will appear and all will be changed they substitute a programme of self-help and a policy of *Realpolitik*, such as the one which was practised by the Maccabaean heroes. The one Messianic shepherd is replaced by a plurality of heroes who will 'shepherd (rule) the land of Assyria with the sword and the land of Nimrod (Babylonia) with the naked blade'. It is they who will deliver Israel from Assyria 'when it comes into our land and tramples over our boundaries'. 'Assyria' and 'Nimrod' are ciphers for foreign invaders.

Verse 7 returns to the topic of the remnant, not the remnant returned from exile and re-assembled in Jerusalem, but the remnant 'in the midst of many peoples'. They live in a dangerous world which, however they dominate 'like a lion among wild beasts, like a young lion among flocks of sheep'. This triumphalism is reinforced by the address to Yahweh in v. 8, 'Your hand will be lifted up over your foes and all your enemies will be cut off.' The primary emphasis of 'Like dew from Yahweh, like showers on the grass' is that they depend on Yahweh and not on man, though the simile may have the subordinate function of representing that their influence on the Gentile world is benign. They 'fertilize' it; they are Yahweh's missionaries. This would project an attitude to the Gentile nations less hostile than the one which otherwise prevails in vv. 6–8 and which is comparable with that in 4.1–3.

Verses 9–13 contain a promise which is conveyed by expressions which have the appearance of menace and which might be mis-interpreted as threat, but the drift of 'I shall cut off' (vv. 9–12) or 'I shall pull up' (v. 13) is salutary and v. 14, 'I shall wreak vengeance with hot anger on the nations which disobey (me)' makes this plain. Verses 9–13 are both a polemic against reliance on military power (vv. 9–10), sorcery and soothsaying (v. 11), idolatry (vv. 12–13) and a promise that Yahweh will free Israel from all of these snares. Israel will serve Yahweh with a single mind and a pure heart and will no longer supplement its trust in him with reliance on the arm of flesh, with a dabbling in the magic arts or with a belief in the efficacy of idols. A trust in Yahweh which needs such crutches to support it is impure and worthless. The implication of the threat against the foreign nations in v. 14 is that they are corrupted by militarism, sorcery, soothsaying and idolatry.

Chapter 6

Both chapters 4–5 and chapters 6–7 represent themselves as part of the book of Micah and by attaching themselves to chapters 1–3 acquire the authority accorded to the eighth century B.C. prophet Micah. They enlarge on chapters 1–3 in different ways and 4–5 expand the horizons of 1–3 more than 6–7 do. They take a big leap from doom to hope on the assumption that the prediction of Micah has been fulfilled and that what the Jerusalem community now needs is the assurance that though Yahweh has punished them, he has not abandoned them. He has brought them into darkness, but he will lead them into light. They are not marooned, doomed to stagnation, and they have a future into which he will lead them and a destination they will reach.

There is no concealing the circumstance, however, that the different times in which they lived does not account completely for the transition from woe to weal. They leaned towards optimism; they were hopeful. The doom prophet was inclined to take a more sombre view, to paint the future in darker colours and to condemn the defective Yahwism of the present. That there were such prophets in the centuries after Micah is shown by chapters 6–7. Perhaps they regarded themselves as having more right to be regarded as the successors of Micah, to wear his mantle, than the *Heil* prophets had. The question is whether the degree of their dependence on him reduces their status and makes them into mere imitators. They lay themselves open to this charge especially in 6.9–12, but the difference of their proclamation from that of Micah has been noted and the general disorder and disintegration which they describe in 7.5–6 is a prime example. They should be given the benefit of the doubt. They were not literary scribblers and copyists, but were prophets in the mould of Micah who lamented the state of affairs in their community as he had done in the eighth century B.C. and attached to them indictments and threats of dire consequences. They were aware only of defects and deterioration in their community and of a fall from grace, of apostasy, ingratitude and disobedience. Their mind was so full of these things, so concentrated on gloom that there was no room for hope. That they succeeded in establishing their prophecy as part of 'The Book of Micah' is an indication that they commanded an audience for it in the exilic and post-exilic periods in Jerusalem and that it met a need.

The opening verses of chapter 6 (vv. 1–5) are an account of legal proceedings which Yahweh institutes against Israel, which he instructs his advocate to pursue and to which he summons the mountains as witnesses. Israel is convinced that it has been badly treated by Yahweh, that he has imposed heavy burdens on them and that their well-being has been neglected by him. He asks them to produce evidence in support of these charges: 'My people, what have I done to you? What excessive demands have I made on you? Bring forward your evidence' (v. 3). However, the account of the law-suit is incomplete and we hear nothing of Israel's side of the case. Despite the invitation in v. 3 ('Bring forward your evidence), vv. 4–5 contain a refutal by Yahweh of their charges, a statement that he delivered them from slavery in Egypt and provided the leadership which made their march to the promised land possible. He countered through the agency of Balaam the plans which Balak laid to ensnare them and he urges them to remember the last lap of the journey, from Shittim to Gilgal, 'that they may discern Yahweh's saving acts'. It is as though he would overwhelm them with a recitation of the *Heilsgeschichte*, silence them before they have the chance to speak. At any rate it is a one-sided legal process. Yahweh asks them to bring forward their evidence but does not give them the opportunity to do so.

The question of vv. 6–7 and the answer of v. 8 is a didactic technique, a *genre* which bears no resemblance to the law-suit in vv. 1–5. Wolff's conjecture (150) that vv. 6–8 is generated by a wrong exegesis of v. 3aβ may be correct: the excessive demands to which v. 3aβ refers were thought to be cultic demands. Even if this were so it would explain only the adjacency of vv. 6–8 to vv. 1–5 and would not establish an intrinsic connection between them. The questions then are asked (so Wolff) with the intention of expressing disagreement with v. 3aβ, and contain an element of hyperbole (a thousand rams; ten thousand rivers of oil). The prime requirement of Yahweh is not such an excess of cultic devoutness, not burnt-offerings, calves of a year old, rams and rivers of oil. It is justice, mercy and a modest walk with God. The answer accords with the teaching of the pre-exilic prophets, especially Amos.

Verses 9–12 condemn dishonesty and deceit in trade, in the manner of Micah. The 'city' which is addressed (vv. 9, 12) is probably Jerusalem. Yahweh warns that his patience with false measures, short bushels, untrue scales and misleading weights is at an end. The dependence on Micah is heavy and is accentuated by the polemic against the wealthy men of the 'city' who are full of violence and its inhabitants who utter lies (v. 12). There is a concluding threat that severe punishment will be inflicted and that the 'city' will be laid waste because of its sins (v. 13). Verse 16 may contain a further indication that Micah's scheme in chapter 1 of passing from Samaria (v. 6) to Judah (v. 9) has been adopted. The northern kingdom has exercised a fateful influence on Judah and Jerusalem. They have observed the decrees of Omri and adopted the practices of the house of Ahab. They have conformed to their policies and they are threatened with ruin in vocabulary which Jeremiah used to describe the consequences of the fall of Jerusalem ('You will evoke whistles of horror and endure the jeers of the nations').

The remaining verses (14–15) deal with a curse of non-success with which the inhabitants of the 'city' will be dogged in any activity in which they engage or endeavour which they undertake. Promising beginnings will be overtaken by unnatural final failures and their efforts made null and void. They will eat but not feel well fed, remove from danger but not save, sow but not reap, press olives but not be anointed with oil and tread grapes but not drink the wine.

Chapter 7

7.8–20, containing three separate psalms which serve as a conclusion to the book of Micah, will be considered in another connection and, for the present, only 7.1–7 need notice. These verses have the form of a lament ('Woe is me!', v. 1) for what has come to pass rather than a threat of judgement and 'the day of judgement which has come' (v. 4b) is perhaps the advanced state of strife and decay which has overtaken the community. 'Judgement' is the dissolution of the bonds of common life, the disappearance of integrity from the land (v. 2), the rifeness of violent malevolence, the demise of trust between man and man and between a man and his wife, so that even the most intimate relationships are tainted. It is the fracture of the solidarity of the family and presence of enemies within a man's own household (vv. 5–6).

It is the appalling depth to which human relations have sunk, the terminal illness of the community, which is the judgement (cf. Wolff, 181) rather than a national calamity inflicted as a punishment by Yahweh. Only in v. 3 are those in high places singled out for special blame. They have made themselves expert at wrong-doing and they discharge their offices crookedly: the statesman asks for money, the judge for a bribe and the great man governs capriciously. Apart from this singling out of those exercising power and incurring special responsibility (cf. 3.1, 11) the picture is one of a community which is everywhere falling to pieces. The person making the lament is like a gleaner when there is nothing to glean: 'there are no grapes to glean, no early figs which I desire so passionately' (v. 1). He can find no crumbs of comfort, no ray of light in the darkness which surrounds him, but his unmitigated gloom provokes a secondary riposte which rejects his hopelessness: 'But I shall watch for Yahweh, I shall hope in God, my saviour. My God will hear me.'

REDACTION HISTORY OF MICAH 1–7

This has been touched on in respect of Wolff's contention that 1.2 is closed by the redactional bracket at 5.14 and chapters 1–3 thereby united by the redactor with chapters 4–5. I have suggested a more precise form of this: at 1.2 Yahweh bears witness against the Gentile world and at 5.14 he exacts vengeance on them in hot anger. The process by which his punishment of the גוים was reached begins at 1.2 and ends at 5.14. It comprehends the fulfilment of Micah's doom prophecy uttered against Judah (1–3, especially 3.12), the awakening of hope in the exilic and post-exilic periods (4–5) and a prediction that Yahweh will act in hot anger against the heedless גוים (5.14).

Wolff (xxxvi) sets out the proclamation of the prophet Micah (1.6, 7b–13a, 14–16; 2.1–4, 6–11; 3.1–12) and identifies Deuteronomistic activity in chapters 1–3, an expansion at 1.1, an insertion at 1.3f., commentary at 1.5, 7a, 13b and additions and alterations at 2.3–5, 10b; 3.4, 5, 8. He detects (xxxiv) fainter traces of Deuteronomistic vocabulary in 6.3–5, 8, 16.

The collection of prophecies of weal (so Wolff) in chapters 4–5 (4.9–5.1, 3, 4a, 5b) are to be dated in the early exilic period, from 587 onwards. In the late exilic period promises that the exiles will return

(2.12–13; 4.6–7a) begin to appear. They are followed by a passage which deals with relations between the remnant of Israel and the גוים (5.6–14) which is followed in turn by another (4.1–8; 4.1–3, according to my analysis) whose topic is the future of Jerusalem. In this connection words of *Heil* are developed by secondary editing and are given an exegetical tendency: 4.6–7a by 4.7b and 5.9–12 by 5.8, 13cj. and 14. My translation of v. 8 is different from that of Wolff, I have not accepted his conjecture at v. 13 and I have interpreted v. 14 in another way, so I have disposed of this final point.

The reference to the streaming of the nations to Jerusalem and their homage to Yahweh (4.1–3) is not earlier than the dedication of the temple in 515 B.C. (xxxi). This is the *terminus a quo* for the extant collection of the material in chapters 4–5 and the incorporation of 1–3 in the *corpus* 1–5 (xxxvi). The post-exilic redaction of chapters 1–5 is the result of a literary movement whose span extends from the early-exilic period to post-exilic times and whose *Sitz im Leben* was the public days of lament which were held in Jerusalem for the fall of that city in 587 B.C., where lections from Micah 1–5 were read, where threats of judgement (1–3) alternated with predictions of *Heil* and oracles concerning the גוים (4–5) and where there were congregational responses to these readings from the prophetic word (4.5; 5.8; see further below).

In order to understand the redactional history of the book of Micah we have to reckon with a school of tradition of universalistic *Heil* prophecy in the early Persian period (Wolff, xxxvi). This is what Wolff says, but, the trend of the attitude towards the גוים in chapters 4–5 is, for the most part, informed by Israelite triumphalism (4.13) or is an affirmation that they are Yahweh's enemies (4.11; 5.8) and that he will act against them in anger to exact vengeance on them (5.14). Only in 4.1–3 is there an unequivocal expression of universalism and this, according to Wolff (xxx), is the latest piece in chapters 4–5, presupposes the dedication of the temple in 515 B.C. and cannot have been composed earlier than this date.

These Jerusalem traditionists transmitted not only the proclamation of Micah with its Deuteronomistic commentary (1–3), but extended the range of the book of Micah with prophecies on the future of the diaspora, of Jerusalem and of the גוים (xxxvi). Moreover, they must have had in their ranks a group who, in loose connection with Micah, engaged in a polemic against social and economic abuses which they discerned in the early post-exilic period. Their contribution (6.2–7.7) was stitched to chapters 5 by the graphical identity of שמעו (5.14; 6.1), אשר לא שמעו 'heedless' at 5.14 and שמעו 'listen' at 6.1.

Finally the Jerusalem school of traditionists adapted the proclamation of Micah (1–3), the new prophecies of *Heil* (4–5) and the piece from the circles of the critics of social and economic abuses (6.2–7.7) for liturgical use as lections in connection with public laments for the fall of Jerusalem and the three psalms with which the book concludes (7.8–20) are responses made by the congregation to these lections. Thus Micah 1–7 acquired liturgical significance in Jerusalem in the exilic and post-exilic periods and the authority of the prophet Micah was transferred to the enlarged version of the book of Micah (1–7).

The aspect of Wolff's admirable outline of the redaction history of the book of Micah which gives me most cause for doubt is his account of the redactional devices by which chapters 4–5 were incorporated in 1–3 and 6.1–7.7 were linked to 4–5. Was an ancient redactor responsible for these archtectonic operations or are they the perceptive conjectures of a modern scholar? The case for deliberate redactional techniques is stronger in respect of the incorporation of 4–5 in 1–3, since the appearance of שמעו at 5.14 and 6.1, with different senses, only has significance if 6.1 is identified as a redactional link. The mention of foreign nations at the beginning of chapter 1 (after the superscription) and at the end of chapter 5 has to be taken more seriously as the opening and closing brackets of a redaction, a calculated attempt to define the scope, the beginning and the end, of a piece of literature. Yet I am not altogether persuaded.

SITZ IM LEBEN OF MICAH 1–7

The fall of Jerusalem in 587 B.C. fulfilled the predictions of doom which Micah had uttered against Judah and Jerusalem in the eighth century B.C. The Jerusalem community interpreted it, along with the other pre-exilic prophecies of doom, as a judgement imposed by Yahweh and Micah 1–3 acquired a liturgical function in the days of lamentation for the fall of Jerusalem which were observed by the community in a cultic setting. Micah 1–3 supplied the lections for these events and in connection with them a school of traditionists with a prophetic bent developed the message of the eighth century prophet, bringing it up to date without changing it much (6–7.7) or transforming it from a message of doom to one of hope (4–5). The literary work of these traditionists was seen by them as a building raised on the foundations of Micah 1–3 and they did not hesitate to include their supplements in the 'Book of Micah' and to claim the authority of that prophet for their work. Hence the lections which were read in a public setting came to consist (among others) of Micah 1–7 and this activity, reflecting the different moods of the Jerusalem community in the centuries after 587, continued throughout the exilic and into the post-exilic period.

It is noteworthy that what began as public laments after the fall of Jerusalem supplied a hospitable pulpit to the new prophets (4–7.7) as well as to the old (1–3) and this is particularly so in the case of chapters 4–5 which were more of a new departure, a different kind of prophecy, as compared with 1–3, than were 6–7.7. The latter were singing the same song as Micah had in the eighth century B.C., taking up the same refrain with variations to describe the ills of their times, and the transition from one to the other does not involve a radical change of subject or mood. Chapters 4–5, however, are more of a turn around. They are necessarily preceded by the discernment that the doom predicted by Micah had been fulfilled in the fall of Jerusalem and that a new chapter was now being written in the relations between Yahweh and Israel. That the prediction of doom must now be set aside and that hopeful prospects must be opened up was a seminal theological insight, a decisive change of direction, a stentorian about-turn. They had been judged by Yahweh, but he had not passed a life sentence on them, for a society which labours under the sense of immutable doom is one which has suffered capital punishment and which will surely die. The message that Yahweh planned a future for Israel had to be sounded and hope had to be reborn.

Chapter 7.8–20 has been discussed (chapter 7) and Rudolph's description of it (following Gunkel) as a 'Post-exilic Liturgy' assessed. My conclusion there was the neither Gunkel nor Rudolph establish that it is all of a piece: it does not have the structural coherence of a liturgy. By classifying it as a 'liturgy' they also imply that it contains both a prophetic proclamation in oracular form (vv. 11–13, which are deleted by Wolff) and the responses of a congregation. Chapter 7.8–20 are not a unity with the shape of a liturgy, but are three separate and discontinuous psalms which served as congregational responses to prophetic lections from the book of Micah made in a public liturgical setting. It is difficult to determine whether the place which they now occupy at the end of the book supplies a clue to the liturgical use to which they were put. Wolff discusses this matter without coming to firm conclusions and his is a wise decision. The attempt to demonstrate that the three psalms have each a particular appropriateness to separate parts of Micah 1–7 is inconclusive and the conjecture that the three responses were made by the congregation when the reading of the book of Micah had come to an end raises awkward questions. Were the lections so lengthy? Were readings not made from other prophetic books besides Micah? It appears that we must rest content with the statement that 7.8–20 were psalms which served as congregational responses and are pointers to a public liturgical use of the book of Micah.

WORD OF GOD

Wolff (1978, 409) has sought to establish that כה אמר יהוה is secondary at 2.3 and 3.5 and that the messenger formula, or any other explicit indication that Micah speaks words which Yahweh has uttered, is absent from Mic. 1–3, the only part of the book which he assigns, for the most part, to the prophet Micah (following Stade, 1881, 162). In his commentary (61, 68f) he has no reservations about the text of 2.3, but he questions the originality of כה אמר יהוה in the prose of 3.5. The earlier form of these observations appears to be directed towards the contention that in chapters 1–3 Micah nowhere claims to have heard the word of Yahweh or to be transmitting words which Yahweh had uttered. Wolff's purpose in making these observations is that Micah, though claiming prophetic authority, does not say explicitly that he speaks the word of Yahweh. He is reinforcing his thesis that Micah held the office of a district elder at Moresheth, that he rose to prophetic status by his discerning critique of the Jerusalem establishment and that his prophetic discourse is couched in language which betrays his provincial sympathies and which rests on the same basis of authority as that on which he had relied in discharging his duties as an elder at Moresheth.

I am attracted to this and I would widen the discussion by asserting that the proposition 'God speaks Hebrew' is never to be taken literally (McKane, 1995), but Wolff's handling of the matter is puzzling, especially if כה אמר יהוה is accepted as genuine at 2.3. In any case, with or without the messenger formula, there is no doubt that Yahweh is the putative speaker at 2.3–5 and the position is the same at 1.6–7 (as Wolff allows, 1982, 16, 26f.). Micah, in his own person, would not have made an assertion in the first person that Samaria would be destroyed, that the towns of Judah would be reduced to ruin and that its inhabitants would lose their tenure of the land.

It could be supposed that by introducing a speech of Yahweh without כה אמר יהוה (assuming that the formula is a later insertion in the text) Micah is deliberately exercising a theological reserve, that he is stopping short of the assertion that Yahweh speaks Hebrew. This is a thought not worth pursuing and the thesis that Micah speaks authoritatively as an elder rather than a prophet should not be conducted with reference to the absence of the messenger formula at 1.6 or its presence at 2.3. At 1.6–7 and 2.3–5 the prophet must be purporting to reproduce words which he has received from Yahweh and the absence of כה אמר יהוה at 1.6 or its alleged secondary insertion at 2.3 does nothing for the contention that Micah was a district elder at Moresheth, that he intervened in the wider context of Jerusalem and that the prophetic authority which he assumed is expressed in terms which betray his provincial sympathies: that his patterns of speech, even as a prophet, are founded on the kind of authority which he exercised at Moresheth as an elder of the people.

It is unlikely that דבר יהוה in the superscription at 1.1 has any contribution to make to the foregoing discussion, though it has a bearing on the wider question which I have raised. Wolff's conclusion (1982) is that the superscription is editorial and that, in its present form, it is not earlier than the exile. It was the later version which altered 'the words of Micah' to 'the word of Yahweh which came to Micah'. According to the superscription in its extant shape the דבר יהוה which Micah received was 'seen' and not 'heard'. Too much should not be made of this, though it should be noticed that חזה and חזון occur in the superscriptions of other prophetic books. The combination of חזון

and כה אמר אדני יהוה (Obad. 1.1) could be taken to indicate that the 'word of Yahweh' is heard by the prophet in the context of visionary experience. That prophetic oracles are the product of such experience is also stated by Amos 1.1, where, however, they are described as 'words of Amos' not 'word of Yahweh'. דברי ירמיהו occurs at Jer. 1.1, but it is clear from Amos 1.3 (כה אמר יהוה) and Jer. 1.2 (דברי יהוה) that no antithesis between the word of Yahweh and the words of a prophet is intended. Nahum's prophecy is described as 'the book of the vision (ספר חזון) of Nahum from Elkosh' (1.1) and Habbakuk's משא (also in Nah. 1.1) is said to have been seen (חזה). Both חזון and חזה occur in the superscription of the book of Isaiah (1.1) and the statement that the דבר יהוה came to Ezekiel (1.3) is followed by וארא 'and I saw' (1.4). It is perhaps not overworking this evidence to draw the conclusion that at a later time the converse of a prophet with Yahweh was thought to have taken place when the prophet was in an abnormal visionary state of mind. The use of ראי in Jer. 2.31 in combination with דבר יהוה points in a different direction. It is probably a marginal comment which has entered the text (McKane, 1985, 51f.) and its sense is something like, 'Discern the word of Yahweh.'

The principal thing is that I am more confident in the truth of the proposition that 'God does not speak Hebrew' than I am in the validity of the efforts to plumb the psychological states or the beliefs of the Hebrew prophets when the language which we have been considering is used of them. To hold that it was a later theological doctrine which imposed the formula כה אמר יהוה or the like on their words encounters the insuperable obstacle that some of them can only be taken as putative words of God, so that the problem is not limited to the formulae which describe them. The prophets make utterances which are appropriate only if Yahweh is the speaker, but it is difficult to press this statement further so that it produces positive results. We cannot rule out the possibility that prophets may have converted their psychological states into converse with Yahweh, that they may have believed that they heard the speech of Yahweh. Or the answer may be literary and theological. They fell into the oracular style to express the depth of their conviction that they spoke the truth and to claim Divine authority for what they said. At any rate certainty should not be claimed where there is none and it should not be supposed that the imposition of כה אמר יהוה or like formulae in a later age solves all the problems.

CHAPTER 1

v. 1 THE SUPERSCRIPTION

Micah is described as המרשתי and, if מרשת is to be equated with מרשת גת (1.14), it is to be located in the Shephelah, the hill-country of south-west Judah, in the region where the other towns mentioned in vv. 10–15 are located. Micah is not entitled a prophet (נביא), but he is said to have received the word of Yahweh (דבר יהוה) and Targ. has פתגם נבואה for דבר and אתנבי for חזה. Micah is said to have engaged in prophetic activity in Judah in the reigns of Jotham (742–735 B.C.), Ahaz (735–715 B.C.) and Hezekiah (715–687 B.C.) and the range of his predictions extended from Samaria to Jerusalem. He is identified with מיכה המרשתי who prophesied (נבא) in the reign of Hezekiah (Jer. 26.18) in connection with a legal precedent introduced by the elders at Jeremiah's trial before Jehoiakim.

Sept., Vulg., Pesh. and Targ. represent MT. Wellhausen (22, 131) reduces the superscription to 'The word of Yahweh which came to Micah, the Moreshite', as the only part of it which rested on tradition, the rest being a product of literary elaboration and conforming to the pattern of Hos. 1.1, Amos 1.1, Isa. 1.1 and Jer. 1.1. Robinson's suggestion (130) that two superscriptions have been combined in the extant text is taken up by Wolff (2), though the content of the two superscriptions set out by him differs from that of Robinson whose second superscription consists of 'The word of Yahweh which came to Micah, the Moreshite, which he saw concerning Samaria and Jerusalem.' Wolff, on the other hand, identifies אשר היה אל יהוה, and בימי ... יהודה as an elaboration of the original form of the superscription which was 'The words (emending דבר to דברי) of Micah, the Moreshite, which he saw concerning Samaria and Jerusalem'.

In preferring the second relative clause Wolff parts company with Wellhausen and Rudolph (31–32) who choose the first. Rudolph supposes that the second may have been triggered by the mention of Samaria and Jerusalem in v. 5. Wolff notices that the extant superscription is not connected syntactically or thematically with what follows and that the mention of Samaria and Jerusalem, in this respect, is an improvement on that of the kings of Judah.

That the superscription, whatever its original shape, is the work of an editor (Hillers, 14) goes without saying, but Wolff (2) is concerned to distinguish between its earlier form and one which is not earlier than the fall of Jerusalem and the exile. The description of a collection of pre-exilic prophetic sayings as 'the word of Yahweh which came to Micah, the Moreshite, in the reign of Jotham, Ahaz and Hezekiah' is a product of lengthy theological reflection typical of that undertaken by Deuter-onomistic collectors and editors in connection with pre-exilic prophetic sayings after the fall of Jerusalem (so Wolff).

> 1. The word of Yahweh which came to Micah, the Moreshite, in the reigns of Jotham, Ahaz and Hezekiah, kings of Judah, which he received in visions concerning Samaria and Jerusalem.[1]

vv. 2–7 SAMARIA AND JUDAH DENOUNCED

Who is being summoned in v. 2? Is it the Northern Kingdom or is it the world of nations? Sept. and Vulg. translate ארץ as 'earth' (γῆ, Vulg. *terra*), Pesh. '*r*' and Targ. ארעא reproduce MT. Sept. and Vulg. indicate that the whole world was summoned and this is the view mostly accepted (Wellhausen, 22; Duhm, 82; Donner, 92; Wolff, 8), though the prob-lem created by such an assumption is acknowledged. The topic of vv. 5–7 is not a judgement of the world, but a punishment which is to be exacted on Samaria and Jerusalem. בכם (v. 2) is resistant to the rendering 'against you', although this is preferred by NEB (cf. Wellhausen and Donner *gegen euch*). Duhm is aware of the difficulty and notices that בכם is translated ἐν ὑμῖν by Sept. (also REB; Weiser (231) and Wolff (8) *unter euch Zeuge*). The contention of Willis (82) that ἐν ὑμῖν εἰς μαρτύριον means 'for a witness against you' and confirms the sense 'against you for בכם is not to be granted. Duhm prefers either 'among you' (cf. Vulg *vobis* or the deletion of בכם. Pesh. and Targ. reproduce MT.

Wellhausen (132) had remarked that in v. 2a Yahweh addresses the whole earth, whereas the threat issued by בכם (v. 2b) apparently refers to Israel only. He supposes that there is no way of reconciling v. 2a with

---

[1]Reading וחזקיהו (cf. *BDB*, 306).

v. 2b other than by assuming that בכם *nicht auf den Israeliten beschränken.* Hence Wellhausen tends to conclude (*contra* Duhm) that nations have been assembled to hear a threat. Jepsen's proposal (1938, 96) disposes of the vexatious בכם by deleting v. 2b (ויהי ... קדשו) as an addition which interrupts the continuity between v. 2a and v. 3.

The apparent grammatical incongruence of שמעו ... כלם (v. 2a) was noted by Kimchi (also Wolff, 10), but the latter defends the combination of imperative and third person suffix as a use which is attested in biblical Hebrew (GK 135r). Wolff explains כלם as *ingesamt* or *in toto.* Sept. has λόγους 'words' in place of כלם which Wolff explains unconvincingly as a consequence of the the tramsfer of כלם to the end of v. 2a (ארץ ומלאה; Sept. καὶ πάντες οἱ ἐν αὐτῇ). For כלם Vulg. has *omnes,* Targ. reproduces MT and Pesh reads *klkwn,* an emendation adopted by Duhm (82) and Robinson (130). A similar incongruence might be thought to exist with the association of the imperative הקשיבו with the third person suffix of מלאה, but it strikes a less jarring note than the other, literally 'the earth and its fulness' (Donner, 92, *und was sie erfüllt*; KJV, 'O earth and all that therein is'). NEB (REB is better, 'the earth and all who are in it' (Wolff, 8, *und wer sie bewohnt*; Sept. καὶ πάντες οἱ ἐν αὐτῇ.

More important is the contention of Kimchi that there is no reference to the Gentile world in v. 2. The plural עמים is explained as a reference to the tribes of Israel and ארץ ומלאה as 'the land of Israel and the people who live in it'. This is the exegesis favoured by Ehrlich (272): עמים is not a reference to heathen people, only to Judah and northern Israel; ארץ ומלאה has only the Holy land in view not the whole earth. If this exegesis were accepted, the discontinuity between v. 2 and vv. 5–7 and the disconcerting change of subject would be removed.

The conclusion that עמים and ארץ ומלאה refer to all the people of the earth is irresistible. What remains unclear is why the nations are summoned to hear a threat of judgement which is not directed against them. Wolff (8) translates בכם לעד as 'among you as a witness' (also Rudolph, 32), but his exegesis is obscure. On the one hand he holds that the representation is not one of world judgement and this agrees with his translation. On the other hand he contends (14) that all the people of the world are assembled so that Yahweh may witness against them (*gegen sie Jahwe selbst Zeuge sein will*) and he holds that עד (compare his translation) has the sense of *Kläger* (24) 'plaintiff'. They are to hear Yahweh's words, because he has a complaint to lay against them.

The trouble, as Duhm (82) discerned, is that there is a hiatus between the beginning of the poem and its continuation—the latter does not seem to require the presence of the Gentile world. The dichotomy is more severe in Donner, because he renders בכם לעד as *Ankläger gegen euch* (also Fritz, 319), 'an accuser against you' and yet he states that Yahweh makes the threat against Samaria (96). Only if בכם is translated 'against you' can it be concluded that Yahweh is issuing a threat against the nations (KJV, 'witness against you'; NEB, 'bear witness against you'). If this is adopted, the judgement which Yahweh purposes is to involve all the nations of the world whom he has summoned to accuse them and establish their guilt. But is this correct? It reinforces the disconnectedness between v. 2 and the threat which is subsequently made against Samaria and Judah.

Willis (377) also opts for 'against you', but his account is more straightforward than that of either Donner or Wolff. He asserts roundly that the peoples of the earth are the accused in a law-suit, that Yahweh's intention is to warn them with the horrific prospect of the judgement which is to fall on Israel and that a variant pattern of Amos 1.3–2.8 is perhaps to be detected: if Yahweh does not spare his own people, they are not to expect that he will spare them (378f.).

The best that can be done is to render בכם as 'to bear witness among you' (Sept., REB; Wolff in his translation) in which case the nations are assembled so that Yahweh may produce irrefutable evidence of the guilt of Judah and, especially, Samaria. Why he should do this remains obscure. Donner (96) states that the threat of judgement levelled against Samaria and Judah had significance for all the nations of the world, but he does not throw light on what this significance is. Moreover he renders בכם לעד *als Ankläger gegen euch* (Smith, 32, 'to witness against you'; H. Schmidt, 131, *als Zeuge wider euch*; Robinson, 130, *gegen euch als Ankläger*) and this is incompatible with the view that Yahweh's design in summoning the nations was to rehearse evidence which would prove the guilt of Samaria and Judah. Weiser (234) leaves both possibilities open, either *gegen euch* or *unter euch* (his translation). Yahweh is making public to the world the guilt of Samaria and Judah or else he is indicting the nations.

Wolff's explanation (36) of v. 2 is an admission that the entrance of the nations is a source of discontinuity in the chapter: it is the latest Deuteronomistic supplementation of 1.1–5 and its function is to represent that Micah's words of judgement against Samaria and Judah is an anticipatory model of the legal process which he will conduct against the world to secure its guilt and intimate its punishment.

Jepsen's proposal (1938, 96) that v. 2b should be deleted needs some consideration. It is an unconvincing line: אדני יהוה followed by אדני, the difficulties created by בכם לעד and the redundancy of מהיכל קדשו which untimeously anticipates יצא ממקומו (v. 3). If בכם לעד disappeared, this would remove the reason to urge that Yahweh is represented as levelling accusations against the nations of the world whom he has summoned. מהיכל קדשו can refer only to Yahweh's descent from heaven with a view to his appearance on earth (v. 3) and Kimchi glosses it with מן השמים. If v. 2b were deleted, the summons to the nations would be followed by the announcement of the theophany (כי הנהו or כי הנה יהוה with Duhm [82] and others) and then v. 2a and v. 3 would be well connected. This would reinforce the claim that vv. 3–4 are a continuation of v. 2 (Fritz, 324) and would weaken the contention of Wolff (21) that v. 2 (including 2b) is continued in v. 5 and that the link between v. 2 and v. 3 has been made by a secondary stitch (כי הנהו).

Even without the deletion of v. 2b, it should be held that vv. 2–4 are a unit (Fritz) rather than vv. 2 and 5 and that כי הנה יהיה or כי הנהו, though it has been anticipated oddly by מהיכל קדשו, is not to be explained as a redactional device which erroneously connects with v. 3 a verse (v. 2) which is continued in v. 5. Otherwise the only textual matter in v. 3 is that Sept. does not represent ודרך (καὶ καταβήσεται = וירד) and Duhm (82) remarks that וירד and ודרך are variants. That ודרך is the secondary variant (Sept.) is confirmed by a fragment of Hebrew text from Qumran Cave 1, where ודרך is a minus (Barthélemy and Milik, 77). Donner (94), on the analogy of Amos 4.13, prefers ודרך while Elliger (BHS) and Wolff (10) opt for וירד, Wolff because he concludes that ודרך is a secondary equalization which connects with Amos 4.13 and Deut. 33.29.

NEB translates v. 4, 'Beneath him mountains dissolve like wax before fire, valleys are torn open, as when torrents pour down a hillside' (REB has 'at his touch' for 'beneath him', but is otherwise the same). This rendering establishes correctly that the first simile (כדונג מפני האש)

connects with ונמסו 'dissolve' and the second (כמים מגרים במורד) with יתבקעו 'are torn open', but it does not retain the word-order of the Hebrew. NEB and REB are altering the form of the Hebrew for what they judge is a more natural kind of English, but they are not proposing an alteration of the Hebrew word-order and so an emendation of the Hebrew text (cf. Wolff, 25). The first simile is apposite, but the point of the second is not so obvious: dissolving mountains and melting wax by fire is a match, but valleys which are torn open and torrents which pour down a hillside is not so transparent a simile. Ibn Ezra has endeavoured to improve it it by suggesting that יתבקעו 'disintegrate' has the sense 'become liquid': the valleys will become liquid and flow like water down a hillside.

Kimchi treats the theophany imagery in vv. 3–4 as a משל, a symbol of the terror of the judgement which Yahweh will execute against Samaria (similarly Ibn Ezra, the 'fire of God' is his anger against Samaria). Wolff (24f.) identifies the theophany imagery as traditionally a component of Yahweh's threat directed against nations with whom Israel is at war. Yahweh appears as a victorious warrior exerting irresistible power in Israel's defence and scattering their enemies. It is then best explained with reference to v. 2, if the assumption that Yahweh has summoned the nations to accuse them (בכם לעד) prior to inflicting defeat (judgement) on them is accepted (Fritz, 323f.). But Wolff (20f., 35f.), who supposes that v. 2 is a later insertion than vv. 3f., suggests that the function of vv. 3f., which celebrates Yahweh's sovereignty over the powers of nature, is to encourage the post-exilic Jerusalem community, facing hard times, to submit to Yahweh's judgement.

Fritz connects the combination of themes (summoning of the nations to judgement and theophany) in vv. 2–4 with a cultic celebration and holds that the vocabulary and imagery point to an ideology which was rooted and developed in the Jerusalem cult. He is far removed from the critical position of Beyerlin (30–42), because Fritz has in mind a post-exilic Jerusalem milieu for 1.2–7 (also Wolff for vv. 2–5), whereas Beyerlin is portraying Micah as an eighth century Jerusalem prophet who availed himself of a Sinai theophany tradition. On the theophany imagery Fritz (326) is distant from the view of Kimchi that it is simply a משל which indicates the severity of the punishment that is to fall on Samaria. Fritz supposes that it is formulated as a precise *ex eventu* prediction: Samaria will be destroyed not by enemies but by a natural catastrophe launched by Yahweh.

Donner's perception (96f.) that 1.5b is a secondary addition to v. 5a is an important pointer to the the sense of בית ישראל in v. 5a. Ibn Ezra's treatment of v. 5b assumes that it is a continuation of v. 5a and that יהודה (v. 5b) refers back to בית ישראל in v. 5a. Wellhausen (132f.) had asked whether v. 5b connected credibly with v. 5a and had raised doubts about its genuineness. He did not reproduce it in his translation (22). It is unclear whether he questioned the equation of בית ישראל (v. 5a) with יהודה (v. 5b), but he urged that בית ישראל should replace יהודה in v. 5b and he baulked at the juxtaposition of the במות of Judah with Jerusalem in the same verse, though he did not question the general appropriateness of the representation that Micah compared Samaria with Jerusalem (cf. Budde, 79f. who identifies v. 5b as secondary). Jepsen (97) considers the idea that בית ישראל should be emended to יהודה (Smith, 34, so emends), and so brought into agreement with יהודה in v. 5b. He advances a counter-consideration, namely, that in Micah 3.1, 8, 9 both יעקב and ישראל refer to Judah. He concludes that v. 5a and v. 5b do not hang together.

במות is strange, but, for the assessment of the status of v. 5b in relation to v. 5a, it is not the major consideration. The versions (Sept., Pesh., Targ.) were puzzled by its lack of correspondence with חטאות in v. 5a. Sept. represented חטאת (ἁμαρτία) in both v. 5a and v. 5b; Pesh. (*ḥṭyt*) and Targ. (חטו) have חטאת in v. 5b. It should not be thought that these readings have text-critical significance. They do not point to a Hebrew text different from MT, but arise from a felt need for a better word than במות to match חטאות or חטאת (Sept.) in v. 5b. Ehrlich (273) was certain that בית ישראל (v. 5a) stood for Judah (also Wolff, 35) and Elliger (BHS) proposed that it should be emended to יהודה.

The crucial contribution of Donner is the realization that v. 5b is parasitic on v. 5a: it is a secondary gloss and its exegesis of בית ישראל is wrong. Hence the indictment of v. 5a is delivered against the Northern Kingdom and the parallelism of יעקב and בית ישראל is synonymous (so Robinson, 131; Fritz, 324; *contra* Wade, 5 who retains v. 5b and equates בית ישראל with Judah). It is only the פשע of Samaria against which the prophet inveighs in v. 5a and Judah is not in his sights. The secondary exegesis of v. 5b, which supposes that it was, is false. H. Schmidt (131, n. 2) agrees, but retains מי פשע ... שמרון (also Rudolph,

41). Weiser (236) remarks that the parallel question relating to Judah and Jerusalem appears to be an insertion, perhaps encouraged by the mention of Judaean kings in the superscription and by the felt appropriateness of including a word against both kingdoms in the first saying. He does not expand on this, but its implication is that both יעקב and בית ישראל in v. 5a refer to the Northern Kingdom.

The interpretation of vv. 5a, 6–7 is complicated by the reference to Judah and Jerusalem. It may be urged that this is an indication that the prophet's concern was already embracing both the Northern Kingdom and Judah in v. 5. Such a riposte has weight only if it is assumed that both v. 5 and v. 9 were spoken by the prophet Micah. It is not part of Donner's case that בית ישראל or ישראל is always to be equated with the northern Kingdom in the book of Micah and he holds that ישראל in 1.13, 15 is a reference to the old unbroken Israel of the twelve tribes. No attempt is being made to dispute that Micah was concerned primarily with the fate of Judah and Jerusalem (1.9) and especially with the region around Moresheth which would be devastated if the Assyrian advance progressed beyond the Northern Kingdom into Judah (1.8–16).

Sept. εἰς ὀπωροφυλάκιον ἀγροῦ (v. 6) for לעי השדה, 'into the field of a garden-watcher', may have been influenced by Isa. 1.8, where ὡς ὀπωροφυλάκιον translates כמלונה and where בכרם occurs. Pesh. *byt dbrʾ dḥqlʾ*, 'a shack in a field in the open country', may have been influenced by Sept. Vulg. *quasi acervum lapidum*, 'as a heap of stones' is followed by Rashi and Kimchi (עי = גלי) and NEB, 'a heap of ruins in open country'. Wellhausen (133) remarks that עי and השדה is an unlikely combination, though he translates (22) *zu einer Wildnis im Felde*, 'into a wilderness in open country'. He notices the conjecture עיר השדה 'rural village' which is adopted by Ehrlich (273). Donner (94), following Marti, emends לעי השדה to לשדה, 'I shall make Samaria into a field, a place for planting vines.' Wolff (11) supposes that לעי השדה is a secondary stitch that sets up a comparison between the fate of Samaria and that of Jerusalem which, according to 3.12, will be ploughed up like a field (שדה) and reduced to a heap of ruins (עיין). The absence of the copula with למטעי כרם is evidence (so Wolff) that השדה לעי is secondary (cf. Duhm, 82, who conjectures that השדה is a corruption of ירושלם. On והגרתי לגי אבניה (NEB, 'I will pour her stones into the valley'; REB, 'I shall hurl her stones into the valley') Kimchi explains that Samaria was set on a hill so that the stones from the ruined city tumbled into the valley.

There are three matters in v. 7 on which attention should be focused: (a) קבצה which is vocalized by MT as Piel (קִבְּצָה) (b) The sense which is to be attached to אתנן which occurs three times (c) The contention of Wolff (11) that v. 7a (שממה ... וכל פסיליה) is a secondary addition to an earlier text of v. 7. On (a) it should be noticed that קבצה is rendered by Vulg. (*congregata sunt*), Pesh. *'tknšw*, and Targ. (אתכנשו) as קֻבְּצוּ 'are amassed', whereas Sept. (συνήγαγεν) follows MT. The emendation קֻבְּצָה requires only a different vocalization of the consonantal text (cf. Duhm, 83), but קבעו with Vulg., Pesh. and Targ. is more favoured (Welllhausen, 133; Duhm, 83; Elliger [BHS]; Donner, 94). Rashi retains MT and assumes an object which is not explicit (כל ההון הזה 'all this wealth') and this is the assumption of Wolff (9), NEB and REB: the subject of קבצה is 'Samaria' and the object to be understood is 'them', 'She amassed them' (NEB, REB).

אתנן (v. 7b according to NEB and REB, is a prostitute's fee, whether a common prostitute (cf. Deut. 23.19, אתנן זונה) or a temple prostitute (קדשה) is not specified. The other uses of אתנן or אתנה (Hos. 2.14) do not connect it particularly with a fee given to a קדשה. In any discussion of this a distinction should be made between the figure of speech itself and the interpretation which is placed on it. Wellhausen (133) concentrates on the interpretation and urges that the exegesis of the verse should not focus on the fee given to prostitutes. The point of the verse is that wealth derived from the patronage given to the Baal cult will vanish as quickly as it accumulated. This, even it it were right, is an interpretation of the idiom which is used and does not engage with the lexicography of אתנן 'gift', 'fee'. If this aspect of the matter is attended to, we shall find that אתנה (Hos. 2.14) is the fee given to a married woman who plays the harlot; אתנן is the fee which a woman with an insatiable sexual appetite pays to men (Ezek. 16.34, 41). Tyre, the great trading nation, which earns her wealth from commerce, is likened to a prostitute who sells her services to all-comers for a fee (Isa. 23.17).

The thoroughgoing cultic character of v. 7a has been taken as an indication that v. 7b refers to temple prostitutes from whose fees the temples of Samaria accumulated wealth (Wellhausen, 133, *Hierodulen*; Weiser, 237; Robinson, 131), though other uses of אתנן refer to the fee given to a common prostitute (Van der Westhuizen, 1973, 54–61).

The matter is complicated by Wolff's claim that v. 7a is a secondary elaboration which concentrates the indictment of Samaria on her idolatrous cultic practices. The vocabulary of v. 7a, according to Wolff, is Hoseanic-Deuteronomistic and, if it is a later addition to v. 7, v. 7b connects with v. 6 and not with v. 7a. In that case it was on the splendid buildings of Samaria that the wealth amassed from the fees of prostitutes were spent. Even so, it is more probable that v. 7b has in mind the consolidated wealth of temples gathered from the fees paid to temple prostitutes than it has the earnings scattered among common prostitutes.

אתנניה (v. 7a) must be related to the occurrences of אתנן in v. 7b. It is a lexicographical puzzle and Wellhausen (22) leaves a blank in his translation, suggesting that אתנניה be emended to אשריה, 'her Asherim' (133; also H. Schmidt, 132; Weiser, 232; Robinson, 130). Watson's explanation (1984, 105) of v. 7, which equates the first occurrence (v. 7a) of אתנן with 'sea-serpent' (prosthetic *aleph*), is far-fetched. With the deletion of אתנניה ... באש as a metrically superfluous addition to v. 7a (Elliger [BHS]; Fritz, 320, n. 27; Rudolph, 33) אתנניה disappears. It may be conjectured that it was אתנן in v. 7b which triggered אתנניה in v. 7a as something of a *tour de force*, cultic furniture derived from harlots' fees. Sept. and Vulg. do not distinguish between the meaning of אתנן at v. 7b and its meaning at v. 7a: v. 7a, τὰ μισθώματα αὐτῆς, *mercedes eius*; v. 7b, ἐκ μισθωμάτων (twice); *de mercedibus, ad mercedem*; Pesh. *dhlth* and Targ. טעותהא, 'its idols' indicate that אתנן is being overworked at v. 7a.

On יכתו (v. 7a) Kimchi suggests that the iconoclastic fury of the victors was not simply vandalism but was an endeavour to extract the gold and silver components of the images as loot. That v. 7a describes the sack of Samarian temples by the Assyrian soldiery and the booty which they used to hire prostitutes is the view of Donner (97f.; *contra* Wellhausen, 133).

Wolff (16) holds that Mic. 1.6, 7b are the words of the eighth century prophet Micah and Fritz argues (329f.) that Mic. 1.2–7 derives from a post-exilic circle in Jerusalem. Wolff (35f.) agrees that Mic. 1.2–5 is of post-exilic origin. According to Fritz (329f.) Micah was not concerned with cultic infringements, with idolatry or with the infiltration of the Canaanite cult into Yahwism and 1.7 was not his work. Micah (so Fritz) lambasted the oppressiveness and inhumanity of rulers, the corruptness of the judiciary and the greed for gain with which judges, priests and prophets were obsessed. The priest interpreted the Torah capriciously and the prophets falsified Yahweh's will. Micah mind was filled not with cultic matters, but with human (or inhuman) behaviour within Judaean society and it was this which supplied the content of his message.

It might be thought that Wolff's relegation of v. 7a to a secondary status is a complete answer to Fritz. If v. 7a is secondary, the passage vv. 6, 7b is emptied of its cultic content. It is against the wealth which is advertised by Samaria's grand buildings that Micah inveighs and it is they which he threatens with ruin. This answers a part, and not the more important part of Fritz's case which is not only that Micah did not focus his message on idolatry, but also that he prophesied to Judah and not to Samaria (330). Hence בית ישראל (v. 5a) becomes an important consideration and it has been argued by me that both יעקב and ישראל refer there to the Northern Kingdom (cf. Fritz, 324).

This does not create difficulties for Fritz, because he does not suppose that the eighth century prophet Micah is responsible for v. 5a and he recognizes that v. 5b is a secondary and false exegesis of v. 5a. That בית ישראל or ישראל in chapters 1–3, the part of the book which Wolff assigns, for the most part, to Micah, refers largely to Judah (the same holds for בית יעקב or יעקב) is not a problem for Fritz. In 1.13, 14, 15 ישראל is associated with towns in the Judaean Shephelah which are under threat. In 2.7, 12 and 3.1, 8 ישראל or יעקב refers to Judah and in 3.9 בית יעקב and בית ישראל are linked to a threat against Zion and Jerusalem (3.12). For Fritz this is a confirmation that Micah is a Judaean prophet and that 1.6–7, words against Samaria, were not spoken by him.

Is Mic. 1.9 a fly in the ointment? Is it a piece of evidence which runs counter to that which has been produced? The nature of the problem will be illustrated by the differing translations of NEB and REB, both of which apparently read מכתה with the versions instead of מכותיה (MT), though there is no indication of this in Brockington (254). NEB, 'Her wound cannot be healed, for the stroke has bitten deeply into Judah'; REB, 'Israel has suffered a deadly blow and now it has fallen on Judah'.

The different translations are not accounted for by a different Hebrew text and they are uninfluenced by the choice between מכותיה

(MT) and מכתה (the versions). So the adoption of מכתה (Wellhausen, 133; Smith, 35; Robinson, 131; Donner, 94; Elliger [BHS]) does not achieve clarification. According to NEB, the מכות or מכה are those of Judah and the concern of the prophet is concentrated on Judah (agreeing with Wellhausen, 133). It might be supposed, however, that עד יהודה later in the verse indicates that the מכות (or the מכה) are those of the Northern Kingdom and that now they have reached Judah (REB). NEB avoids this conclusion and reconciles מכתה with עד יהודה by referring מכתה to Judah also.

The importance of the difference between NEB and REB is that it has a bearing on v. 5a. If כי אנושה מכתה (v. 9) is rendered 'For Israel (the Northern Kingdom) has suffered a deadly blow' (REB; probably Kimchi's exegesis) and, if בית ישראל (v. 5a) refers to Judah (cf. 5b), v. 9, with its movement from the Northern Kingdom to Judah, is resuming the juxtaposition of יעקב (the Northern Kingdom) and בית ישראל (Judah) in v. 5a and is weakening the contention that in v. 5a יעקב and בית ישראל both refer to Samaria. Thus Smith (34f.) emends בית ישראל to יהודה (v. 5a), retains v. 5b and reads מכתה (v. 9). The position of Robinson and H. Schmidt is different. Robinson (131) judges that v. 5b is secondary and Schmidt (131, 133) deletes ומי ... ירושלם in v. 5b. Hence the suffix of מכותיה or מכתה (v. 9) refers both to יעקב and בית ישראל (v. 5a) and Schmidt makes this explicit, *Denn unheilbar ist der Schlag, der ist (Samaria) getroffen* (also von Orelli, 112 [מכותיה = *Die Samaria treffenden Streiche*]). Van der Woude (1976, 31, 37) argues that יעקב and בית ישראל (v. 5a) both refer not to the Northern Kingdom but to the old unbroken Israel. Since he holds that vv. 8ff. are continuous with vv. 6–7 and that v. 5a is a prelude to vv. 8ff., the suffix of מכותיה or מכתה (v. 9) connects with both יעקב and בית ישראל.

Even if מכותיה or מכתה is read, NEB's (Wellhausen's) interpretation of v. 9 should be preferred and the verse should not be thought to throw doubt on the conclusion reached in respect of v. 5a. It should be noticed that Duhm's objection (83) to מכותיה or מכתה is that the suffix hangs in the air: he does not entertain the idea that it might resume יעקב and בית ישראל in v. 5a. The problem in v. 9 disappears entirely if מכותיה is emended to מכת יה, 'stroke of Yahweh' (Duhm, 83; Weiser, 238; Elliger [BHS]) or מכת יהוה (Rudolph, 34; Wolff, 12; noticed by Donner, 94). Wolff further suggests that יהוה is the subject of נגע and the emendation of נגע to נגעה (Wellhausen, Duhm, Donner) is unnecessary.

Why is an oracle against Samaria assigned to Micah of Moresheth near the beginning of the book which bears his name? According to Fritz (330) the Northern kingdom may have been destroyed prior to the time of his emergence as a prophet. Here we are reduced to speculation. Lescow (82f.) holds that the reason for this was a particular historical event. Fritz supposes that it was the felt need for a more comprehensive theology. Lescow conjectures that a chronic anti-Samarian *animus* in some circles in post-exilic Jerusalem was fanned by the Samaritan schism, the setting up of a rival cult on Mount Gerizim in opposition to Zion, and that this generated 1.6–7. Fritz (319, 324, 330f.) traces 1.5a, 6–7 to the quest for a more complete theodicy. Since Micah directs Yahweh's threat of judgement against Judah and Jerusalem, the whole story should be told. When the book of Micah was being collected, an entry should be made which would make it clear from the outset that Samaria's fall had also been a consequence of Yahweh's judgement.

2. Listen all you peoples,
    be attentive, O earth, and all that it contains,
    that Lord Yahweh from his temple may be among you as a witness.
3. For look! Yahweh is coming out of his dwelling-place
    to descend and walk on the heights of the earth.
4. Mountains dissolve beneath him,
    valleys are split open,
    like wax before fire,
    like torrents pouring down a hillside.
5. All this stems from Jacob's transgression and Israel's sin.
    What[1] is the transgression of Jacob?
    Is it not Samaria?
    What[1] is the high place[2] of Judah?
    Is it not Jerusalem?
6. So I shall make Samaria a heap of ruins in open country,
    a place for planting vines;
    I shall cast her stones into the valley
    and lay bare her foundations.
7. All her carved figures will be smashed,
    all her images burnt.
    I shall break her idols to pieces;

---

[1]The use of מי for מה is strange (cf. GK 137a).
[2]Reading במת for MT במות.

she gathered (them) out of fees for harlots
and they will become harlots' fees once more.

vv. 8–16 A LAMENT FOR THE TOWNS OF JUDAH

Sept. (v. 8) has third person verbs (κόψεται; θρηνήσει; πορεύσεται; ποιήσεται) instead of the first person verbs of MT, but the first person fits the lament better than the third. κόπτομαι means to beat the breast as a sign of grief. Presumably the third person singular verbs of Sept. refer to the inhabitants (יושבת) of the succession of towns which follow in vv. 10–15. Sept. renders כתנין as ὡς δρακόντων 'like serpents' or 'like dragons', a reading which arises from the confusion of כתנין (singular) with כתנים (plural). σειρήνων 'sirens' for יענה is a mystery, since בנות יענה is regularly translated as 'ostriches' (Smith, 32, 38, 'daughters of the desert' = 'ostriches'; NEB 'desert owls'). σειρήνων has been traced to a supposed connection between יענה and ענה 'sing' (Rudolph, 34; Hillers, 22), hence 'daughters of the sirens' (θυγατέρων σειρήνων).

Vulg. *velut draconum* simply confuses תנין with תנים and for בנות יענה is has *struthionum* 'ostriches'. It follows MT with first person verbs. Pesh. has a series of second person feminine singular imperatives instead of the first person singulars of MT and this has the effect of making the prophet issue an instruction to wail and howl to the cities which he addresses in vv. 10–15 rather than expressing a personal anguish at the prospect of the disasters which will overtake them. With 'as a jackal and as the daughter of a jackal' Pesh. shows *yrwr* twice. Targ., with third person plural verbs, extracts a similar sense from the verse as Sept.: 'Because of this they (the towns which are listed) will weep and wail and go about bare-foot and naked. They will make lamentation like jackals and mourning like ostriches.' Pesh. and Targ. follow Sept. (ἀνυπόδετος) in rendering שולל (Qere) as 'bare-foot' (Wellhausen, 22; Smith, 32; Weiser, 238; Robinson, 130; Rudolph, 34; Wolff, 9; Hillers, 22), while Vulg. (*spoliatus*) prefers 'despoiled', 'stripped' (so KJV, RSV, REB).

Rashi cites Isa. 59.15 (משתולל) and Ps. 76.6 (אשתוללו), 'whoever shuns evil is thought to be a madman' and 'the stout-hearted are distraught' respectively. שולל (Qere) is taken in the sense of losing the

light of reason (cf. Hillers, 22). At Mic. 1.8 NEB 'naked and distraught'
reverses the word-order of שׁוֹלָל and עָרוֹם. REB ('he makes counsellors
behave like madmen') follows NEB's philology of שׁוֹלָל at Job 12.17
(NEB, 'He makes counsellors behave like idiots'), but, unlike NEB,
does not adopt it at Isa. 59.15 ('and those who shun evil withdraw'), Ps.
76.6 ('the bravest are despoiled') and Mic. 1.8 ('despoiled and naked').
At Isa. 59.15 NEB renders 'and whoever shuns evil is thought a
madman' and at Ps. 76.6 'men that lust for plunder stand aghast'.

אֲנוּשָׁה (v. 9) 'incurable' is rendered by Vulg. as *desperata*, by Pesh. as
kybʾ 'painful' and by Targ. as ממרעה 'terminal'. Sept. has a free
translation which achieves the sense of אֲנוּשָׁה: κατεκράτησαν, the
wound has gained an ascendancy, is beyond healing. The incongruence
between אֲנוּשָׁה and מכותיה (MT) is removed by Sept. (ἡ πληγή αὐτῆς;
מכתה), Vulg. (*plaga eius*), Pesh. (*mḥwth*) and Targ. (מחתה), Wellhausen (133), Smith (35), Robinson (130), and Hillers (22) follow the
versions. 'Her wound' is 'Israel's wound', with 'Israel' = 'all Israel'.
Weiser (238), Rudolph (34) and Wolff (12) read מכת יהוה and suppose
that מכותיה (MT) is a corruption of מכתיה with יה an abbreviation of
יהוה. Rudolph and Wolff then explain the shift from באה to נגע, from
feminine singular to masculine singular, by assuming that מכת יהוה is
the subject of באה and יהוה is the subject of נגע. The choice of באה may
have been influenced by the predicate אֲנוּשָׁה (Wolff).

The problem of lack of agreement between באה and נגע, which is
concealed by Sept. (ἥψατο) and Vulg. (*tetigit*), is repaired by Pesh.
(*qrbt*) and Targ. (קריבת). It is improbable that באה and נגע have
different subjects as Rudolph and Wolff suppose (cf. Hillers, 22).
Weiser, who reads מכת יהוה, assumes that it is subject of both באה and
נגע, but does not indicate any emendation of נגע to נגעה. נגע should be
emended to נגעה with Pesh. and Targ. (Wellhausen, 133). Wellhausen
deletes עד ירושלם at the end of the verse.

Rashi comments on אֲנוּשָׁה 'for it (Judah and Jerusalem) was sick with
its wounds', citing 1 Sam. 12.16, 'and the child was grievously sick'.
Kimchi explains מכותיה (MT): it refers to ailments of different kinds,
those caused by wounds, those by famine and those by pestilence. אֲנוּשָׁה
denotes severe pain and terminal illness. He comments further: 'The
king of Assyria (Sennacherib) advanced against all cities of Judah and
seized them. He came to the gates of Jerusalem (so Targ. בתערי) and it
is Jerusalem which is called the gate of my people, for it is unique in all

the land of Israel to the glory of God who dwells in it,' Ibn Ezra explains אנושה similarly: it is distributive in force and each one of the sicknesses is incurable (dealing with the lack of agreement between it and מכותיה).

MT of v. 10 is, for the most part, plain sailing. בגת אל תגידו is an allusion to 2 Sam. 1.20 (אל תגידו בגת). בית לעפרה, with word-play on עפר, is an unusual form of a place-name, noted by Hillers (25) but adopted in his translation (24) and also in that of Wolff (9). התפלשו (Qere התפלשי) should be read with Sept., Vulg. and Pesh. (Targ. also has a plural imperative, namely, חופו 'cover'). Wellhausen (133), Ehrlich (273), Smith (43), Weiser (238), Robinson (132), Rudolph (34f.), Wolff (12) and Hillers (25) follow the versions. התפלשתי (Kethibh), 'I have sprinkled', is a secondary adjustment which produces word-play with פלשתים 'Philistines' (Wellhausen, 133; Rudolph, 35) and, according to Ibn Ezra, has the effect of making the prophet the speaker.

Sept. has a text which differs from MT in puzzling details. μὴ μεγαλύνεσθε has been thought to point to אל תגדילו (Wolff, 12; Hillers, 25), but it is perhaps unnecessary to conclude that the Greek translator has read a different Hebrew text from MT which should be rendered 'Do not broadcast it in Gath', a sense to which μὴ μεγαλύνεσθε approximates, 'Do not make a big thing of it.' Again the case for emending בכו in order to create a second place-name is not strong, whether οἱ ἐν ᾿Ακιμ (Sept.; ᾿Ακιμ = Akko?) or one which repeats the word-play of גת/תגידו, namely תבכו/בבכא, deleting אל before תבכו (Robinson, 132; cf. Wellhausen, 22, 133 and Ehrlich, 273) or replacing it with אך (Weiser, 238; Wolff, 12). Sept.[OC], which Rudolph (34) holds is secondary, supports בבכא (ἐν βαχειμ, Ziegler, 207).

Rudolph (34) has suggested that either בבית ל or מבית ל (Sept. ἐξ οἴκου) is a prepositional phrase 'within' and this deals with the awkward בבית לעפרה which becomes 'within Aphrah'. Instead of עפרה or לעפרה Sept. has the obscure καταγέλωτα 'derision' and the equally obscure καταγέλωτα ὑμῶν 'your derision' occurs at the end of the verse. To speculate on what Hebrew text may have produced these readings is perhaps an idle occupation, neither חפר nor פער (Rudolph, 34) explains the Greek.

In v. 10a Vulg. reproduces MT and in v. 10b it renders בבית לעפרה

as 'in the house of dust'. Either it does not identify בית לעפרה as a place-name or it conceals this in order to make the word-play explicit, 'in the house of dust sprinkle yourself with dust'. Pesh. reproduces the place-name (*bbyt d'wpr'*), but is no doubt aware of the word-play ('*wpr'/'pr'*). It renders אל תגידו (MT) by *l' taḥdwn* 'do not rejoice' (= תגילו אל; Robinson, 132). Weiser (238) emends בגת to בגנות גלה 'in the gardens of Gilo' in order to achieve word-play between תגילו and גלה. This brings about an antithesis of 'rejoicing' and 'weeping', but it does not capture the nuance of the Hebrew, where 'making public' and 'excess of weeping' contribute to the sense 'keep it dark'. Targ. reproduces MT at v. 10a and v. 10b is a paraphrase, 'You that live in Beth Aphrah cover your head with ashes.'

Rashi's comment on 'Do not tell it in Gath' is 'lest the Philistines rejoice over us' (also Ibn Ezra) and this reveals that he is aware of the provenance of the tag (2 Sam. 1.20). He notices the word-play (עפר/בית לעפרה) and observes that in the language of the lament עפר התפשי (Qere) is the equivalent of עפר התגלגלי 'roll yourself in the dust' (Hillers, 24). Kimchi also notices that the language is that of the קינה and comments, 'The news is so terrible that it should not be spoken of or grieved for' and this takes the right sense of MT. Ibn Ezra comments, 'The prophet laments over Israel and weeps at the vengeance taken by the Philistines and their rejoicing over Israel. There is a tradition that the occasion of the prophecy was the capture of Jerusalem by the Chaldaeans.' He reads התפלשי and remarks that, according to the Kethibh (התפלשתי), the prophet is the speaker.

עברי לכם (v. 11) 'take to the road' is a minus in Sept., but לכם may have some relation to ὑμῶν, an element of καταγέλωτα ὑμῶν which Sept. attaches to v. 10. κατοικοῦσα καλῶς τὰς πόλεις αὐτῆς means something like 'those who inhabit its towns in style', but it is obscure. καλῶς derives from a failure to recognize that שפיר is a place-name. בשת is a minus which is deleted by Smith (43), Weiser (238) and Robinson (132) and emended to תשב by Rudolph (35). τὰς πόλεις αὐτῆς shows that the punctuation of MT has been observed and that עריה has been vocalized as עֶרְיָה. Sept. reads, 'The inhabitants of Zanaan (so Ziegler, 208; Sept.[B] Σεννααρ 'Shinar'?, cf. Gen. 10.10) have not gone out to mourn its adjoining house.' מספד is rendered as an infinitive (κόψασθαι), בית האצל is associated with אצל 'beside' and interpreted as 'adjoining house'. MT מכם has been read as מכה and

rendered as πλήγην ὀδύνης 'a grievous wound'. Hence מכם has been
translated twice in Sept. (Wellhausen, 134) as ἐξ ὑμῶν and as πλήγην
ὀδύνης and MT עמדתו is a minus. Rudolph's attempt (35) to find a
word in the Hebrew text which the Greek translator read, of which
עמדתו is a corruption, is not worthwhile. Among the modern commentators Wolff (12) and Hillers (26) have retained the punctuation of
MT (also KJV and RSV). Hillers translates, 'Pass on, inhabitants of
Shaphir in shameful nakedness.' Wellhausen (22) and Weiser (238)
leave blanks in their translations and Ehrlich (274) gives up the verse as
hopelessly corrupt.

Vulg. renders שפיר *habitatio pulchra* and this may be a word-play on
שפיר (a place), namely, 'fair habitation'. Otherwise, like Sept., it follows
the punctuation of MT and attaches עריה בשת (*confusa ignominia*) to
שפיר ... ערבי. It detects word-play between יצאה and צאנן (*in exitu*),
domus vicina betrays the same connection between בית האצל and אצל
as was found in Sept. and it translates מספד as *planctum* 'lamentation':
planctum domus vicina does not construe. For עמדתו it has *quae stetit
sibimet*, 'one takes from you what is free-standing'.

Pesh. has a different punctuation from MT. It connects עריה בשת
with what follows rather than what precedes and it represents MT as ʿrṭl
npqt wlʾ bhtt, 'The inhabitants of Zanaan have gone out naked and
unashamed.' עברי לכם is rendered as עבדי לך (ʿbdy lky). לך is a
correction of לכם which restores grammatical agreement with עבדי and
עבדי arises from the confusion of ד with ר (cf. Vulgate which secures
agreement [*transite vobis*], and similarly Targ. [עברו לכון], by making
both imperative and suffix plural). שפיר (špyr), צאנן (sʾn), and בית האעל
(byt ʾwṣl) are identified as places and מספד בית האצל is given as
mrqwdtʾ dbyt ʾwṣl—a defective clause. *tsb mnkwn mḥwth* for
יקח מכם עמדתו is difficult to make out, but *tsb* in conjunction with
mnkwn can only represent the third feminine singular imperfect (תקח)
and *mḥwth* represents מכתה, 'she receives from you her wound' or 'it
receives from you its wound'. This makes poor sense. מכם has
apparently been translated twice by Pesh. (*mnkwn* and *mḥwth*; so Sept.)
and יקח has been read as תקח. עמדתו is a minus.

Targ. reads, 'Take to the road, inhabitants of Shapir, who go into
exile naked, stripped and ashamed. The inhabitants of Zanaan do not
go out as those who have been delivered. Make bitter mourning for
those of your heroes who were slain, O Beth Ezel. Your desirable houses

were seized and joined together, whether in separate expropriations(?), whether when the best parts of your land were taken from you.' The punctuation of MT is kept and there are two extensive paraphrases of מספד בית האצל and יקח מכם עמדתו.

Rashi, who punctuates as MT, notices the mixture of singular (עברי) and plural (מכם) and explains עברי as collective (the town is an entity), while the prophet is addressing individual members (לכם) of the community (also Wolff, 12). עריה בשת refers to those who went into exile (also Targ.). Rashi comments on לא יצאה ישבת צאנן: 'They will not go out as those who have been delivered' (likewise Targ.). On מספד he remarks, 'The mourning was decreed for the loot which was taken and for the land which was seized, the adding of house to house, field to field, one thing and another.' On יקח מכם עמדתו he comments, 'The foundations of the buildings which you put up and established on your land.' He takes עמדתו as 'foundations' and this recalls the sense which Robinson (132) achieves by emending מספד to מוסד and מכם to מכון: 'The foundations of Beth Ezel are no more, the ground on which it stood.' Kimchi notices the word-play between שׁפיר 'beautiful' and Shaphir (a place name), 'They were עריה בשת because they went into exile.' He makes the same point as Rashi about עברי לכם and assumes that both צאנן and בית האצל involve word-play, without indicating how it works. Ibn Ezra identifies שׁפיר, צאנן and בית האצל as the names of towns and he also links עריה בשת with exile and bondage as Targ., Rashi and Kimchi do.

Weiser (238) follows Duhm in emending עברי לכם to העבירו שופר לכם, 'Give a blast on the trumpet' and a variant of this is הריעו שופר (Robinson, 132). עריה is emended by Weiser and Robinson to מעירה which is connected with לא יצאה, 'The inhabitants of Zanaan have not gone out of their city.' בוש is deleted. An alternative emendation of עריה is עירה an accusative of place 'in their city' (Rudolph, 35; Brockington, 255). Weiser and Robinson depart from the punctuation of MT as do Rudolph, NEB and REB. Rudolph (35) emends בשת to תשב, 'The inhabitants of Zanaan remain in their city, they do not go out (from it)', and מספד בית האצל into a nominal clause (also NEB and REB), 'Beth Ezel is a place of lamentation'. Rudolph emends מכם to ממך and עמדתו to עמדתך 'One takes away from you your support' or 'Your support is taken away from you.' NEB and REB retain בשת, 'Have not the people of Zanaan gone out in shame from their city?' Wolff (9, 12f.) and Hillers (24) keep the punctuation of MT and Wolff the text of MT. Hillers (26) inserts ספדי before מספד ('Make mourning') and emends עמדתו to חמדתך, 'he takes away your treasures'. The emendation does not improve the sense. NEB and REB 'she can lend you support no longer' is an idiomatic transformation of 'one takes away from you its support'.

Sept. has τίς for כי (v. 12) and ἤρξατο εἰς ἀγαθά for חלה לטוב, but 'Who has begun with respect to good things'? is obscure. For MT לשער Sept. gives εἰς πύλας (לשערי), and ὀδύνας 'pain' may be either an indication that מרות is not identified as a place-name or else it is word-play on מרות (מרר 'to be bitter').

Vulg. derives חלה (infirmata) from חלה 'to be sick' and translates MT quia infirmata est in bonum, a, more or less, literal rendering. quae habitat in amaritudinibus 'who dwell in bitterness' is a rendering of ישבת מרות, 'For those who dwell in bitterness have no energy for what is good.' in amaritudinibus like ὀδύνας may be a word-play on מרות or an indication that it is not recognized as a place-name. in portam reproduces MT לשער. Rudolph (36) concludes that Sept., Vulg. and Pesh. do not identify מרות as a place. Perhaps they do without explicitly playing on it.

Pesh. (mṭl d'tkrht ltbʾ), like Vulg. derives חלה from חלה 'to be sick' and for ישבת מרות has ʾmwrtʾ dmrrt, a construction identical with that of Sept. mrrt probably has the sense 'bitterness', though it can denote 'poison', 'snake venom' in Syriac. With trʿyh dʾwršlm Pesh. and Targ. (בתרעי ירושלם) follow Sept. and some modern commentators have made this emendation (Wellhausen, 134; Weiser, 238; Rudolph, 36; Hillers, 24). Rudolph explicates MT (לשער) as a haplography of yodh and and Wolff (13) accounts for Sept. as a dittography of yodh.

Targ.'s paraphrase continues v. 12: 'whoever was living in the best of the land and was expecting good, refused to return to the Law, to which you are subject; hence evil came down from Yahweh to enter the gates of Jerusalem'. The most significant textual point is that Targ. apparently represents חלה לטוב as יחלה לטוב (ומסברא לטב), 'and was expecting good'. This has been influential. Rashi glosses חלה with קותה (cf. Kimchi's comment) and modern scholars have emended חלה to מיחלה or יחלה, 'the inhabitants of Marot expected good' (Wellhausen, 134; Smith, 43; Weiser, 238; Robinson, 132; Rudolph, 35f.; Wolff, 13;

Hillers, 26). Weiser and Robinson substitute אך for כי and Rudolph and Wolff מי (Sept. τίς). KJV's translation is 'For the inhabitant of Maroth waited carefully for good' (similarly RSV).

Rashi comments, 'They hoped for (קותה = חלה) good, but because of מרותה evil came down on them.' מרותה is presumably 'their rebellion' *ex* מרה, though I have not found evidence that there is a form מרות 'rebellion'. If I take Rashi correctly, the word play is on the place name מרות and מרות 'rebellion'. Kimchi derives חלה from חיל 'to writhe' (also Ibn Ezra) and links it with 'pain'. It is another item of the vocabulary of the lament. The inhabitants of Maroth were committing evil and yet experienced good. He identifies Marot as a place; it will suffer, because of the good times it enjoyed. Ibn Ezra draws a distinction between מרות (a place—a proper noun) and a common noun which has a sense—which denotes.

Wellhausen (134) discerns further word-play in v. 12, in the circumstance that מרות and ירושלם are joined to fates which are the antitheses of their names. Marot ('bitterness' expects 'good' and Jerusalem (שלום 'peace', 'prosperity') experiences 'evil'. Ehrlich (274) emends חלז לטוב to חלה למות 'sick unto death', 'mortally sick' (2 Kgs 20.1). According to Hillers (24) the first כי is asseverative ('surely') and the second is to be rendered 'yet'. REB (cf. NEB) translates v. 12, 'The people of Maroth are in the depths of despair, for disaster from the Lord has come down to the gates of Jerusalem' and this nuance of חלה לטוב deserves serious consideration. The meaning of the phrase is that the inhabitants of Marot are in such low spirits, so sick with despair, that they cannot entertain the hope of well-being and prosperity. Hillers' (24) proposal that טוב has the sense 'sweet' is cogent only if the emendation יחלה לטוב is adopted. It produces the antithesis of sweetness and bitterness (מרות *ex* מרר) and there is no difficulty in taking טוב as 'sweet' (*BDB*, 373; Driver, *CML*[1], 151; Von Soden, 3, 1377–8).

Both Sept. (ψόφος) and Vulg. (*tumultus*) render רתם (v. 13) as 'din' (Rudolph, 36, = נהם?). Sept gives ψόφος ἁρμάτων καὶ ἱππευόντων 'din of chariots and horses' for רתם המרכבה לרכש and Vulg. *Tumultus quadrigae stuporis habitanti Lachis*, 'The bewildering din of chariots is the lot of the inhabitants of Lachish', is further removed from MT. *stuporis* represents לרכש and *habitanti Lachis* יושבת לכיש (vocative)

with which Sept. (Swete and Ziegler) opens a new sentence. Pesh. has
pgdt for רתם of which יושבת לכיש is the subject, 'The inhabitants of
Lachish have harnessed the horses to the chariots.' Targ. fills out MT,
'Prepare (טקיסו) the chariots for war; attach them (רמו על) to the
horses, O inhabitants of Lachish.'

The punctuation of Sept. (a new sentence at κατοικοῦσα Λαχεὶς)
indicates that ראשית (ἀρχηγός) is to be attached to יושבת לכיש not
המרכבה לרכש and NEB, with MT's punctuation, so translates:
'Harness the steeds to the chariot, O people of Lachish, for you first led
the daughter of Zion into sin.' Vulg. renders ראשית as *principium* and is
to be rendered rather as 'It (horses and chariots) is the major sin of the
daughter of Zion.' Pesh. and Targ. probably maintain MT's punctuation and their renderings of ראשית, *rš* and ריש respectively, point to
'first' in the sense of 'principal' and attach it to horses and chariots
(Wellhausen, 22 'arch-sin'; Wolff, 10 'main part').

Vulg., Pesh. and Targ. agree in this respect against Sept. The final
motive clause, 'for the sins of Israel are found in you' is a reference to
the reliance on military power (המרכבה לרכש).

Rashi glosses רתם as אסרי and comments, 'Yoke the chariots to the
horses, for they can go fast and you will escape' (cf. Kimchi, 'רכש is an
animal which moves at speed'). Kimchi likewise gives אסר as an
equivalent of רתם and guesses from the context (לפי מקום) that
ראשית חטאת means 'principal sin' and is an allusion to Baal worship
which Lachish learned from the northern kingdom (ישראל) and
introduced to Judah, even to Zion. Ibn Ezra notices the lack of
grammatical agreement between רתם (for which he suggests רתמי) and
יושבת לכיש. Ehrlich (274) also remarks on this incongruence which he
removes by vocalizing רתם as רְתֹם, an infinitive absolute with the force
of an imperative (also Weiser, 238; Robinson, 132; Rudolph, 36;
Wolff, 13; Hillers, 27). Ehrlich describes רתם, which is a *hapax
legomenon* (*BDB*, 958) as 'obscure' and Wellhausen (22) leaves a blank
in his translation.

Kimchi's equation of ראשית חטאת with Baal worship imported from
the northern kingdom has been noticed and this is an indication that
ישראל has been taken as denoting particularly 'Samaria' (Weiser, 242)
rather than 'all Israel' (Ehrlich, 274; Rudolph, Wolff and Hillers assume
that ישראל is an equivalent of 'Judah'). Hence Kimchi does not associate
ראשית חטאת with the acquisition and show of military equipment,

whereas Ehrlich discerns a connection between המרכבה לרכש and ראשית חטאת and between both and פשעי ישראל (a reference to Judah's parade of weaponry). Ehrlich has given another reason for not making ראשית ... ציון continuous with כי ... ישראל, namely that the transition from היא to בך is decisive: היא resumes המרכבה לרכש and כי בך begins a direct address to יושבת לכיש.

Wellhausen (134) agrees that היא would more naturally be referred to the horses and chariots which are frequently described as Israel's deadly sin were it not for the following כי clause which attaches ראשית חטאת to יושבת לכיש. He discusses the question whether פשעי ישראל is an allusion to the sins of the northern kingdom and rejects the idea (also Smith, 48). He holds that the distinction between the northern kingdom and Judah is not maintained in Amos and Hosea and that in Micah 3.14–15 ישראל denotes Judah which is Micah's practice elsewhere. Ehrlich (274) had noticed that 'horses and chariots' are linked with Lachish (2 Chron. 11.9) in the time of Rehoboam before the division of the kingdom and that such garrison towns (ערי הרכב; ערי מרכבות, 2 Kgs 9.19) were established by Solomon.

Weiser (241), Robinson (133), Rudolph (36), Wolff (13) and Hillers (27) discern a play on words between לרכש and לכיש. Weiser (238), Robinson (132), Rudolph (36) and Hillers (24) translate ראשית as 'beginning' ('You are the beginning of sin for the daughter of Zion'). Weiser differs from the others in equating ישראל with the northern kingdom rather than Judah and Smith (47), Weiser (242), Robinson (133) Rudolph (44, 48) and Wolff (18f.) identify v. 13b as secondary. A threat of judgement is out of place in the context of a lament and Weiser supposes that v. 13b is a continuation of the threat against Samaria in vv. 6–7 (ישראל = Samaria). The 'beginning' of Jerusalem's sin is illustrated by the presence of horses and chariots, taken over from the northern kingdom, in Lachish. This is the sense of the secondary v. 13b when it is accommodated to v. 13a.

Rudolph (36) eases the transition from היא to בך by inserting אַתְּ before היא and so makes v. 13b into an address to יושבת לכיש: ראשית חטאת means 'the beginning of punishment' and the punishment of Lachish is an intimation of what will be meted out to בת ציון. 'For in you are found the sins of Judah (ישראל)' refers to the concentration of military power, the evidence of reliance on the arm of the flesh (47). The addition in v. 13b makes the point that Jerusalem will be the next to be punished. Wolff (19) similarly identifies v. 13b as a commentary on v. 13a. It contains neither word-play nor a cry of distress and its function is to expose the sin of the daughter of Zion.

Neither Sept. nor Vulg. (v. 14) follows the punctuation of MT (*athnach* at גת). Sept. places בתי אכזיב in apposition with מורשת גת and then construes לאכזב למלכי ישראל as a nominal clause (Ziegler, 208, prefers ἐγένετο to Sept.[B] ἐγένοντο). Thus 'the possession of Gath' is explicated as οἴκους ματαίους 'senseless houses' and this is followed by 'They have been a vanity to the kings of Israel.' Vulg., with *domus mendacii* 'house of falsehood' for בתי אכזיב, also takes it as an epithet of מורשת גת rather than a second place-name, but it extends the apposition to the end of the verse, 'the house of falsehood which has deceived the kings of Israel'. Hence neither Sept. nor Vulg. identifies אכזיב or בית אכזיב as a place-name.

שלוחים 'marriage gift' (1 Kgs 9.16) is not rendered by either Sept. (ἐξαποστελλομένους) or Vulg. (*emissarios*) as 'a parting gift' or 'a dowry'. Sept. 'Therefore he (δώσει) will give those who are being sent out as far as (על = ἕως) the inheritance of Gath' is obscure. Vulg. also takes שלוחים as masculine plural, 'Therefore he will post (*dabit*) spies (to keep surveillance) over the inheritance of Gath'. *emissarios*, if it is a survival of the Old Latin, may be a translation of ἐξαποστελλομένους and a clue to the sense of Sept. If there is word-play, it is between Moresheth as a place name and מורשת 'inheritance' (also Pesh. *yrtwt*; Targ. מחסני).

Pesh., 'Therefore you will grant a release (*šwbqn*) to (MT על = *l*) the inheritance of Gath' or 'You will sever relations with the inheritance of Gath.' Pesh. renders בתי אכזיב ... ישראל as a nominal clause, 'The houses of deceit were a source of deceit to the kings of Israel.' Since Pesh. does not show 'the houses of deceit' in apposition to מורשת גת, it may be a second place name with word-play. Targ., with קורבין 'offerings' for שלוחים 'gifts', captures the sense of the Hebrew and interprets 'houses of Achzib' as a reference to the land of Judah. Otherwise it paraphrases MT· 'Therefore you will send offerings to the inheritances of Gath. The houses of Achzib will be given up to the Gentile nations, because of the sins of idolatry which the kings of Israel perpetrated with them.' Achzib is identified as a place name and לאכזב has a double interpretation: it is a surrender of Achzib to the Gentile nations and it is the practice of idolatry by the kings of Israel.

It is not clear that Targ. is indicating word-play between אכזיב and
לאכזב.

According to Rashi, 'the houses of Achzib' is an allusion to the land
of Judah (Targ.) which defected to Pekah, son of Remaliah, (king
of northern Israel) and played false with the house of Ahaz (king of
Judah). Thus 'kings of Israel' = 'kings of Judah'. Kimchi renders
לכן תתני ... גת as 'For you give offerings to (אל = על) Moresheth-Gath'
and comments, 'For you serve idols (cf. Targ.) and you teach others to
supply the needs of idolatry and to give offerings in Philistine country.'
He notices the word-play between מורשת and 'inheritance' (ירושה) and
remarks that, now enemies have occupied מורשת, Judah makes gifts (he
cites 1 Kgs 9.16) to secure its help. אכזיב is a town in Judah (Targ. and
Rashi) and לאכזב is a play on it which alludes to the manufacture of
idols (Targ.) in the houses of Achzib. Kimchi comments that when
ישראל is used of all Israel, as it is here, it includes Judah and so 'kings of
Israel' = 'kings of Judah'. Ibn Ezra glosses שלוחים with מנחות 'gifts',
'offerings' and identifies מורשת גת as a place in Philistine territory. Gifts
were made to it to secure its help (Kimchi). Ibn Ezra cites an opinion
that בית אכזיב is a town in Judah and discerns word-play between אכזיב
and לאכזב, noting the prosthetic *aleph* in both. בית אכזיב (MT
בתי אכזיב) was a broken reed in Judah's time of need.

Wellhausen (22, 134) translates גת as a vocative and so Moresheth
and Gath are different places: 'Therefore, take your leave of Moresheth,
O Gath.' That there is word-play between מורשת and מארשת 'bride' is
indicated by שולחים, yielding the alternative translation: 'You must take
leave of the bride, O Gath.' The second half of the verse is rendered as a
nominal clause, 'The houses of Achzib have become a source of deceit
to the kings of Israel.' Achzib is a Judaean town (so Rudolph, 36; Wolff,
33; Hillers, 27) and ישראל = Judah (according with Micah's practice,
Mic. 3.1, 8, 9, Wolff, 33). Moresheth is a different place from מרשה (v.
15).

Ehrlich (274) vocalizes תתני as תִּתְּנִי and supposes that Lachish is
addressed: 'Therefore you (Lachish) will be given as a dowry to
Moresheth Gath' (cf. Smith, 'Thou (Lachish) givest a parting-gift to
Moresheth Gath' [41, 48]) Moresheth Gath had passed into the
possession of a non-Israelite people (Ehrlich) and the anticipated loss of
Lachish is expressed as a figure of the marriage between Lachish (the
bride) and Moresheth Gath. ישראל is 'all Israel' and here Judah. Ehrlich

emends מלך ישראל to מלכי ישראל 'the king of Judah' (Smith, 44; Weiser, 238; Robinson, 132) and בתי אכזיב is explained on the assumption that בתי is an allusion to two towns with the name בית אכזיב, one in northern Israel (Josh. 19.29) and the other in Judah (Josh. 15.44). Hebrew does not form plurals of proper names and בית appears as a plural in order to indicate that there are two Beth Achzibs.

Weiser (238) emends לכן תתני to לָךְ נִתְּנוּ, 'To you has been given a farewell present (שלוחים, 1 Kgs 9.16), O Moresheth Gath.' על arises from the erroneous תתני and is to be deleted. בתי אכזיב is to be rendered 'houses of Achzib' (Wolff, 10; Hillers, 27). Wolff (32) identifies these with workshops in which royal pottery was made, so that the loss of Achzib would incommode Davidic kings. Robinson (132) emends תתני to יְתְּנוּ . על to ל, and בתי to בית (Rudolph, 37). He explains שלוחים as 'letter of divorce': 'Therefore they will give a letter of divorce to Moresheth Gath.' He translates אכזב as *Trugbach* 'a stream which runs dry' (cf. Kimchi אכזב מים; Weiser, 238; Rudolph, 36; Hillers, 24, 'a dry watercourse') and emends למלכי to למלך.

At לכן Rudolph postulates a dittograph of the ל of ישראל (v. 13) and emends it to כֵן. He changes תתני to תִּתְּנוּ (a general address) and על is an equivalent of אל: 'With reason you must give a parting gift to Moresheth Gath. Beth Akzib (reading בית) has become as a stream which has run dry for the kings of Israel' (= 'kings of Judah'). Wolff (13) emends תתני to יִתֵּן or יִתְּנוּ and על to אל, 'A parting gift is to be given to Moresheth Gath. The buildings of Achzib are a source of deceit to the kings of Israel' (= 'kings of Judah', 32). Hillers (27) retains MT תתני and supposes that Zion is being addressed. He renders שלוחים as 'dowry' (Ehrlich) and discerns word-play between מורשת and מארשת 'betrothed', 'bride'. Why should Zion give a dowry to Moresheth Gath? Is the 'daughter of Zion' the bride? Word-play between מורשת and מארשת can be postulated even if שלוחים is rendered as 'farewell gift' (Weiser, Rudolph, Wolff) rather than 'dowry' (Ehrlich, Hillers). It becomes word-play of a different and more grisly kind if שלוחים is taken as 'letter of divorce' (Robinson): not a wedding-present but the unexpected shock of a letter of divorce.

Moresheth Gath is explained by Weiser (242) and Wolff (32) as 'daughter city of Gath' and Hillers (27) has suggested that the proximity of Moresheth to Gath may be indicated—Gath is part of its 'postal address'. Weiser (242), Rudolph (48) and Wolff (32), who notice the word-play מארשת/מורשת, note that the 'parting-gift' (שלוחים) is given, not in connection with the final departure of a bride from her family, but as a present to a place which will be lost to Judah and whose inhabitants will go into exile.

Sept.[B] ἀγάγωσιν (v. 15) and τους κληρόνομους, 'Until (ἕως = עַד; MT עֹד) they bring the possessors (or 'dispossessors') differs from MT אבי לך (=אביא) and הירש, 'I shall yet bring the possessor (or 'dispossessor') to you'. It is unlikely that ἀγάγωσιν is a deliberate avoidance of the first person because it does not suit the context. Rather it is a scribal error for ἀγάγω σοι (Sept[Qmg, L]) which is adopted by Ziegler (208) and represents MT. Λαχείς is a puzzling plus as is κληρονομία. Smith (44) explains Λαχείς as a dittography of לך and the first two consonants of ישבת. כבוד ישרלא is given as ἡ δόξα τῆς θυγατρὸς Ἰσραήλ, 'the glory of the daughter of Israel'. 'Daughter of Israel' is an unusual expression and 'daughter of Zion' ('daughter of Jerusalem') appears in some Greek manuscripts (Ziegler, 209). Both occurrences of עד are vocalized as עַד (ἕως), whereas MT has עֹד followed by עַד, 'until the daughter of Israel will come to Adullam'.

Vulg. reproduces MT with adhuc (עֹד), adducam tibi, usque ad (עַד) and veniet gloria Israel. Pesh., like Targ., shows עֹד (twb; Targ. עוד) and עַד ('dm' l; Targ. עַד). Pesh represents MT עד עדלם by 'dm' l'lm 'for evermore' and עד עדלם יבוא כבוד ישראל is rendered as 'the glory of Israel will be in the ascendant (n'l') for evermore'. 'I shall yet bring to you an heir' becomes 'There will yet be an heir to you' or 'You will yet have an heir' and the construction of Targ. (עוד איתי) is the same as that of Pesh. Targ.'s paraphrase offers a similar sense for עד עדלם יבוא כבוד ישראל as Pesh., but retains MT עדלם: 'As far as Adullam the borders of the land of Israel will extend and grow.' Hence, since v. 15b contains a promise, it is probable that v. 15a is similarly interpreted by Pesh. and Targ. and that it is thought to contain the promise of an heir (הירש; Pesh. yrwt'; Targ. מחסנין 'heirs').

Rashi, however, belies this interpretation of Pesh. and Targ., since he glosses הירש (v. 15a) as 'the enemies who will dispossess you'—a threat, whereas he interprets v. 15b as a promise like Pesh. and Targ.: Adullam, once the border of Israel, will become the border again. Israel will overcome the idolaters and its territory will extend as far as Adullam. He notices the word-play between הירש and מרשה, as does Kimchi, but

לשון נפל על הלשון (Rashi and Kimchi) probably refers only to a play on similar sounding words (Kimchi, קרובים בלשון; Weiser, 242 'assonance'; Hillers, 28) rather than to an etymological play, a claim that ירש and מרשה are derived from ירש and are linked in sense (so Smith, 49; Wolff, 10, 33).

Kimchi departs from Pesh., Targ. and Rashi in supposing that v. 15 is entirely threatening. On v. 15a he comments, 'I shall bring to you an enemy who will possess your land and exile you from it'. Mareshah and Adullam are identified with Judaean towns and he remarks 'as far as Adullam will come a possessor of the land of Israel'. The ירש is Sennacherib who advanced on all the fortified cities of Judah and took them (2 Kgs 18.13). The entire verse is a threat. Ibn Ezra equates הירש with האויב and appears to agree with Kimchi that the verse has a threatening aspect throughout.

Wellhausen (134f.) vocalizes both occurrences of עד as עֵד on the ground that הירש is a place-name or the corruption of a place-name corresponding to עדלם. The point which he makes is somewhat blunted by his admission that the sense of v. 15b, and especially עד עדלם is impenetrable.

Ehrlich (275) questions the appropriateness of the first person (א)אבי (v. 15a). In a lament which encloses a threat Yahweh should not be the speaker and so a first person verb offends against the context. Ehrlich emends (א)אבי to יבוא (also Weiser, 239; Robinson, 132; Rudolph, 37; Wolff, 13) whose subject is הירש. יבוא[2] has the same subject and כבוד ישראל is in apposition with עדלם (also Robinson, 132): the dispossessor will penetrate as far as Adullam, the glory of Israel.

Smith (41; Weiser, 239) emends עד עדלם to עד עולם (Pesh.) and Weiser translates v. 15a as a question which requires a negative answer. 'Will an heir yet (MT עֹד) come to you?' receives the reply 'The glory of Israel has perished (יבוא emended to אבד) for all time coming.' Robinson (132) vocalizes עד as עֹד (MT) and renders, 'Once more the dispossessor will come to you, O people of Mareshah.' עֹד[2] is deleted and יבוא[2] emended to יאבד (also Smith, 44), 'Adullam perishes, the glory of Israel.

Rudolph (37) interprets both v. 15a and v. 15b as a threat (Kimchi), 'The dispossessor will come to you, O people of Maresheth' emends אבי to יבוא, but his translation of v. 15b is novel and is reached by a process which Hillers (28) describes as 'fantastic'. Rudolph connects his translation, 'The glory of Israel approximates to Adullam', with a folk etymology of עד עדלם יבוא. עדלם was analysed as עד לים and עד לים יבוא taken as 'The glory of Israel is submerged in the sea'—is irrecoverably sunk. 2 Sam. 23.19 ועד השלשה לא בא, 'but he did not rival the three' (NEB, REB) is cited in support (49).

Wolff (13, 33) holds that עדלם is a historical allusion and a reference to David's hiding-place in the cave of Adullam when his fortunes were at a low ebb (1 Sam. 22.1)—a possibility rejected by Rudolph (49) on the ground that מערה is absent from the text. The sense of v. 15b is then that the glory of Israel has been reduced to a hole in the ground, where David concealed himself *in extremis* from his enemies. The Davidic kings in Jerusalem will be reduced to a flight whose outcome will be a humiliation as great as David's concealment in the cave of Adullam. Wolff conjectures that עד may indicate that there had been an earlier enemy invasion and is a threat that it will be renewed.

Hillers (24, 28) retains MT throughout (Smith, 44 also retains אביא) and describes v. 15b as 'lexically impeccable', though the concession that it 'defies explanation' (Smith, 52) apparently causes him no exegetical concern.

Micah 1.16 is a general summons to engage in mourning for the 'beloved sons' (תענוגיך), the inhabitants of the towns which had been ravaged, who had been carried off as prisoners. Sept. has ἐμπλάτυνον τὴν χηρείαν σου, 'Make your widowhood wide', perhaps 'Display your widowhood', that is, as a sign of mourning. Sept. apparently fixes on the widow as the typical mourner (cf. Hillers, 28) and the state of widowhood as characteristically sorrowful. Schleusner (Ziegler, 209) conjectures that χηρείαν should be replaced by κουρείαν 'shearing', 'Cut your hair very short' and Rudolph's κουράν gives the same sense. Rudolph's objection to κουρείαν is that the word is not attested in Greek. Vulg. reproduces MT.

For קרחי וגזי Pesh. has *mrwty wgwzy* 'Tear out (your hair) and cut (it) off' and Targ., similarly, תלישי ורמא, 'Tear out (your hair) and cast it away (?)'. Targ. paraphrases הרחיבי קרחתך כנשר as 'Like an eagle (or vulture) whose feathers have fallen out, so pluck out all your hair.' Wellhausen (22), Weiser (239), Robinson (132), Rudolph (37), Wolff (13), NEB and REB have 'vulture'. G. R. Driver's proposal that ראשך should be inserted after גזי, which is dismissed by Rudolph (37), should be compared with Targ.'s אסגא מרט ברישיך for הרחיבי קרחתך.

Rashi explains קרחי וגזי differently from Pesh. and Targ. To קרחי he appends the comment רושך and to גזי the comment שערך: 'Make your head bald and cut off your hair.' Kimchi supposes that the command קרחי וגזי is made either to Mareshah and Adullam or to Judah as a whole (Wellhausen, 133) and Ibn Ezra's remark is that the shearing of hair—a sign of mourning—is urged on city after city. קרחה, according to Kimchi, is the pulling out of the hair (agreeing with Pesh. and Targ.).

Ehrlich (275) holds that shearing of the head is not a sign of mourning (*contra* Ibn Ezra), and that the severe cutting of the hair does not produce baldness. Hence קרחי וגזי means 'Make yourself bald by tearing out your hair' and גזי, here as at Job 1.20, refers to the pulling out of the hair which produces baldness. גזז is never used of the shearing of the head and the beard, גלה is the word for that. But גזז is given by *BDB* (159) and KB[3] (179) as 'shear' at Mic. 1.16 and Job 20.1 and קרחי וגזי should be translated 'Shave (your head) and cut off your hair' (so Rashi; NEB [REB], 'Shave the hair from your head in mourning').

Rudolph (37) conjectures that קרית דוד 'city of David' is omitted by haplography at the beginning of v. 16 (cf. Weiser, 239, who inserts בת ציון after וגזי; cf. Wolff, 14, בת יהודה). Wolff (239) is influenced by the plus θυγατρός (בת) at Sept. v. 15 whose correct position is thought to be at the beginning of v. 16.

Word-Play

Word-play or assonance are too general terms with which to describe the literary devices which are used in Mic. 1.10–15. These are not occupied, for the most part, in establishing etymological connections between similar sounding words, though Wolff's translation (9–10) creates this impression for צאנן/יצאה, *Ausbach* (v. 11), לכיש/לרכש, *Spannburg* (v. 13), מורשת/מורשת, *Besitz* (v. 14) and מרשה/הירש, *Besitzstadt* (v. 15). The principal distinction which has to be made is a play on words which involves both sound and sense and a play which involves only sound and a majority of the cases in 1.10–15 fall under the latter. The form of words used by Rashi and Kimchi describe assonance, word-play founded on a similarity of sound, and support this statement. Kimchi's phrases are לשון נפל על הלשון and קרובים בלשון (vv. 11, 13, 15). Rashi uses לשון נפל על הלשון in respect of מרשה/הירש (v. 15).

There are two kinds of exception to this classification, where the word-play rests on both sound and sense and where it rests on sense and not sound. The first is represented by עפר/בית לעפרה (v. 10) and אכזב/בתי אכזיב (v. 14), the second by מרות/לטוב (v. 12) and שׁפיר/ עריה בשׁת (v. 11). For the first pair Wolff is justified in rendering *Staubhausen/Staub* and *Trugstadt/Betrug*, since the author's intention was probably to play on both sense and sound. Wolff (33) holds that his intention was the same with מרשׁה/הירשׁ and it not clear how far Rudolph (48) is disagreeing with him when he says that the etymology (both derived from ירשׁ) is false (cf. Hillers, 28). This could mean that either the author relied on a false etymology or that he did not intend to establish any etymological connection.

The second pair in vv. 11 and 12 have no element of assonance but have an antithetic relation of sense expressed so sharply that it is a kind of play: not beauty but shame and not goodness (or 'sweetness', Hillers, 26) but bitterness. Rashi comments בית הבשׁת כאשׁר נקרתה שׁפיר, 'house of shame just as it was called beautiful' and Kimchi remarks, 'Instead of being beautiful they have been transformed into צריה בשׁת, for they have gone into exile.'

חגידו and גת (v. 10aα) may be a calculated assonance, but the principal question to be asked is whether the pattern of v. 10aα is repeated in v. 10aβ. There is no doubt that Sept. supposed that it was (ὅι ἐν Γεθ; ὅι ἐν Ἀκείμ), but Ἀκείμ = Akko is not in the right geographical area and, on the strength of 'ἐν βαχείμ (Ziegler, 207), Wellhausen (133) has conjectured בבכים for בכו—a place-name whose location he does not indicate. Ehrlich (273) also holds that v. 10aβ was a pun similar to that of v. 10aα and that כו is a corrupt place-name introduced by ב. Smith (42) and Robinson have emended בכו to בכא (accusative of place, cf. Ps. 84.4) which, according to Hillers (25) is 'possibly near Jerusalem'. Rudolph (34), Wolff (12) and Hillers (25) have set their faces against this search for a place-name and for the continuation of assonance in v. 10aβ by adhering to the dictum that a half-verse should contain only one place-name, but 'Do not circulate it in Gath, do not weep in—' is attractive, the blank being filled with a place-name which plays on תבכו.

In v. 14 there is, according to Wolff (10), word-play between מורשׁת, a place-name, and מורשׁ, a common noun meaning 'possession' (*Besitz*) or 'inheritance'. מורשׁת גת 'possession of Gath' describes מורשׁת

as a satellite of Gath whose location is fixed with reference to the larger
city, so that Moresheth Gath is a kind of 'postal address'. Moresheth
and Gath are shown as two separate locations on Hillers' diagrammatic
map (29), with Moresheth Gath due south of Gath. If this is the correct
elucidation of מורשת גת, מורשת is to be correlated with המרשתי (1.1)
and is Micah's home town. The other places mentioned in vv. 10–15,
in so far as they can be identified (Hillers, 25–28) are located in the
Shephelah, in the area around Moresheth.

Rashi and Kimchi explain the name מורשת גת differently. They
connect it with David's capture of Gath from the Philistines (1 Chron.
18.1) and his giving it as an 'inheritance' to Israelite settlers. Rashi
comments, 'The kingdom of David caused you to inherit Gath and you
(Lachish?, cf. Ehrlich, 274) give שלוחים to it'. Rashi, Kimchi and Ibn
Ezra suppose that מורשת גת is the name of one place and that Gath
acquired the sobriquet מורשת when it was taken by David from the
Philistines and given to the Israelites by him.

The other play discerned in v. 14 is that of מארשת/מורשת and
שלוחים is then explained as a 'wedding-present' or 'dowry' (Wellhausen,
134; Ehrlich, 274; Weiser, 242; Robinson, 133; Rudolph, 48; Wolff,
32; Hillers, 27). According to Ehrlich, Lachish will be given (תתני) as a
dowry to (אל = על) Moresheth Gath, that it to say, Moresheth Gath
has passed into the hands of non-Israelites and this state of affairs is
figured as a marriage between Moresheth Gath and its new possessor.
Lachish gives a dowry to the bride, that is, Lachish is about to suffer the
same fate as Moresheth Gath. If תתני is emended to יתנו (Rudolph, 36),
and v. 14 treated as a general address ('they will give' equivalent to 'will
be given'), the sense is the same, except that the reference to Lachish
disappears: the capture of Moresheth Gath is represented as a marriage
between the place and its new owner, so that the bride receives a dowry
or a wedding-present. Wellhausen (22) takes גת as a vocative: Gath is
required to give a wedding-present to the bride (מארשת/מורשת),
'Therefore you will give a wedding-present to the bride, O Gath'
(134).

Mic. 1.10–15 does not sit easily with the high moral seriousness of
the remainder of chapters 1–3 which are usually attributed to the
prophet Micah. The prophet of doom is not easily reconciled with the
man of letters who engages in elaborate literary decoration and throws
off puns in verse after verse. Verses 8–16 are, however, a lament and the

question arises whether the difference in style has a connection with the
genre. Chapters 1–3 consist otherwise of indictments and threats
uttered by a prophet of doom. Was word-play a convention in the
context of the lament? Was it thought to add pathos or power to it, to
magnify the dimensions of the catastrophe which was being lamented?
Kimchi refers at intervals in his comments on vv. 8–16 to the special
vocabulary of the lament; he does not, however, connect these particularly with paronomasia or word-play. There is something Gilbertian in
suggesting that literary fun, playing with words, was admitted as a
fitting convention for a lament, but the question begged is whether it
was simply employed as a show of skill and verve or whether it was
thought to make a more serious contribution to the effectiveness of the
lament. It may have had functions whose identity we can no longer
confidently recover; it may have been intended to create effects which
are beyond our ken.

8.   This is why I lament and wail,
       go about despoiled and naked.
       I howl like a jackal
       and make mourning cries like an ostrich.
9.   Her wound[1] will not heal,
       for it has reached Judah;
       it has arrived[2] at the gate of my people;
       it has come as far as Jerusalem.
10. Do not broadcast it in Gath;
       Do not weep extravagantly;
       in Beth Aphrah[3] roll yourselves[4] in dust.
11. Take to the road, inhabitants of Shaphir, naked and in shame!
       Have not the inhabitants of Zanaan been expelled?
       Beth Ezel is a place of mourning;
       its support[5] is taken away from you.
12. The inhabitants of Marot are in the depths of despair,
       for evil has come down from Yahweh to the gate of Jerusalem.
13. Harness the horses to the chariots, inhabitants of Lachish.
       [It is the principal sin of the daughter of Zion
       for in you the transgressions of Israel were found[6]]

[1]Reading מכתה.
[2]Reading גגעה.
[3]Reading בבית עפרה.
[4]Reading התפלשו.
[5]Above, p. 43.
[6]Above, pp. 46f.

14.   Therefore a parting-gift will be given[7] to[8] Moresheth Gath.
Beth[9] Achzib is a source of deceit to the kings of Israel.
15.   The dispossessor will again come[10] to you, inhabitants of Mareshah.
The glory of Israel will extend as far as Adullam.
16.   Shave your head and cut off your hair for your beloved children.
Make yourself as bald as the vulture, for they have gone into exile.

[7]Reading יתנו.
[8] אל = על.
[9]Reading בית.
[10]Reading יבוא.

CHAPTER 2

vv. 1–5 WOE TO THOSE WHO STEAL FIELDS
AND HOMESTEADS!

'Woe betide those who plan evil while they lie in their beds!' (v. 1, deleting ופעלי רע). Micah breathes strong indignation, condemnation and threat (cf. Wolff, 47, by using the הוי of the lament he is signalling that the high-handed methods of the oppressors are a way to death). ופעלי רע is represented by the versions (Sept. καὶ ἐργαζόμενοι κακά; Vulg. *et operamini malum*; Pesh, *wʿbdyn byšt*; Targ. למעבד דביש), but its deletion was proposed by Wellhausen (135) and he has been followed by H. Schmidt (138), Smith (53), Weiser (244) and van der Woude (68). Duhm prefers the deletion of און ו, 'Woe betide those who plan evil deeds!', with פעלי pointed as פָּעֳלֵי. This leaves intact the scheme of hatching plans while lying in bed and carrying them out the next day.

Other ways of doing this are proposed by Ehrlich (275) and Wolff (38f.). Ehrlich holds that פעלי רע refers to no more than the hatching of evil, the laying of plans to do evil, and so he concludes that חשבי און and פעלי רע are synonymous phrases, 'Woe betide those who plan mischief and hatch evil!' Wolff urges that חשבי is the *nomen regens* of both און and רע and that פעלי should be vocalized as פָּעֳלֵי (so Robinson, 132; cf. Rudolph, 51 who favours פָּעֳלֵי = 'deeds' and so keeps the pointing of MT; so Hillers, 31): 'Woe betide those who plan mischief and plot to do evil deeds!' Willis (1967, 537–539) holds that פעלי רע means 'to do evil in their dreams': 'Woe betide those who lay wicked plans and dream of doing evil!'. Kimchi's comment has the same effect as this: he glosses פעלי רע with בלבבם 'in their heart' and so preserves the pattern, plotting by night and action in the morning (cf. Rashi, 'Turning over in their minds all night how they might commit evil in the morning').

באור הבקר may have the sense 'as soon as it is light': they waste no time and rise early to implement their plans. Vulg. *in luce matutina* reproduces MT, but Sept. καὶ ἅμα ἡμέρᾳ perhaps means 'as soon as day breaks' and both Pesh. and Targ. suppose that an early rise is indicated. Those who plan the next day's programme at night in their beds do not

59

allow the grass to grow beneath their feet. They set out to implement their plans early the next morning.

The final clause of v. 1 כי יש לאל ידם certainly indicates that they have the power to implement their plans. If there is any obscurity, it belongs to the idiom in which the phrase is couched. Sept. and Vulg. found the clause difficult. Sept. rendered לאל as πρὸς τὸν θεόν and Vulg. as *contra Deum*. Sept inserted οὐχ ἦραν, 'because they did not lift their hands to God (in prayer)' [so Smith, 53]. The evil plans which they implement are traced to godlessness and impiety. Vulg. conveys the same sense but with a different translation, 'because their hands are set against God'. Pesh. follows Sept. in respect of the insertion of ἦραν, but it renders כי as 'and': *wšqlyn'ydyhwn lwt'lh'*, 'and (yet) they lift their hands to God'. According to Pesh. they are hypocrites rather than godless; their thoughts and actions are evil, but they go through the motions of prayer. Targ. ארי אית חילא בידיהון, 'because there is power in their hands' is the sense which has been largely followed and Kimchi comments 'for there is power (כח) in their hands to oppress the poor' (so KJV; Wellhausen, 23; Smith, 53; ; Weiser, 244; Robinson, 132; Van Der Woude, 68; Rudolph, 51; Wolff, 37 ; Hillers, 31).

The connecting of לאל with 'God' (Sept., Vulg., Pesh.), a lexicography which Wolff (47) rejects, is found in Duhm (84), Brockelmann, 1906, 29–32 Ehrlich, 1908, 15 and H. Schmidt (137). Duhm translates כי יש לאל ידם 'for their hand is as (the hand of) God'. There is no danger that they will fail in their designs for lack of power. Brockelmann connects the expression with a primitive stage of Israelite religion which is unrecorded and is lost. An idiom, derived from religion, indicative of power or powerlessness, survived in the language (Gen. 31.29; Deut. 28.32; Micah 2.1; Prov. 3.27; Neh. 5.5), though its origins were no longer recoverable. The idiom comes down from a time when a God (a *Geist*, a *numen*) was believed to energize the blood or a member of the body, when the hand (יד) had its own אל, its own source of power. Ehrlich also maintains that in these passages אל does not have a sense other than 'God' and, he holds that כי יש לאל ידם has the sense 'Their power is equal to the power of God.' Schmidt, with *Denn ihre Faust ist ihnen Gott* highlights rather the naked 'Fist' as the only religion which they have, the only Absolute to which they give recognition. They are devoted to the law of the jungle. Might is right.

Verse 2 is free of textual difficulties and the versions do not differ significantly from MT. Why the coveting of the fields should be coupled with the seizing of orphans (Sept. ὀρφανούς is influenced by Job 24.9) is not clear and the object which has to be supplied is rather 'They covet fields and acquire (them) by force' (וגזלו; Vulg. *violenter tulerunt*). Vulg. represents איש (Leningrad manuscript ואיש) with some Hebrew manuscripts. In Sept. καὶ κατεδυνάστευον (= ועשקו) has been transposed with καὶ διήρπαζον (= ונשאו), though the διαρπάζω does not render נשא anywhere else in Sept. Pesh. translates MT freely. It supplies an object for *wnsbyn*, namely *lhwn*, and adds *bqtyʾ*: 'And they covet fields and houses and seize them with violence' (cf. Vulg.); it renders וביתו with *bqnynh*: 'They act oppressively against a man with his possessions and his property' (*wbyrtwth*). איש is a minus. Targ. follows MT.

We have to ask what state of affairs is described by this very strong language. It appears that the foundations of a society are being shaken, that its structure is disintegrating, that nuclear institutions on which its stability depends, homesteads, families, fields, little communities rooted in the soil, are being swept away by robbery with violence. It is unlikely, however, that the situation is one where dispossession and eviction are being effected at the point of the sword, where a rabble is running riot and confiscating the homesteads and fields of small farmers. What is happening is violent oppression, but it is not this kind of violence.

On the other hand, these are not infractions of law, outrages stemming from covetousness, which can be regarded as not unusual evidences of a measure of criminality to be expected in any society, which are forbidden by law and counselled against by the *dicta* of proverbial wisdom. The circumstance that חמדו is used here and that the tenth commandment (Ex. 20.17) prohibits covetousness ('You are not to covet your neighbour's household') or that wisdom sentences (Prov. 14.31; 22.16; 28.3) deprecate the oppression of the poor (cf. Wolff, 48) throws little light on the fragmentation of society which is alleged by the prophet and it should not be thought that Micah is making a big thing of this. In the circumstances which are described this would be a lame statement of the obvious with which we should not burden him.

Nor should Wolff's supposition (44, 48) that these are the depredations of 'king's men', of royal officials and the military, stationed in the fortified cities around Moresheth, a likely explanation. No doubt such were not above high-handed action and were capable of seizing property and land which they coveted at the expense of the small farmers who were the owners, but the disintegration of Judaean society which is portrayed requires the assumption of structural collapse and social mayhem of a different order from this. We are not to suppose that the homesteads and fields were surrendered to a show of physical force, a *force majeure*, and that the small farmers were evicted by a kind of robbery with violence, so that they were dispossessed by a greedy and ruthless bureaucracy which was abusing its power. The pressure which was exerted was irresistible and in the prophet's view it was socially destructive and inhuman. It was a seizure of homesteads and fields which broke up nuclear communities, but it was not done by means of physical violence. It was the exercise of a different kind of power, more refined but no less cruel than physical violence.

What then was the pressure which swept all before it? Kimchi comments that covetousness was in the heart of the aggressors and robbery was in their hands: 'They ask their colleagues to sell fields to them and, if they are unwilling to sell their fields, they take them by force. If a man will not give up his homestead and his field they beat him and imprison him.' According to Kimchi, the small farmer was offered a price for his property, but the pressure which was exercised if he refused was perhaps more usually financial than physical and this is how Ibn Ezra presents the matter. Loans which have been granted to a debt-ridden peasantry are called in, the property is seized when the loan cannot be paid and the peasant loses possession of his homestead and his field (cf. Smith, 57; Robinson, 133; Hillers, 33). Such tactics, according to Micah, amount to robbery, the seizure of property and a kind of violent dispossession, an exercise of financial power. We are in the presence of conditions of economic change, 'the adding of field to field' (Is. 8.5): 'Woe betide those who add house to house, field to field until everyone else is displaced.' The process is causing great social damage; it is destroying rural homesteads, a means of subsistence, a way of life, a cultural asset and a source of stability. It is creating rural depopulation and a class of displaced persons; it is giving rise to great human suffering.

This would be a correct account of the matter, even if we were to conclude that the tides of economic change were irresistible and were to add that it is sadly true that such changes inevitably cause social dislocation and human suffering. We would then be saying that the heat of the prophet's moral indignation has in it something of a vain Luddite resistance to change. Yet this does not draw the sting from the prophet's polemic and the claim that a moral critique may not be applied to the inhuman consequences of the economic changes which are taking place, 'the agrarian reform', should not be granted. Those who carry out such changes are required to take into consideration the amount of social damage and dislocation which their measures cause, to act responsibly and mercifully and to minimize human suffering and despair.

What then were these events which were taking place in the second half of the eighth century in Judah? The few in that community were wealthy and the many were poor. The acquisition of wealth and its possession by the few was connected with the institution of the monarchy and the creation of a class of 'king's men', of high officials, though there were others who had acquired their wealth outside this circle of royal patronage. It is likely that these officials along with great property owners sought to increase their wealth by investment in land and by creating an agriculture of large fields to the detriment of the small holders of land. They were in a strong position and they exercised their financial power ruthlessly on a debt-ridden peasantry.

Alt's account (1959, 373–381) is more complicated and its contents are a combination of economic and political history. On the economic side it connects Micah's polemic with the making of large farms out of smallholdings (Isa. 5.8) and the eviction of peasants saddled with debt and faced with the foreclosure of mortgages. It explains this state of affairs as a consequence of the relationship established by Davidic kings between the city state of Jerusalem and the territory of Judah. They considered Judah an appendage of Jerusalem, claimed its land as crown property and made grants of land to Jerusalem notables in their entourage. A long process of development has to be supposed as a consequence of these arrangements and a detailed history of it is not recoverable. It has to be assumed that the notables residing in Jerusalem had at first only a passive interest in their grants of land in Judah, but that at some point in time they began to exploit their ownership actively and to develop large farms out of smallholdings. To do this they had to evict the peasants and they made new laws, became moneylenders, foreclosed the loans which they had granted and drove the small farmers from their homesteads and their land.

Hence Alt pinpoints those who were responsible for replacing the smallholdings of Judah with large farms and he connects the process with the claims made by the city-state of Jerusalem on the territory of Judah. The Jerusalem nobles were driven by economic motives, but the power which was in their hands derived from political benefit which they enjoyed, not from wealth gained in trade. It was not a straightforward case of financial pressure, the oppression of the poor by the wealthy who bought up land and employed new methods of farming as a means of acquiring more wealth.

Bardtke (1971, 244–250) has a different explanation, with special reference to Is. 5.8f., but one which also has a bearing on Micah 2.1f. The protest which is raised in these two passages is related to a special situation of danger which faces the Judaean state, when Judah was threatened with Assyrian invasions in the reigns of Ahaz and Hezekiah. There was an influx of refugees from the Northern Kingdom, traders of Canaanite extraction, who brought bars of gold with them and used them to buy town houses and agricultural land. They purchased land which was farmed in small pieces by peasants, the growth in the numbers of whose family or clan had resulted in smaller and smaller allocations to each of its members. The traders bought such land in its entirety and made it into a single, economically viable farm: they added field to field. Some of the Judaean peasants were employed as farm labourers, but more of them became landless and displaced persons.

The sale of such land was encouraged by the Judaean state, since it helped to fill its war chest in the face of the Assyrian threat and since more efficient farming increased agricultural wealth which was needed to meet the demands of Assyrian tribute. The prophetic interventions of Is. 5.8f. and Micah 2.1f. reflect this temporary period in the history of Judah, the sharp danger represented by the Assyrian threat and the social dislocation which it produced, rather than a development of smallholdings into larger farms, a process of agrarian change.

Bardtke trawls widely in the Old Testament to support his thesis, but two comments will suffice. (a) The view that the 'houses' in the two passages are 'town houses' and are spatially distant from the 'fields' is very improbable. The houses are not to be separated from the fields in this manner: they are the homesteads where the peasants live. (b) According to Bardtke's thesis the small farmers who are made homeless and landless do not sell their holdings. There is then no question of forced sale or debt-ridden peasants. Their land is sold above their heads 'by the state or by private citizens' who have the disposal of it in their power. The proceeds fill the coffers of the state, the sale brings about more efficient farming and creates more agricultural wealth. With the passing of the time of special danger to Judah conditions return to normal in the countryside and the peasant resumes the cultivation of his small fields. In a more settled period the Canaanite traders resume their trading and find more profitable investments for their gold than land. All of this is difficult to swallow.

Verse 3 contains Yahweh's threat (לכן) which follows on the indictment of vv. 1–2 and the Hebrew text is mostly straightforward. The action which Yahweh threatens is a rejoinder to the evil plans which have been hatched (v. 1, חשבי און; v. 3, חשב רעה), assuming that על המשפחה הזאת whose originality is questioned, refers to the miscreants of vv. 1–2. Both על המשפחה הזאת and כי עת רעה היא at the end of the verse are represented by Sept., Vulg., Pesh. and Targ. They are taken as secondary by Smith (53) and Wolff (39), על המשפחה הזאת by the latter on the ground that it interrupts the connection of חשב and רעה. Wolff (39) and Robinson (133) also suppose that כי עת רעה היא at the end of the verse transforms a threat issued against a particular group into a general epoch of doom.

The main exegetical point is the sense of רומה which is a *hapax* and those versions which take it to mean 'erect' are to be followed (LXX ὀϱθοί; Pesh. *bqwmt' pšyṭ'*; Targ. בקומא זקופא). Kimchi glosses it with קומה טובה. Vulg, on the other hand with *superbi* understands the 'erect stature' as a reference to a proud mien as does KJV 'go haughtily' and REB 'walk haughtily'. NEB 'walk upright' is to be preferred (so Schmidt, 137; Smith, 53; Rudolph, 51; Wolff, 37). Ehrlich (276) emends רומה to קומה.

The assumption that the evil planned by Yahweh is likened to a yoke on the necks of those who are threatened by which their freedom to pursue their designs will be destroyed, which will restrict and cramp them intolerably and from whose constraint they will be unable to shake themselves free, is widespread. Their subjection will be unremitting and, with the yoke of servitude on their necks, they will never be able to raise their heads. Kimchi comments, 'When your necks are under a yoke of evil, you will be in subjection (נכנעים) and will not be able to walk with an upright carriage.' Hence Kimchi concludes—and many have followed him—that the yoke is a figure of the servitude which will be imposed by a foreign invader who will conquer and occupy Judah and stamp his rule on the erstwhile oppressors, so that they in turn will be enslaved and will suffer unrelieved oppression (cf. Robinson, 134).

Alt (377), on the other hand, argues that a background of invasion and conquest (the Assyrians) is not to be sought for v. 3 or for vv. 4–5. Robinson (133f.) posits the discontinuity of vv. 1–3 and vv. 4–5. He describes v. 4 as a 'fragment' to which an editor or annotator has added a prose verse (v. 5), so that v. 4 and v. 5 are also discontinuous. The lament (v. 4) is raised by Judaean farmers whose land has been seized by an invading conqueror.

The most-favoured opinion is that vv. 4–5 are continuous with vv. 1–3 and that עליכם in v. 4 refers to the oppressors of vv. 1–3 who are represented as speaking the lament of v. 4. In that case ישא ... נהי means 'one will put a lament into your mouth' or 'a lament will be put into your mouth'. Verse 4 is still 'word of Yahweh' (v. 3) and Yahweh states that others (unspecified) will put a lament into the mouths of the oppressors of vv. 1–2—'a satirical dirge' (Smith, 58; cf. Hillers, 31 'a taunt-song'). But Smith supposes that it is the exultant Assyrians who utter the mock lament and so it is their identity which is concealed behind ישא and עליכם refers to the Judaeans who have been defeated and conquered. It is they who are mocked in this pseudo-lament by a triumphant foe. So Smith, like Robinson, but in a different manner, separates v. 4 from vv. 1–3 and, like Robinson, he separates v. 5 from v. 4. Verse 5 cannot be construed as an address by the enemy (Assyria) to the Judaeans and it means that neither the oppressors nor the oppressed will have any land or that the notables (vv. 1–2) will not be able to take land from the poor, because they will have none. Thus Smith (58) connects v. 5 with vv. 1–3 rather than with v. 4. Weiser (246) holds that v. 4 is allegedly spoken by the oppressors of vv. 1–3, but that לכם which he adopts at v. 5 (MT לך) does not refer to the same group as עליכם (v. 4). Verse 5 is directed against the Judaeans in general. The consequence of the greed for land displayed by the notables (vv. 1–2) will be the entire loss of Judah to a foreign conqueror. By their sins they have plunged themselves and all the inhabitants of Judah into poverty.

Likewise Kimchi does not connect vv. 4–5 with vv. 1–3, but he assumes that the person who makes the lament in v. 4 is a false prophet (נביא השקר) and that it is he who is subsequently threatened in v. 5.

This deals with the problem of the singular לך (v. 5). This prophet is false not because of his shallow optimism (the usual complaint against false prophets), but because of the blackness of his pessimism which is construed as a refusal to believe that the land seized from the people of Judah by the notables and then by a foreign conqueror will be restored by Yahweh to his people. Kimchi does not suppose that משל is an indication that the lament which is uttered is also a satire (*Spottlied*) as some scholars do (Smith, 58; Robinson, 134; Rudolph, 51; cf. Wellhausen, 23 *Lied*; Schmidt, 137 *Spruch*; Wolff, 37 *Spruch*; NEB 'poem', REB 'verse'). Rather he couples משל with חידה and takes it as a reference to the content of the lament: it consists of 'cryptic words' (דברים סתומים), words which are clouded in obscurity.

Kimchi's exegesis of v. 4 is founded on MT which is almost certainly corrupt (especially v. 4b), but on which he undertakes to comment. The pessimistic false prophet bemoans the scene of devastation which he surveys, the consequences of an invasion, a conquest, an occupation and an exile, and then he says, 'He (God) has exchanged us for another owner, for what was the land of my people has become the land of the enemy.' On the obscure איך ימיש לי (v. 4b) he comments, 'How can this be that he (God) takes aways from me what was mine!' On לשובב . . . יחלק he remarks, 'When I reckoned that God willed to restore to us our fields, which the enemies had taken, at that time the enemy strengthened his grip on them and divided them among the enemies.' According to Kimchi the lament assumes conquest by an invading enemy and exile. The excessive pessimism of the false prophet consists in his assertion that Judaeans will not regain their land when they return from exile. It will continue in possession of the conqueror and his subordinates.

The threat delivered in v. 5 is that the person who has disseminated such gloom and has advertised such a lack of trust in Yahweh will not have a share in the land when the redistribution is effected. The thought that invasion, defeat and occupation are mirrored in v. 4 has been influential in the history of exegesis. 'Restore' in Kimchi's comment shows that he has understood לשובב as an infinitive construct Poel of שוב and two modern commentators (Rudolph, Wolff, see below) have returned to this opinion, though they have suggested the sense 'to pay back' and have rendered לשובב *als Heimzahlung* (Rudolph) or *zur Vergeltung* (Wolff), 'as retribution'.

Rudolph (51–55) may be taken with Kimchi, since he, for the most part, is founding his exegesis of vv. 4–5 on MT. He differs from Kimchi in that he supposes vv. 4–5 to be continuous with vv. 1–3. The lament which is raised is put into the mouths of the oppressors who are accused in vv. 1–2 and threatened in v. 3, but it is a lament with a satirical content (*Spottlied*) and this is the force of משל. Rudolph incorporates נהיה in the text as another term for 'lament', a synonym for נהי, and he notices that it is so attested in one of the Qumran scrolls (Carmignac, 1955, 351). He renders נהי נהיה as 'most doleful lament' and this recalls Kimchi's treatment of the cluster משל, נהי, נהיה—a piling-up of synonyms.

In order to achieve his interpretation Rudolph (p. 53) makes one crucial emendation of MT לך to לכם (v. 5). In this he follows Ehrlich (276), Smith (55), Weiser (244), Alt (378 n. 2) and BHS: a haplography of *mem*. He thus harmonizes עליכם (v. 4) with לכם (v. 5). Those in whose mouths the lament, with satirical overtones, is put are none other than those who are threatened in v. 5, namely the oppressors of vv. 1–3. Otherwise Rudolph retains MT: על המשפחה הזאת and כי עת רעה היא at v. 3, ימיר, איך ימיש לי and לשובב שדינו יחלק at v. 4. The erstwhile oppressors complain that their fields are now in the ownership of the conquering enemy and ask indignantly how it is that they have been alienated from the land which they once possessed. But then, according to Rudolph, they admit that the redistribution is a retribution.

Rudolph (54f.) acknowledges that there are passages in the lament, so constructed, which could not credibly have been spoken by those whose nefarious activities are described in vv. 1–2. They would not have referred to the loss of their fields as 'retribution' (לשובב) and it is difficult to reconcile חלק עמי (v. 4) with the circumstances in which they are assumed to have made the lament. Clearly 'land of my people' does not mean 'land of the people of Judah' in the mouths of the oppressors, since it was they who had seized the smallholdings and converted them into large farms. Hence with חלק עמי and לשובב we may have to reckon with cases where the voice of the oppressed breaks through and the fiction of a lament, satirically conceived, spoken by the oppressor, is not successfully carried out.

Rudolph has thus detected in elements of this mixture of the form of lament with a satirical content an artistic dichotomy. The representation that the oppressors raise a lament is fashioned as a device for combining lament with satire and the attempt is made to achieve this with appropriate literary gusto, to take off the notables who, because of invasion and conquest, are hoist with their own petard, but there is a failure to retain the lightness of touch needed to keep up such literary fun. Hurt and gloating break through and it is the sentiments of the oppressed rather than the deflation of the oppressors, and the display of them as ridiculous figures, which is communicated. The comical and absurd aspect of men who are aggrieved and feel themselves badly done by because they have been deprived of land which they stole is blurred.

Returning to the text of v. 4 we find that Sept. substitutes ἐν μέλει 'in song' for MT נהיה and that Vulg. has *cum suavitate* 'pleasantly'. Targ. ובעיניתיה 'and with his lament' and Pesh. *wbqynt* 'and with a lament' (with a different word-order from MT) are also related to נהיה by Rudolph. It is unlikely that any of these readings support Rudolph's opinion (52) that נהיה has the sense 'lament' (cf. Carmignac, 1955, 349). They are rather all expansions of MT, but they probably have no bearing on נהיה. The latter should be explained either as a dittography of ונהה נהי (Wellhausen, 135; Schmidt, 138; Ehrlich, 276; Smith, 54; Weiser, 244; Robinson, 134; Hillers, 32) or as a dittography which has become a secondary comment in the light of defeat and exile: 'It has happened' (Wolff, 39). Duhm (84) explains נהיה as an integral part of the Hebrew text, 'The word is fulfilled.' אמר (MT) is rendered by Sept. as λέγων, by Vulg. as *dicentium*, by Pesh. as *wn'mr* and by Targ. as יימר. לאמר has been widely preferred (Wellhausen, 135; Schmidt, 138; Robinson, 134; Duhm, 84 אמר; Ehrlich, 276 ואמר; Weiser, 244 ואמר; Rudolph, 52 אמר; Wolff, 39 ואמר or לאמר).

Sept. has κατεμητρήθη ἐν σχοινίῳ 'is measured out with a line' for MT ימיר and similarly Pesh. represents ימיר as *bšwyt nplg*. The Hebrew equivalent of Sept. is עמי ימד בחבל and of Pesh. חלק עמי בחבל יחלק. On the basis of either κατεμητήθη or κατεμητρήθη ἐν σχοινίῳ MT has been emended to ימד (לחבל). Alt (377 n. 2) prefers חלק עמי יחלק because of the assonance of חלק and יחלק (cf. Pesh.). יחלק is recovered from v. 4b which he supposes is otherwise made up of corrupt dittographies and variants of v. 4a (p. 377 n. 2). Vulg. has read MT *pars populi mei commutata est* 'the portion of my people has been exchanged (cf. Targ. מעדן להון, 'they dispossess them'). In v. 4b καὶ οὐκ ἦν ὁ κωλύσων αὐτὸν τοῦ ἀποστρέψαι 'and no one prevents them so that they turn aside', does not appear to be an attempt to render MT (איך ימיש לי), though τοῦ ἀποστρέψαι may be a rendering of לשובב. Vulg. translates איך ימיש לי as *quomodo recedo a me* and לשובב hopefully as *cum revertatur*. Pesh. and Targ. are not close to MT. Pesh. has *wly dmhpk ḥqltn bšwyt*, 'and there are those who alter our fields with a measuring line'. *bšwyt* is repeated (cf. v. 4a) and otherwise v. 4b may be a free rendering of לי לשובב שדינו יחלק. In that case איך ימיש is a minus in Pesh. Targ. translates v. 4b as 'They banish them from their heritage, redividing their fields' which does not correlate well with MT. It is evident, however that יחלק has been read by Targ.; Vulg. (*Qui regiones nostras dividat*) also follows the vocalization of MT (יחלק), whereas Sept. has vocalized יחלק as יְחֻלָּק. Cathcart (1988, 195) has introduced new philology and derives שדד from Akkadian *šadadu* 'to measure out'. שדוד נשדנו is rendered as 'We have been measured out for sale completely', לשובב is emended to שודד and ימיש לי to ימשל, 'How the measurer rules!'.

Verse 5 is plain sailing compared with v. 4. Sept. reproduces MT literally and the other versions render it more or less exactly. Vulg. has *sortis* for בגורל. Pesh. has the rendering, 'who measure with the line and divide by lot' and Targ. is similar. All the versions support לכן and בקהל יהוה at v. 5, but it is deleted by Duhm (85) on the ground that it is inappropriate to a lament (v. 4) and is the contribution of a copyist. Schmidt's deletion (137) of לכן is connected with his assumption that v. 5 is a rejoinder to v. 4 which is made by the notables of vv. 1–2.

One cannot be confident that the versions are reading a different Hebrew text from MT and, in particular, that Sept. read ימד בחבל at v. 4a or Pesh. יחלק בחבל. The occurrence of חבל at MT v. 5 increases the possibility that it is a supplementation which has been supplied by Sept. at v. 4a and Pesh. may be dependent on Sept. for this item. The emendations which have been offered for v. 4 should be acknowledged as conjectural and the likelihood is that v. 4b is corrupt in MT.

Stade's reconstruction (1886, 122f) has been a model for later scholars (Schmidt, 138; Smith, 55). He emends (a) אמר to לאמר (b) לשובבינו to לשובב (c) ימד בחבל to ימיר (d) ואין משיב to איך ימיש לי (e) יְחֻלָּק to יחלק (f) He locates שדוד נשדנו at the end of the verse:

> The land of my people is measured out with the line
> and there is no one to restore (it).

Our fields are allotted to our captors;
We are utterly despoiled.

Wellhausen (135) emends אמר to לאמר, ימיר to ימד, איך ימיש לי to
אין המשיב לי and יחלק is pointed as יִחֲלֵק. לשובב he gives up as
unintelligible and leaves a blank in his translation (cf. Weiser, 244 and
Robinson, 134 who delete לשובב):

We are utterly despoiled;
the land of my people is measured out.
There is no one to restore it to me;
Our fields are divided.

Duhm (84f.) vocalizes MT אמר as אֹמֵר, emends ימיר to ימד,
וחלק עמי to חלק עמי on the ground that יחלק is a corrupt dittography
of וחלק. Verse 4b is otherwise unintelligible (also Ehrlich, 276). Duhm
emends איך ימיש לי ל to אין מושב לו, 'no dwelling-place remains for it'
(לו refers to עמו?) and conjectures that שובב שדינו יחלק is a corrupt
dittography of שדוד נשדנו חלק. He translates:

We are utterly despoiled
and the land of my people is measured out;
no dwelling-place remains for it.

The sense of v. 5 is, 'None of us will in the future participate in the
general assembly which redistributes the land, because we shall have
been carried off captive and the conquerors of Judah will share it among
themselves.' Duhm emends לך to לו, deletes לכן and בגורל (as a gloss
on or variant of בקהל). Hence Duhm makes the common assumption
that the background of the lament in vv. 4–5 is the invasion of Judah
by a foreign conqueror and the oppressors of vv. 1–2 do not appear in
his exegesis. It is the people of Judah who are lamenting the depredations of an invader who has seized their land, as well as the circumstance
that they will be absent exiles when the land is redistributed.

Weiser (244) and Robinson (134) both adopt ימד and ואין משיב.
BHS has ימד (בחבל) and לשובינו (with Stade). In his statement that v. 5
is directed towards the Judaeans in general Weiser is tending towards
Duhm, but in saying that the consequence of the greed for land shown
by the landlords (vv. 1–2) would be the entire loss of Judah to a foreign
conqueror he is incorporating the oppressors of vv. 1–2 in his exegesis:
their rapacity had pushed themselves and the entire population of Judah
into poverty.

Remarks made on Rudolph's interpretation of vv. 4–5 focused on
the difficulty of reconciling 'land of my people' and 'retribution' with a
lament which is put into the mouths of the notables of vv. 1–2. 'Land
of my people' remains a difficulty for Alt, whereas v. 4b does not feature
in his interpretation of v. 4 as a lament which these notables are
represented as uttering. The second threat against them in v. 5,
emending לך to לכם, is made more credible by the deletion of
בקהל יהוה (378 n. 1). By proposing that בקהל יהוה should be attached
to חלק עמי ימד (v. 4a, 'the land of my people is measured out in the
assembly of Yahweh'), Alt is ameliorating the problem of 'my people' in
a lament allegedly spoken by the oppressors of vv. 1–2. 'My people'
then refers to those who joined field to field and the complaint they
make is that this land is now redistributed 'in the assembly of Yahweh'.
This is in line with Alt's contention that v. 4a and v. 5 are complementary to vv. 1–2 and that their background is not an invasion by a
foreign conqueror (Assyria). There is no element of threat to the general
population of Judah in v. 4a and v. 5, but there is a covert promise that
the land taken by the oppressors of vv. 1–2 will be redistributed among
the Judaean farmers from whom it was wrested. Alt (377–379)
identifies those who expropriated land as the ruling class in Jerusalem.
The power of Jerusalem nobles over the ownership of land and the
management of agriculture followed from the personal union between
the kingdom of Judah and the city-state of Jerusalem and the prece-
dence of the latter as the seat of the king, his court and his officials who
constituted the Jerusalem ruling class. These Jerusalem notables may
have become money-lenders and thereby exerted the pressure on the
small farmers of Judah which drove them from their fields. At any rate
Judah lost the position it had hitherto occupied as an independent state
with its own social and economic order and became an appendage of
the city-state of Jerusalem.

NEB ('We are utterly despoiled, the land of the Lord's people
changes hands. How shall a man have power to restore our fields now
parcelled out?') emends MT in the following respects (Brockington,
1973, 255): (a) עמי to עם יהוה (י an abbreviation of יהוה?) (b) ימיש לי to
ימשל (c) יחלק to יחלקו (Sept. διεμερίσθησαν). שובב is taken as an
infinitive construct Poel (so Rudolph and Wolff) with the sense 'to
restore' and MT ימיר is retained. ימיש לי to ימשל is a bold emendation
and the change of 'my people' into 'people of Yahweh' does not increase

the credibility of this being part of the landlord's lament. Presumably we have to interpret 'the Lord's people' as a reference by the oppressors of vv. 1–2 to themselves: it is a claim that they are 'Yahweh's people'. They lament that the large areas of land which they have acquired are being parcelled out and that they have no power to obstruct the redistribution.

REB, 'We are utterly despoiled, for our people's land changes hands. It is taken away from us; our fields are parcelled out to renegades' is emending יחלק to יְחֻלָּקוּ but is otherwise undertaking to translate MT and is attaching the sense 'apostate', 'renegade' to שובב (*BDB*, 1000; Smith, 59, 'to a rebel'; Hillier, 32, 'to the apostate'). The translation 'our people's land' for חלק עמי is an attempt to ameliorate the difficulty caused by the appearance of such a phrase in a lament put into the mouths of the oppressors.

According to Wolff (39f.; 49f.) the original text of 'the landlord's lament' consists of 'We are utterly despoiled, one divides our fields' (= MT שדינו יחלק) and this is the only part of v. 4 which is to be assigned to the prophet Micah. This has been interpolated with a commentary by an editor in the period of the Babylonian exile: 'The land of my people is measured out. (ימד with Sept.). How (the soil) has been taken away from me in retribution. Our fields have been divided up.' The landlord's lament spoken ostensibly by the notables of vv. 1–2 has a satirical intent and is a kind of mocking (*Spottlied*). The editor has changed a particular form of oppression into a general period of doom. Verse 5 is a prosaic editorial addition which connects with the secondary part of v. 4. It apparently addresses those who complain, 'The land of my people is measured out. How (the soil) has been taken away from me in retribution.' This refers to a sacral redistribution of land (גורל; קהל יהוה) and is an effort to make Micah's threat relevant to the generation of the exile.

The editorial supplementation has the effect of shifting the historical background from the eighth century (vv. 1–3) to the time of the Babylonian exile when a more widely distributed evil overwhelmed the whole community, and the threat of v. 5 (retaining MT לך) is not directed against particular oppressors, the landlords of vv. 1–3. 'For it is an evil time' (v. 3) and 'In that day' (v. 4) mark the transition from the eighth century to the period of the Babylonian exile which has been made by the editorial infiltrations. Wolff supposes that 'We are utterly despoiled, our fields are divided' has as its background a situation of invasion, warfare and conquest and, especially, of the laying waste of land. It is a prediction of an Assyrian onslaught (pp. 48–50).

The conclusion to be drawn is that vv. 4–5 are not all of a piece and that they contain secondary elements which articulate a lament of the small farmers of Judah rather than a landlord's lament. If v. 5 is to be integrated with the lament of these notables, לך must be emended to לכם (v. 4, עליכם; v. 5, לך) and בקהל יהוה deleted. With this done 'We are utterly despoiled, our fields are parcelled out' encounters the unconsoling rejoinder 'You will not have any land allotted to you.' This part of vv. 4–5, assigned to Micah, would be a continuation of vv. 1–3, whether the oppressor's lament reflects a background of invasion and disorder and it was this which caused the loss of lands of which they complain (Wolff) or whether the landlord's lament is a covert promise that the land which had been expropriated would be redistributed to the Judaean farmers (Alt).

1. Woe to those who plot evil
   and plan evil deeds[1] in their beds!
   They rise early to do them,
   for they have the power.
2. They covet fields and take them by force;
   they desire houses and seize them;
   they rob a man and his household;
   they violate private property.
3. Therefore these are the words of Yahweh:
   I am planning evil against the lot of you
   from which you will not shake free your necks
   nor walk erect, for it will be an evil hour.
4. On that day a saying will be taken up about you
   and a lamentation[2] raised:
   We are completely devastated,
   the land of my people changes hands.
   How I have been dispossessed!
   Our fields have been divided up[3]
5. Therefore you will have no one
   to allot land to you with the measuring-line[4].

---

[1]Reading פֹּעֲלֵי.
[2]Deleting נהיה.
[3]Deleting לשובב and reading יְחַלְּקוּ.
[4]Deleting בקהל יהוה.

vv. 6–11 A COMPLAINT AND A THREATENING REJOINDER

Since Rashi and Kimchi comment on a difficult Masoretic text and do not resort to emendations, it will be convenient to begin the study of Micah 2.6–11 with them. The passage is represented as spoken by Yahweh (v. 7, דברי) but it does not have the literary form of an oracle. It is a mixture of indictment (vv. 8–9, v. 10b?) argumentation (vv. 6–7, v. 10a?), threat (v. 10?) and reflection (v. 11). Yahweh reports the *ipsissima verba* of the adverse reaction of his community (vv. 6–7) to the interminable 'dripping' of the prophets of doom and indicates that the response of the former is equally a tedious reiteration of their contentions: they confront a litany of doom with the tiresome, repetitive assertions that they are sick to death of the gloom generated by the doom prophets: '"Do not go on dripping", they drip.'

Kimchi comments: 'Israel rants to the prophets of God, "Do not remind us of the words of God, for we are not listening to you".' That נסף is a pejorative metaphor (Kimchi; Smith, 53; Weiser, 247) and not a straightforward synonym of נבא (Rashi; Wellhausen, 135; Robinson, 134; Rudolph, 56; Wolff, 38; Hillers, 34) is a presupposition of this rendering of אל תטפו יטיפון (v. 6). However there are indications in the commentaries of Rashi and Kimchi that Yahweh himself is not persuaded of the wisdom of the tirades of the doom prophets; they exacerbate the divide in the community and fan the flames of opposition and hostility. The doom prophets speak the truth, but they should not stoke up opposition to their message of doom by dwelling on it too much. לא יטפו לאלה (v. 6) is taken by Kimchi as, 'They (the prophets of doom) should not din their message into the ears of these men' (those who disagree with it sharply). לא יסג כלמוח (v. 6) is translated, 'One should not multiply calamities'—יסג is derived from הסגה. Kimchi comments: 'The prophets of God should not overdo their prophecies to these men (לאלה) and then they will not receive calumnies, for, if they din them into their ears, they will heap calumnies on themselves.' Rashi remarks, 'Lest calumnies from them overtake you' (deriving יסג from נשג). Another interpretation of לא יטפו לאלה takes לאלה as 'concerning these things' and renders לא יטפו לאלה as a question asked by Yahweh: 'Are not those who oppose prophecies of

doom equally obsessive?': '"Do not go on and on", they go on. But do
they not go on and on about these things?' (cf. NEB and REB).

Kimchi supposes that the ה of האמור (v. 7) is the definite article, but
it is probably an interrogative particle (GK 100n): 'Can it be said, O
House of Jacob, "Has Yahweh's anger been roused or are these his
deeds"?' Here Yahweh cites a complaint made by the House of Jacob
(his community) about the tone of doom prophecy and a claim that
doom prophets have misread the state of affairs. The trouble does not
lie in the circumstance that they have become unresponsive to Yahweh,
but rather in his change of attitude to them. They encapsulate their
complaint in the question, 'Has Yahweh's anger been roused or are
these his deeds?' If the blows which have fallen on the community have
been struck by Yahweh, then he has changed his nature. But are these
blows correctly interpreted as struck by Yahweh? Verse 7 continues with
Yahweh's response to these questions and with a denial that his attitude
to them has changed (so Duhm, 1911, 86) He is still benevolent, but
he has never been unconditionally benevolent. If there are evidences of
his lack of benevolence, there are also evidences of lack of uprightness in
the lives of his people. To those who are upright in the conduct of their
lives he shows his benevolence.

Yahweh makes a counter-claim—the attitudes of his people towards
him have altered (v. 8). This, however, according to Rashi and Kimchi,
is not a direct counter-claim: he is not saying explicitly that they have
become his enemy: 'Lately ('yesterday'; cf. KJV 'Even of late') my
people rise up as an enemy.' Rashi and Kimchi relate this to the
activities which are described in v. 8 and v. 9. It is the hostile and
vicious deeds of his community against men, women and children to
which reference is made in vv. 8f. and there is no open reference to their
enmity against Yahweh, though their actions against human beings and
the attitudes which they manifest demonstrate an enmity to the will of
Yahweh.

The words which follow in v. 8 (ממול שלמה אדר) are a puzzle which
neither Rashi nor Kimchi elucidates, but there is evidence that they
suppose שלמה to be an equivalent of שמלה (metathesis of מ and ל) and
that they equate אדר with אדרת. Rashi comments, 'In that you plunder
garments and splendid clothing and strip them off travellers on roads
adjoining to you.' The victims are portrayed as עברים בטח and
שובי מלחמה. The former indicates that they were unsuspecting, that

they thought themselves secure, and did not perceive that they had a need to guard themselves against attack and attempted robbery. שׁובי מלחמה is more troublesome. שׁובי is apparently a passive Qal participle in a construct relation with מלחמה. The rendering 'returning from war' makes שׁובי into an equivalent of שׁבי, the active Qal participle (KJV 'averse from war' renders שׁובי as passive—see further below). שׁובי מלחמה then emphasizes the peaceable intentions of the travellers and complements עברים בטח.

Verse 9 recalls the nefarious activities of the oppressors of vv. 1–2: women are driven from their desirable homes and their children are permanently deprived of Yahweh's 'glory'. The degree of intelligibility of v. 9b is not high. What can be meant by the irreversible taking away from infants of Yahweh's glory? Rashi comments, 'חדרי is the glory and wealth which I gave to them' and Kimchi asks the question, What is the meaning of חדרי לעולם? He replies that it is the joining of man to woman and the procreation of children. These infants are cut off early from the possibility of attaining that glorious status.

Yahweh issues an imperious and peremptory threat to these offenders. They are to go into exile forthwith, for the Promised Land is no longer promised to them, is no more a place for them to settle in tranquillity (מנוחה). The reason for their expulsion is not given altogether clearly: their uncleanness (טמאה is regularly 'ritual uncleanness') is not further elucidated and חבל is derived differently by Rashi and Kimchi. Rashi connects it with חבל 'to join' (BDB I חבל, 286) and Kimchi with חבל 'to act destructively', 'to ruin' (BDB II חבל, 287). Hence תחבל וחבל נמרץ means, according to Rashi, 'You band together and it is a grievous mob.' Kimchi glosses חבל with משחתה 'destruction' and gives the word-string as תחבל חבל נמרץ, omitting the waw of MT: 'You have corrupted the land with a destructive corruption.'

At v. 11 Yahweh ruminates on the perversity of those that reject the prophets of doom who make strenuous demands on them and seem to shut out the sunlight. What if they speak the truth? But the people prefer false reassurance and expect that a prophet will always speak good tidings and guarantee them an easy life of plenty, a perpetual feast, a sybarite spread. This is the kind of prophet who would please them, but prophecy is a serious business.

A different structure for Mic. 2.6–11 is indicated by Sept. (v. 7 = דבריו; MT דברי). Vulg. verba mea, Pesh. mly and Targ. פחגמי support

MT. If Sept. is adopted, MT is not speech of Yahweh, but it is spoken
by Micah concerning the nature of Yahweh's words. In that case there
is nothing in vv. 6–11 which requires the assumption that its literary
form is speech of Yahweh and it becomes instead a critique by Micah
of his opponents. They complain of the tedious gloominess of the
prophets of doom. Yet are they not equally repetitive in the recitation
of their counter-litany? (v. 6) To the question which they raise whether
Yahweh is out of temper and acts malevolently towards them, Micah
responds that Yahweh is benevolent but not unconditionally benevolent (v. 7b).

He makes the contrary claim that, of late, it is the community who
has changed its attitude to Yahweh and he cites examples of their
hostility to peaceable travellers and their inhumanity to women and
children (vv. 8–9). עמי is not incompatible with the assumption that
Micah speaks. Micah, no less than Yahweh, could describe his community as 'my people' (Wellhausen, 136). Micah requires and commands those responsible for such inhumane behaviour to depart from
the land which was promised and was given as a final resting-place for
Yahweh's people. They have not contributed to its quietness and
tranquillity; they have polluted it by their destructive behaviour. In v.
11 Micah reflects satirically on the kind of prophet who would be
received with open arms by his people: a wind-bag and a liar, one who
prophesies to them a life of ease, perpetual feasting, a gourmet's and a
toper's paradise.

Wellhausen (23) adopts דבריו at v. 7 (*seine Worte*) and supposes that
v. 7 is not to be explained as a citing by Micah of the words of his
opponents followed by his own rejoinder in which he justifies the ways
of Yahweh. It is rather a continuation of v. 6 and the speakers are
Micah's adversaries. The response of Micah appears in vv. 8–10 (p.
136). In this connection Wellhausen holds that if the second ה (v. 7) is
an interrogative particle (הקצר), the first (האמור) must also be and he
conjectures that the text is corrupt after the first ה and that it should
read 'Is the House of Jacob rejected?' Elliger (BHS) emends האמור to
הארור, 'Is the House of Jacob accursed?' The two questions asked in v.
7 are then sceptical questions which demand a negative answer: the
House of Jacob is not accursed and has not been rejected by Yahweh
and the signs of the times are not read correctly by Micah. Yahweh has
not lost patience with his people and the blows which have fallen on

them have not been struck by him—a repudiation of the premisses of the prophets of doom.

Verse 7 is elucidated differently by Duhm (1911, 85) who comments on an unemended Masoretic text (האמור בית יעקב). This is the questioning of the truth of a saw which had a wide circulation: 'Has the question which you ask substance, O House of Jacob?'. The proverbial form of the question is then produced by the prophet and v. 7b is a rebuttal of the insinuation of the question. Verse 10, according to Duhm, is not spoken by Yahweh (or Micah) to those who are indicted in v. 9, but is spoken by the oppressors to the oppressed. They cloak their greed and ruthlessness in a bogus concern for those whom they drive from their desirable homes: the houses are insanitary and constitute a health hazard (v. 10b) and their inhabitants must vacate them forthwith—an ingenious but improbable exegesis (followed by Weiser, 250).

Otherwise the versions do not make a major contribution to the elucidation of MT, though some of their features deserve notice. Sept. and Pesh. suppose that נטף has a distinctive sense and that it is not simply a synonym of נבא, whereas Vulg. and Targ. incline with Rashi to the view that it is an equivalent of נבא. Neither Sept. nor Pesh. represent יטיפון and they take 'drip' differently from Kimchi: not 'drip' in the sense of tiresome and unendurable repetition (a needle stuck in the groove of a gramophone record) as in Prov. 19.13 ('the nagging of a wife is an unrelenting drip'), but rather as an indication of a lachrymose utterance, of prolonged moping. Sept.: 'Do not weep tears, let them not mope about these things.' Pesh. renders לא יטפו לאלה as *wl' tdmʿwn 'l hlyn*, retaining the second person plural of the first verb, 'and do not mope about these things.' Vulg., on the other hand, gives *ne loquamini loquentes* for אל תטפו יטיפון, but it incorporates a special sense of נטף with its translation of לא יטפו לאלה as *non stillabit super istos*, 'one should not go on dripping about these people'. Targ. treats נטף throughout as a synonym of נבא: 'Do not utter prophecy and do not teach this people' has affinities with Pesh. (repetition of the second person verb) and with Kimchi (לאלה = 'to these men'). כלמות is construed by Sept. (οὐ γὰρ ἀπώσεται ὀνείδη) and Vulg. (*non comprehendet confusio*) as subject. Vulg. is puzzling, but it is clear that both Sept. and Vulg. have parsed כלמות (כלמוח) as a singular form. Sept. 'Reproach will not turn back' (be deflected) recalls RV 'Reproaches do not depart' (*BDB*, 691). This could be the words of the prophet's opponents cited by him, in which case it would be a further comment by them on the bad effects of too much advertising of doom and on the tendency of reiterated warnings to degenerate into recriminations: 'Calumny will not go away.'

Pesh. has *dlʾ ndrkkwn ḥsd* for לא יסג כלמות, 'for no ignominy will overtake you'. This, taken with the second person plural verbs which precede, is a continuous citation of the opponents of doom prophecy: 'Do not shed tears and do not weep for these things, for no ignominy will overtake you.' כלמות (singular) is again subject and only Targ. parses it as object. לא יסג כלמות is rendered ארי לא מקבלין אתכנעו, 'for they will not receive reproach' ('they' = the opponents of the prophets of doom?). Pesh has equated יסג with ישג (Rudolph, 56f.; Wolff, 40), but the use which modern commentators make of Pesh. supposes that יסג = ישג should stand without a suffix (Rudolph, 56), with the first person plural suffix understood (so Wolff, 38) or that a first person plural suffix should be inserted (Weiser, 247; Robinson, 134; Hillers, 34). Hence Pesh. is not taken over lock, stock and barrel and a different sense from that given by Pesh. (*dlʾ ndrkkwn*) is found לא יסג כלמות. This becomes a denial by Micah's adversaries that his gloomy predictions will come to pass: 'Ignominies will not overtake (us).'

Sept. ὁ λέγων (v. 7) takes ה as the definite article (so Kimchi) and represents אמור as אמר. It renders בית יעקב as nominative and in this it agrees with Vulg. *dicit dominus Iacob*. The accusing query made by the House of Jacob against Yahweh is contained in the words הקצר . . . מעלליו. Pesh. is less clear: האמור is translated as *dʾmyr* and *'l* is inserted before *byth dyʿqwb*, 'which is said concerning the House of Jacob'. But the question which follows is asked critically by the House of Jacob. Targ. poses a similar problem by inserting ב before בית יעקב: 'Is it right that they say concerning the House of Jacob?'

Sept. (v. 8) has καὶ ἔμπροσθεν for ואתמול, 'and previously' (cf. KJV, 'and of late'; MT, 'and yesterday'). Pesh. joins ואתמול to v. 7 (*wʾtmly*, 'and I was filled'). Otherwise Sept. and Vulg. translate MT (עמי לאויב יקומם) and Pesh renders לאויב as *'yk gnbʾ*, 'like a thief'. Sept. has κατέναντι for ממול and similarly Pesh. *lwqbl* (cf. Vulg. *desuper* 'above'). Sept. and Pesh. understand ממול שלמה אדר תפשטון in the same way, 'Against his peace they (Pesh. 'you') flay his skin.' שלמה is read as שלמה which is analysed as שלם + ה (suffix) and אדר is explained as Aramaic 'skin'.

תפשסן is given as second person plural by Pesh. in agreement with MT and as third person by Sept. Vulg renders *Desuper tunica pallium sustulistis*: *sustulistis* 'take off' is a rendering of תפשטן and *tunica/ pallium* are doublets (ארר/שלמה) cf. Duhm (1911, 85). For מעברים בטח Sept. has τοῦ ἀφελέσθαι ἐλπίδα 'to take away hope' (cf. Pesh. *dt‘brwn sbrh*) and for שובי מלחמה it has συντριμμὸν πολέμου (cf. Targ. בתבירי קרבא). Vulg. translates 'and those who were innoccuous travellers you involved in war', (*et eos qui transibant simpliciter convertistis in bellum*). The most influential of these textual indications in v. 8 is the reading of שלמה as שלמה (Sept., Pesh.), since this has been used by modern commentators.

If we revert to v. 7, Wellhausen's dissatisfaction with האמור בית יעקב (135f.) may be recalled. The implication of this is that v. 7 is to be assigned to the opponents of Micah and that the prophet speaks in vv. 8–11. Rudolph's exegesis is a variation of this. He agrees that the adversaries of Micah speak in v. 7, but he retains האמור בית יעקב instead of replacing it with הארור בית יעסב or the like. Moreover, he supposes that vv. 8, 9, 10b are represented as the speech of Yahweh (p. 61). The grammar of האמור בית יעקב which is proposed by Rudolph (p. 57) is too complicated and, if it is to be retained at v. 7, בית יעקב should be construed as a vocative: 'Can it be said, O House of Jacob?' (NEB and REB), followed by the saying on which the prophet throws doubt.

This, however, gives a different construction of v. 7 . The verse opens with האמור בית יעקב spoken by Micah and this introduces a stereotype which he cites from his adversaries and which is intended as a rejoinder to doom prophecy: 'Has Yahweh lost patience or are these his actions? Are not his words productive of good to him whose conduct is upright' (emending דברי to דבריו with Sept.; Wellhausen, 23; Ehrlich, 276; H. Schmidt, 138; Smith, 55; Weiser, 248; Robinson, 134; Rudolph, 57; Hillers, 35). The opponents of Micah are questioning the premises of doom prophecy. Yahweh's attitude to his community is the same as it always was and calamities which have overtaken them are not to be interpreted as punishments. His benevolence to those who lead upright lives remains constant.

A modification of this (already noted) sets out from 'Can it be said, O House of Jacob?' (Micah speaking), allocates הקצר ... מעלליו to Micah's adversaries whom he cites and takes הלא דבריו ... הולך as a prophetic rejoinder and this alters the sense of the verse. The question then asks querulously whether there has been a change of attitude on the part of Yahweh to his people, whether misfortunes suffered by them are indeed his judgements. The prophet's riposte is that Yahweh is constant but that they have been fickle. Yahweh maintains his benevolence to those whose conduct is upright.

Wolff (40) rings further change in the interpretation of v. 7. He adopts הארור for האמור so that the verse begins with a sceptical question framed by the opponents of doom prophecy . He retains MT (דברי), but holds that Micah is speaking for himself and not in the oracular style (voice of Yahweh): דברי means 'the words which I (Micah) speak'. Micah's rejoinder is communicated by הלא דברי ... הולך: doom prophecy contains a positive element and he has proclaimed that Yahweh's benevolence is shown to those who walk uprightly. Wolff holds (contra Rudolph) that in vv. 8, 9, 10b Micah continues to speak in his own person and that עמי (vv. 8, 9) does not require the conclusion that Yahweh is the speaker in these verses.

Whether the exegesis of v. 7 sets out from האמור בית יעקב or הארור בית יעקב, from הקצר to the end of the verse should be assigned, with דבריו for דברי to Micah's opponents (so Wellhausen, 135f.; Ehrlich, 277; H. Schmidt, 138; Weiser, 248; Robinson, 135; Rudolph, 60; Hillers, 35). הלא דברי ... הולך is their cosy theology rather than an element of doom prophecy.

Verse 10 is another verse which has been divided up between different speakers and which has a bearing on the structure of vv. 6–11. The main choice is whether v. 10a is a reinforcement of v. 9—the eviction order is given in the *ipsissima verba* of the evictors—or whether v. 10a is the sentence of exile, passed by Micah (or Yahweh) on the oppressors, followed by a combination of explanation and threat in v. 10b. The range of possibilities may be set out as follows: (a) Verse 10 is spoken by Micah (or Yahweh) to the oppressors (Wellhausen, 136, Micah threatens the same people as he does in vv. 1f.; Smith, 62, Yahweh dismisses the guilty summarily to their doom). Wellhausen remarks that v. 10b is corrupt and unintelligible, whereas Smith retains it, though his translation ('Ye shall be destroyed with irremediable destruction') requires the emendation of תחבלו חבל נמרץ to תחבל וחבל נמרץ which is represented by Sept. (διεφθάρητε φθορᾷ). (b) The allocation of v. 10 in its entirety to the oppressors has already been noted.

Verse 10 is then a spurious reason given by them for the eviction of women and children from their homes. The houses are insanitary (טמאה) and continued occupation of them will ruin the health of the occupants (Duhm, 1911, 86; Weiser, 250, reading MT). (c) The callousness and unscrupulousness of the evictors is highlighted by the reproduction of their *ipsissima verba* at v. 10a and the riposte of Micah (or Yahweh) is given in v. 10b (Ehrlich, 278; Robinson, 135; Rudolph, 59; Wolff, 41). These scholars cast doubt on the suitability of טמאה ('ritual uncleanness') to the context. Rudolph emends it to קנאה and redivides תחבל וחבל as תחבלו חבל: 'You create grievous anguish.' Ehrlich emends טמאה to מאומה (Robinson and Wolff to מעט מאומה) and redivides תחבל וחבל נמרץ as תחבלו חבל נמרץ, 'For a small thing you exact a grievous pledge' (also Robinson and Wolff; I חבל, *BDB*, 286). Verse 10b is then construed as a final indictment of the oppressors. It should be noticed that uncertainty as to the nature of v. 10b persists, even where it is assumed that v. 10a is spoken by Micah (or Yahweh). Thus Smith supposes that v. 10b is a continuation of the threat of v. 10a (so KJV and RSV). KJV translates, 'It shall destroy you even with a sore destruction', whereas NEB (REB), emending תחבלו חבל נמרץ to תחבל וחבל נמרץ renders it as a final indictment: 'You that defile yourself would commit any mischief, mischief however cruel' (II חבל, *BDB*, 287). This is the more probable conclusion however v. 10a is taken.

Wolff (p. 41) finds evidence of a Deuteronomistic redaction in v. 10 and suggests that it was this which transformed what was originally an accusation into a threat. The process is found in Sept. διεφθάρητε φθορᾷ, with ἕνεκεν ἀκαθαρσίας (בעבור טמאה) joined to המנוחה: 'You create ruin.' MT, with תחבל וחבל ומרץ, which *ex hypothesi* represents a later stage of the redaction than Sept., can be interpreted only as indictment: 'Because of uncleanness you (singular) cause ruin and the ruin is grievous.' Only with תחבל vocalized as תֵּחָבֵל. does accusation become threat: 'Because of uncleanness you (singular) will be destroyed and the destruction will be grievous' (Weiser, 247). Alternatively תחבל וחבל נמרץ is redivided as תחבלו חבל נמרץ 'You (plural) will be destroyed with grievous destruction' (Smith, 53— without a textual note; H. Schmidt, 138, emending נמרץ to נהרץ 'You will suffer ineluctable destruction'). The final accusation is brought into a more exact relation with v. 9 (eviction for unpaid debt?) and with

vv. 1–2 (devious land-grabbing) if Ehrlich's emendation is adopted: בעבור (מעס) מאומה תחבלו חבל נמרץ 'For a trifle you exact a grievous pledge' (also Robinson and Wolff).

In v. 8a (MT) the prophet (or Yahweh) complains that of late (ואתמול) my people (עמי) have risen up as an enemy, but in v. 9 'the women of my people (נשי עמי) suffer at the hands of merciless evictors. עמי denotes the persecutors at v. 8 (a section of the people; cf. v. 3 המשפחה הזאת) and at v. 9 it denotes the persecuted. This unevenness cannot be tolerated and עמי at v. 8 as at v. 9 must refer to the oppressed. Most scholars have achieved this by emending the obscure ואתמול עמי and Wellhausen's proposal ואתם על עמי תקומו (136) has been influential. This necessitates the emendation of יקומם to תקומו or קמים (Ehrlich, 276; Robinson, 134; Wolff, 40; Hillers, 35). Another emendation which has the same effect is ואתם לא עמי לאויבי קמים, 'But you are no longer my people, rising up (against me) as my enemy.' (Brockington, 1973, 205; cf. Weiser, 247). Rudolph's emendation is unnecessarily complicated (ואתם לו עמי לא אויבי וקמם: 'And you, would that you were my people, not my enemy and their (עם) adversary!'). It, however, changes the sense of v. 8a in the same way as the others and so עמי in both vv. 8 and 9 are those who suffer oppression and they are joined in a fellowship of suffering to those of vv. 1 and 2.

NEB (Brockington, 1973, 255) emends ממול to ממולי and connects it with the preceding part of the verse, 'rising up as an enemy to my face'. Rudolph (580) makes the same adjustment, but respects the punctuation of MT: 'In front of my eyes you strip off garments.' Rudolph accepts that שלמה is a metathesis of שמלה of which he supposes that אדרת (אדר by haplography) is a doublet (also Ehrlich, 277; Weiser, 247 n. 3). An influential emendation has been the substitution of שלמה for שלמה to which Sept. (κατέναντι τῆς εἰρήνης αὐτοῦ) and Pesh. (lwqbl šlmh) lend support. Wellhausen (136) reads שלמים and Wolff (40) שלמים or שלם. ממול is emended to מעל or על (Smith, 50; Weiser, 247, n.3; BHS; Wolff, 40): 'From those who are peaceably disposed you strip off their garments.' The emendation of מעברים בטח 'from unsuspecting wayfarers' to מַעֲבְרִים לבטח 'bringing on the unsuspecting' (Weiser, 247, n. 4; Robinson, 134) is unnecessary (so J. T. Willis, 1970, 84) and the remaining problem is the phrase for which Wellhausen (p. 136) and others (Smith, 56; Ehrlich, 277; Hillers, 35) substitute שבי מלחמה 'booty of war', 'captives in war'

(Hillers). שׁוּבֵי (passive participle) has been taken as an equivalent of שָׁבֵי (active participle), 'returning from war' (Rudolph, 58; NEB 'returning warriors' emending שׁוּבֵי to שָׁבֵי. (Brockington, 1973, 255; REB 'returning from the battle'). שׁוּבֵי should be allowed its passive force (H. Schmidt, 138; J. T. Willis, 1970, 82f., 84; Wolff, 41) and שׁוּבֵי מלחמה is then complementary to עברים בסח: the travellers are not expecting trouble (they are not armed to the teeth), for they have taken an aversion to war—they have renounced war.

ואתמול עמי should be emended to ואתם על עמי, יקומם to תקומו and שׁלמה. ממולי to ממול should be taken as a metathesis for שׁמלה, אדר as a haplography of אדרת and אדרת as a doublet of שׁמלה: 'But you rise up against my people as an enemy. In my sight you strip off the garments from unsuspecting travellers who are turned away from war.'

There is a grammatical incongruence in v. 9 which should perhaps be tolerated (Ehrlich, 277; Rudolph, 58; Wolff, 41; GK 124s), but תענוגיה and עלליה are emended by some to תענוגיהן and עלליהן (Duhm, 1911, 86; Schmidt, 138; Smith, 56; Weiser, 247; Robinson, 134). Otherwise the obscurity of הדרי is the only remaining difficulty in the verse. The oppressors evict the women from the houses in which they delight and take away from their children the 'glory' which Yahweh has given them. Wellhausen (23) has not been followed in supposing that מבית תענוגיה should be translated as 'from their beloved children': mothers are forcibly separated from the children on whom they dote.

It has been noted that Rashi and Kimchi give different accounts as to the content of הדר: Rashi is nearer to modern commentators who retain MT. Wellhausen (236) remarks that that the loss of הדר consists in the sale of children to foreigners and their consequent permanent alienation from Yahweh. Duhm (1911, 85) comments that the loss of הדר is the deprivation of land and citizen rights. Smith (62), Weiser (247), Robinson (134) and Hillers (36) are satisfied with 'my glory'. H. Schmidt (138), following Gressmann, proposes חדרי לעולם, 'final resting-places, 'tombs' (cf. Rudolph, 59), whereas the sense 'bed-chamber' is captured by emending הדרי to חדר (Wolff, 41, *Schlaf-kammer*) (cf. Rudolph, 59). Rudolph favours הדור for הדרי in the sense of 'home': the children are uprooted from the place to which they belong and to which they should have been anchored throughout their lives.

The impression should not be created that vv. 1–10 are a seamless robe and that v. 11 is a problem created by the transition from consistent indictment to reflection touched with irony. Verses 6–7 are argument rather than indictment and, in so far as the voice of the oppressors is introduced (perhaps also in v. 10a), the monotone of accusation in vv. 1–10 is interrupted and there is evidence of the use of a literary device to introduce satire and deflate the oppressors (for example, the cosy theology which they utter at v. 7b—reading דבריו). This satirical note would be enhanced if Duhm's interpretation of v. 10 were adopted. Nor should the discernment of a prosaic character in v. 11 (Smith) be regarded as decisive. The verse is set out as prose by NEB and REB, but others represent it as poetry. Moreover, there are difficulties in linking v. 8 with the earlier part of the chapter. Are those who have taken to a kind of brigandage (v. 8) to be identified with those who are pilloried in vv. 1–2? Verse 8 does not advance Pixley's hypothesis (1991, 53–60) that Micah (2.6–11) had been fomenting a peasants' revolt against oppressive landlords and that vv. 6–7 are an attempt to silence him. The reflective mood and the irony of v. 11 do not disengage it from vv. 1–10, but the circumstance that a different usage of עם appears in it (Rudolph) is a more weighty consideration.

6. 'Do not go on and on', they go on.
'They should not harp on these things.'
Disaster will not overtake[1] (us).

7. Can it be asked, O house of Jacob,
'Is Yahweh's patience exhausted?
Are these his deeds?
Does he not deal benevolently[2] with the upright?'

8. But you rise[3] against my people[4] as an enemy.
In my sight[5] you strip off the robes[6]
from those who are passing by unsuspecting,
with no hostile intentions.

9. You drive the women of my people
from their desirable homes;
you take from their children
my glory for ever.

10. Rise and go;
this is not your final resting-place;

[1] יסג = ישג.
[2] Reading דבריו.
[3] Reading תקומו for יקומם.
[4] Reading ואתם על עמי for ואתמול עמי.
[5] Reading ממולי for ממול.
[6] Deleting אדר (אדרת) as a doublet of שמלה = שלמה.

because you are defiled
you cause[7] irreparable damage.

11.   If a man of wind were to go about uttering falsehoods and saying, 'I
      shall predict for you wine and strong drink', his drivel would be to
      the liking of this people.

vv. 12–13 A GATHERING OF THE DISPERSED AND A MARCH HOME

I begin with MT and with the commentaries of Rashi, Kimchi and Ibn
Ezra. Rashi supposes that vv. 12–13 are a prophecy of hope which looks
to the future and he explains the infinitive absolute אסף in this
connection, 'The days are coming (עוד ימים באים) when I shall gather.'
Targ., on the other hand, like Kimchi, supposes that v. 12 is a
prediction of exile, so that his comment בסוף means something like
'finally'. Rashi comments on כצאן בצרה, 'like a large flock which is
located in a secure fold', deriving בצרה from בצר. He cites Targ. (דירא
בעדרא בגו, 'like a flock in the midst of a fold') for בתוך הדברו and
comments 'a place where it (the flock) is fed', indicating that he
understands דבר as 'pasture'. He notices the suffix with the definitive
article (הדברו). GK 1910, 127i (*BDB*, 1907, 184; Smith, 67; Robinson, 136; Rudolph, 62; Wolff, 42) deals with this oddity by redividing
the Hebrew text (בתוך הדבר ותהימנה). The comment of Rashi on
תהימנה brings him nearer to the exegesis of Kimchi who equates בצרה
with the Edomite town of that name (cf. KJV, RV, 'sheep of Bozrah').
Rashi's elucidation of תחימנה מאדם shows that he interprets the sheep
in the fold as the imagery of a simile which refers to men penned in
towns like sheep. He remarks, 'The towns resound with noise (תחימנה)
from the scurrying about of men in their midst.' Hence תהימנה מאדם is
not a direct continuation of the preceding similes, but is an application
of them (also Kimchi).

   It is difficult to believe that Rashi has siege conditions in mind and
that he takes 'the gathering of Jacob' (v. 12) as a herding into fortified
cities for asylum in conditions of siege, though he portrays the deliverer
(מושיעה) as breaking through the barrier of a thorn hedge (v. 13),
resuming the imagery of v. 12) and pioneering a level road for those
who follow him. The first part of v. 13 could refer to the bursting out of

[7]Reading תחבלו חבל for תחבל וחבל.

a siege, but the level road (Rashi, לישר לפניהם הדרך) rather portrays smooth progress led by Yahweh and recalls the מסלה of Isa 11.16, 40.31, 49.11 etc. (cf. Wolff, 55f.; Mendicki, 1981, 96–99) and the road with a uniform surface along which swift and easy progress can be made (Prov. 2.13; 4.11; Isa. 42.16).

Though there is ambiguity in Rashi's exegesis of vv. 12–13, there is little doubt that he interprets the verses as a prophecy of hope—a prediction of the gathering together of the scattered remnant of Israel from their different places of exile as a preliminary to their safe and triumphant progress home under the leadership of Yahweh (cf. Rudolph, 65, 'fold' and 'pasture' are figures of a gathering prior to deliverance). Kimchi, on the other hand, explains v. 12 as a preparation for exile rather than in association with a prophecy of hope: not a gathering of Israel scattered in exile but a people under siege and on the brink of exile. 'The sheep of Bozrah' are large flocks and the appropriateness of 'Bozrah' derives from the circumstances that Edom is a land of cattle: it has extensive pastures in which large flocks of sheep graze (cf. Hillers, 38). But Bozrah also indicates that the sheep, the fold and the pastures are a similitude which refers to fortified cities under siege, where the population is swollen by refugees who have taken shelter in them: 'They will gather in siege conditions in fortified cities for fear of the enemy' (Kimchi).

Kimchi's presupposition is that those gathered in the fortified cities do not have the power to resist the enemy. Their morale is not high. They do not expect to repulse the besieger and are agitated at the prospect of his attack. The third feminine verb (תהימנה) is elucidated on the assumption that the subject is 'the fortified cities'. Hence Kimchi agrees with Rashi that the simile comes to an end at הדברו and that its interpretation begins at תהימנה: the fortified cities buzz with the throng of anxious refugees (מאדם). Kimchi does not suppose that v. 13 is a prediction of deliverance. He takes it as a description of a scene which was a prelude to exile and identifies it with an allusion to the siege of Jerusalem by Nebuchadrezzar and with the break-out of Zedekiah and his cohort (Jer. 52.1–7). Prior to Zedekiah's flight the שכינה was raised over those besieged and afterwards they went into exile (Kimchi). According to Brin (1989, 118–124) vv. 12–13 are a prediction of doom; v. 12 depicts a defenceless situation and v. 13 is a kind of irony. Yahweh will not go before to lead his people to deliverance, but to ensure that they get their deserts and arrive at their destination—destruction.

The Versions

כלך is represented by Vulg. and Pesh., the plural suffix (כולכון) by Targ., while Sept. (σὺν πᾶσιν) renders כלך more freely. כלך is emended to כלו (Wellhausen, 137; Ehrlich, 5, 278; Smith, 67; Schmidt, 148; Weiser, 251; Robinson, 136; Hillers, 38), but it is retained by Rudolph (64f.) and Wolff (38, 55). If כלך is retained, יעקב is a vocative and שארית ישראל is an accusative. The two are then not synonyms: יעקב is all-inclusive and שארית ישראל refers to the diaspora.

The insertion of suffixes by Pesh ('*knšk; 'qrbk*) has the effect of making both יעקב and שארית ישראל into vocatives, perhaps under the influence of כלך (cf. Hillers, 38). Targ. similarly attaches a suffix to אאסף (אכנשכון) and adds גלותכון after אקבץ (אקריב) and this requires vocatives. Targ. 'I shall surely bring near your exile, O remnant of Israel' shows an understanding of v. 12 similar to that of Kimchi: it is an intimation that exile is imminent and not a description of arrangements which are a preliminary to deliverance. Pesh. connects יחד with what precedes it, contrary to the punctuation of MT. Sept., Vulg. and Targ. follow the punctuation of MT.

Sept. spells out the suffix of אשימנו as τὴν ἀποστρόφην αὐτοῦ (LXX[B] αὐτοῦ; Ziegler, 1943, 211 αὐτῶν; cf. Targ. אשוינון, 'I shall set them'). כצאן בצרה 'like sheep of Bozrah' (MT, KJV, RV) is analysed differently by the versions: בצרה is explained as ב + צרה. On the analogy of בתוך הדברו this is probably correct (so Wellhausen, 1892, 137) and Targ. renders both ב and בתוך with בגו. Sept. (ἐν θλίψει) and Pesh. (*b'wlṣn'*) vocalize צרה as צָרָה (ex צרר) meaning 'affliction', whereas Vulg. (*in ovili*) and Targ. (בגו חטרא) render בצרה as 'in a sheepfold'. The latter have given rise to the vocalization of צרה as צְרָה. (Schmidt, 148; Weiser, 251; Rudolph, 62; Wolff, 42). The form is not otherwise attested in biblical Hebrew. Smith (69) suggests that צְרָה is a by-form of סירה (*BDB*, 377), and Syriac *tyr'* and Arabic *ṣyrat* are noticed (Robinson, 136; cf. Symm. and Theod. ἐν ὀχυρώματι 'in a fortress').

The versions do not explain satisfactorily the phrase בתוך הדברו and only Pesh. represents the suffix (*rb'h*). Moreover, they attach the wrong sense to דבר 'pasture': Sept. κοίλη 'resting-place' and Vulg. *caularum* 'sheepfolds' 'Sheepfold' is also the sense of Pesh. *rḇ'h* and Targ. חטרא. Wolff (38), though he notes דבר 'pasture' follows the versions in his translation (*in der Hürde*). He is perhaps influenced by the assumption that there is synonymous parallelism between צְרָה and דבר.

The versions disagree with Rashi and Kimchi in their interpretation of הדברו תהימנה which should be emended to הדבר ותהימנה. The versions all assume that the imagery of the simile is being continued in this phrase and that Israel is still being likened to a flock of sheep. This rather than its containing an interpretation of the imagery of the simile, as is supposed by Rashi and Kimchi. This is also the tentative view of Wolff (42) who suggests that ותהימנה should be emended to ותהיינה and who treats ותהיינה מאדם as a gloss whose function is to explain that the 'sheep' of v. 12 in a 'fold' are crowds of men in devastated cities. The presence of men (Vulg. and Targ. 'a multitude of men') in the vicinity of the fold, to which the flock is not accustomed upsets the sheep at rest (Vulg. *tumultuabuntur*) and they bleat loudly at this interruption of their privacy. Sept. and Pesh. indicate a different reaction: they shrink from or cringe at the presence of humans. Rudolph's exegesis (65) of ותהמה מאדם (emended) is different. The phrase reinforces the emphasis on the togetherness of the preceding part of v. 12 and the largeness of the assembly gathered is an enhancement of the note of hope (similarly Weiser, 251).

The third person feminine plural is accounted for by assuming a compound subject, a mixture of feminine singular (צרה) and masculine singular (דבר), 'fold' and 'pasture' being equivalents of 'sheep' (GK 1910, 145b; *BDB*, 1907, 223; Smith, 69; Wolff, 42). Rudolph (62f.) rejects this explanation of the third person feminine plural and emends ותהימנה, *ex* הום to ותהמה *ex* המה (so also Hillers, 38). Wernberg-Møller (1958: 307) derives תהימנה from המה as a Qal.

In Sept. at v. 13 the Hebrew verbs, one perfect (פרצו) and the others waw consecutive imperfect, are all rendered as aorists. Wellhausen (137) notes the oddness of the tenses and Smith (69; also Rudolph, 63) explains עלה and פרצו as prophetic perfects which are resumed by waw consecutive imperfects (also future). עלה at the beginning of the verse is a minus in Sept. and διὰ τῆς διακόπης perhaps represents (so Wolff, 42) על הפרץ 'through the breach'. The Hebrew text represented by Sept. may be defective (haplography of ה). Pesh. *slq trw''* represents MT and otherwise produces perfect tenses for the *waw* consecutive

imperfects of MT. It shows פרץ for פרצו and Robinson (136), also
Wolff, 42) has supposed that there is a dittography of ו in MT. Pesh. *tr*ʾ
twrʾt 'make a breach' renders פרץ and שער is a minus. Vulg. translates
the Hebrew perfects (עלה and פרצו) as present tenses and the waw
consecutive imperfects as future tenses. This suits the context better,
since v. 13 is presumably a prediction of which the present tense would
be a graphic portrayal (cf. NEB, 'So their leader breaks out before them,
and they all break through the gate and escape, and their king goes
before them, and the LORD leads the way'). Vulg. follows the
vocalization of הפרץ in MT: *pandens iter* 'the path-finder'.

Targ. renders עלה as ויסקון (סלק) and gives משיזבין 'deliverers' for
הפרץ (cf. Rashi מושיעה). In view of the reference to Yahweh as king
(Smith, 69; Weiser, 252; Robinson, 136; Van der Woude 1969, 257;
Rudolph, 65) there can be little doubt that v. 13 is a prediction of a
triumphant march home. Unlike Kimchi, Targ. has created an antithesis between v. 12 and v. 13: the one is a coralling of Israel for exile, the
other an escape from captivity and a victorious progress to freedom.
Targ. expands MT at v. 13: deliverers will advance in front of them and
a king will lead at their head. He will shatter the enemies who oppresses
them; he will reduce powerful strongholds; he will possess the nations.
Their king will be at their head and the Memra of Yahweh at their
side.

According to Rudolph (65; also Smith, 68; Weiser, 252; Robinson,
137) the figure of 'sheep' and 'fold' is maintained in v. 13a and the
portrayal is that of a bell-wether (*Leithammel*) breaking out of an
enclosure at the head of the flock. In v. 13b the imagery is dropped and
the interpretation appears: Yahweh as king will lead his people out of
their incarceration in a foreign place and they will march home. Wolff's
view (55) is that the figure of the flock does not appear in v. 13a and
that the transition from simile to interpretation occurs at ותהימנה מאדם,
a gloss which explicates the flock of sheep as a throng of men (cf. Rashi
and Kimchi). Verse 13 (so Wolff) depicts a foreign place where
scattered Israelites had been assembled, not a besieged city but a
fortified one, a prison whose outer perimeter they are unable to breach.
Yahweh is the פרץ who breaks through the fortifications and leads his
people through the city-gate (שער) as their king. But the relationship
between v. 12 and v. 13 is then obscured: that the 'gathering' in v. 12 is
represented as a comforting word (קבץ; אסף; so Wolff) sits uneasily

with the assumption that the place of assembly is a prison from which an escape has to be made. On the other hand, the elucidation of בצרה as 'Bozra' (MT) can be connected with the view that vv. 12–13 depict a break-out from a foreign city (cf. Wolff, 46) in which the assembled exiles are immured.

It was noticed that whereas Rashi took vv. 12–13 to be a prophecy of weal Kimchi interpreted it as a prediction of doom and that Brin has recently produced his own version of the exegesis of these verses after the manner of Kimchi. A general division of opinion among modern scholars does not hinge on the choice between weal and woe but on whether the verses are to be assigned to Micah and his age (Schmidt, 148; Van der Woude 1969: 256f.; Rudolph, 65; Hillers, 39f.) or whether they are to be located in a later age and presuppose conditions of exile and dispersion (Wellhausen, 136f.; Ehrlich, 1912: 278; Smith, 66; Weiser, 251f.; Wolff, 46). Both of these groups are agreed that vv. 12–13 predict weal.

Let us consider the first division and begin with Schmidt. He assigns vv. 12–13 to Micah and supposes that the situation in which they are set is the siege of Jerusalem by Sennacherib in 701 (v. 12) and the relief of that siege (v. 13) which enabled the besieged Judaeans to return to their places of domicile in Judah. This, however, is not what vv. 12–13 appears to describe. If we pass over the objection that עלה (v. 13) is unsuitable, since the exit from Jerusalem is a descent, there remains the objection that vv. 12–13 deal with a gathering of the dispersed of Israel in a foreign place and a victorious progress home led by Yahweh. Hillers (39) does not pinpoint the historical situation so exactly as Schmidt, but he urges that vv. 12–13 could well be assigned to Micah and dated in the eighth century: 'But the loss of the Northern Kingdom in 722 and the large deportation of Sennacherib in 701 might easily have suggested in the eighth century that the flock of God was in need of a gathering.' He meets the requirements of the verses better than Schmidt, but his contention that the historical background is the eighth century rather than the exilic period and the dispersion of Israel is improbable.

Van der Woude revives an exegesis of Ibn Ezra and holds that vv. 12–13 are the utterances of false prophets who were Micah's adversaries and that they are a counter-blast to his prophecies of doom. Verse 12 refers to a besieged city (Jerusalem; cf. Schmidt) and v. 13 contains an

assurance that Yahweh will intervene as a deliverer. Van der Woude
urges that שארית ישראל and other features do not necessarily point to
an exilic background, but his contention that the basis of the hope of
the false prophets was their Zion theology, their dogma that Jerusalem
was inviolable, does not seem to have much to do with the depiction of
vv. 12–13.

Finally there is Rudolph who stands somewhat apart from those with
whom he is classed. He acknowledges that vv. 12–13 are a prediction of
the gathering of the dispersed of Israel in exile and a return home. They
are, however, a prediction made by Micah in the eighth century. The
question to be asked is whether such an exact prediction of weal focused
on the distant future could issue from an eighth century prophet of
doom so taken up with the storm-clouds of the present. Rudolph
admits that there is not a continuity between v. 11 and vv. 12–13 and
he explains the position of the latter as an element of a doom/weal
pattern imposed by a redactor on the book of Micah (1/2; 3/5; 6/7).
Doom prophecies are followed by a hopeful conclusion in a regular
sequence. This is the arrangement of a redactor, but these predictions of
a better future are to be assigned to Micah. The judgement which has to
be made is whether vv. 12–13 are better accounted for as a luminous
prediction by an eighth century prophet of a distant future or as a future
hope which arises from the circumstances of exile and dispersion.

Robinson stands apart from the scholars of the second group
(Wellhausen; Ehrlich; Smith; Weiser; Wolff) in that, though he locates
vv. 12–13 in the post-exilic period, he assumes a Palestinian background, not an exilic one, and describes the verses as a kind of
apocalyptic. A visionary surveys a land which is overrun by enemies and
whose inhabitants have been decimated, the survivors having taken
refuge in a strongly fortified city, perhaps Jerusalem, where they are
besieged. The siege is relieved under the leadership of Yahweh. The
verses deal with the last days, the end of time, when great tribulation
issues in final victory. The problems which arise from Robinson's
exegesis are those which were raised in connection with the first group
of scholars. What is portrayed is not the raising of a siege, but a journey
home from a foreign prison which has been breached.

The others in the second group hold that vv. 12–13 presuppose the
exile and the dispersion and this rules out a pre-exilic origin but leaves
open an exilic or post-exilic one. Wolff (55f.) picks out the dependence

on the vocabulary and imagery of Deutero-Isaiah and identifies vv.
12–13 as a prophecy of weal which was attached to the book of Micah
by a redactor in the early Persian period. He acknowledges that the
incohesiveness of vv. 12–13 remains a problem, that the gathering of
the dispersed of Israel, which is a comforting and hopeful word, does
not combine well with escape from imprisonment in a foreign city. He
suggests that v. 13 may have originated as an exegesis of 'fold' in v. 12,
but, if his intention is to say that this is a wrong exegesis of v. 12, the
implication is that v. 13 is secondary. A formal difference between v. 12
and v. 13 which has been noticed (Weiser, 252; Rudolph, 64; Wolff,
56; Hillers, 39) is that v. 12 has the form of 'word of God', whereas v.
13 refers to Yahweh in the third person.

> 12. I shall not fail to gather you, all of you[1], O Jacob
>   I shall assuredly assemble the remnant of Israel
>   I shall muster you like sheep in the fold[2],
>   Like a flock in the pasture[3],
>   [and they will be noisy[4] with men[5]].
> 13. The leader of the flock will advance before them,
>   The flock will break through, pass the gate, and go out of it.
>   Their king will go before them,
>   Yahweh will be at their head.

[1]Retaining כלך with MT.
[2]Reading בצרה as בצרה.
[3]Reading בתוך הדבר.
[4]Reading ותהימנה.
[5] ותהימנה מאדם a secondary gloss.

CHAPTER 3

vv. 1–4 RULERS WHO HATE GOOD AND LOVE EVIL

According to MT (ואמר, v. 1) the speech which follows in vv. 1–4 is direct; according to Sept. (καὶ ἐρεῖ) and Pesh. (wʾmr) it is reported. Hillers (41) adopts וְאָמַר as the original Hebrew text and Rudolph (67) concludes that the vocalization of ואמר assumed by Sept. and Pesh. is erroneous. In both cases the speaker who is introduced is presumably Micah (so Kimchi; Duhm, 86—in contrast to the roisterers of 2.11), since the reference to Yahweh in the third person (v. 4) precludes him from being the speaker.

Wellhausen (137) supposes that ואמר is secondary and that שמעו נא was the original beginning of vv. 1–4 (cf. v. 9) and he is followed by Ehrlich (5, 278) who describes ואמר as a secondary link showing poor taste (also Smith, 72). Wolff (64f.) agrees that ואמר is redactional, but he takes it as a statement that the contents of chapter 3 were dictated or written down by Micah. Weiser (253) suggests that ואמר is evidence of a narrative which is not fully preserved. Robinson (137) calls in question the unity of vv. 1–2a and 2b–4 and points to the transition from 2nd person to 3rd person. He conjectures that v. 2b and ואשר (v. 3) are stitches with which a redactor sewed together vv. 1–2a and 3–4. Willis (54) conjectures that 'And I said' is a signal from a redactor that a new section of the oracles is about to begin (cf. Rudolph, 68f.; Wolff, 65). The sections are specified as chapters 1/2, 3/5, 6/7. 'Jacob' and 'House of Israel' refer to Judah (Wellhausen, 137; Robinson, 137) which may indicate a post-722 date for chapter 3 (Rudolph, 70; see, however, Wolff, 66f.; Hillers, 43). Sept. has καὶ κατάλοιποι for וקציני at v. 1 and v. 9 and Rudolph (67) explains this by supposing that קצין has been connected with קץ 'end' and that 'end' has been taken as an equivalence to 'remainder' (cf. Wolff, 60).

The language in these verses is grisly. The leaders of Jacob (Sept., Pesh., 'the house of Jacob' as at MT v. 9) and the rulers of the house of Israel are appointed to discern and support what is right (v. 1), but they hate good and love evil. Their abuse of the offices which they hold is

95

extreme and inhuman. They murder the people for whose well-being
they should care and then they butcher them and make a meal of them.
The authority and power which they wield they exercise as cannibals
(Weiser, 254; Hillers, 41, 43). Wolff (69f.) contrasts the desperate
hunger which drives mothers to eat their children in conditions of siege
(2 Kgs 6.26–30; Lam. 4.10) with a 'cannibalism' which is a corruption
of power, which goes hand in hand with affluence, and is a matter of the
policy adopted by those who govern a community.

Both Wellhausen (137) and Duhm (86) are inclined to delete v. 2b
(cf. Wellhausen's translation, p. 23). They notice that the 3rd person
plural suffixes of עורם and עצמותם do not refer to anything which
precedes them and Wellhausen adds that v. 2b is a variant of v. 3a (also
Smith, 72f.) and his translation does not show v. 2b (23). Duhm
conjectures that v. 2b is misplaced and that it should come after v. 5a
(Marti). Weiser (254) agrees that the suffixes of v. 2b lack a reference,
but he relocates it after v. 3, emending גזלי to גזלו and interpreting it as
a threat uttered against the rulers which is a preliminary to v. 4. H.
Schmidt (137), on the other hand, deletes v. 3 as an expansion of v. 2b
and Rudolph deletes part of v. 3 (ועורם מעליהם הפשיטו) as a gloss on v.
2b elucidating the unusual sense which is attached to גזל there, 'steal'
< 'strip' < 'flay' (also Wolff, 60). Rudolph (67) explains the 3rd person
plural suffixes in v. 2b as indefinite (*ihr einem*). Wolff (60) appeals to
ואמר (v. 1) in order to justify the 3rd plural suffixes in v. 2b: ואמר is an
attempt to establish that chapter 3 is a continuation of chapter 2 and so
the suffixes in v. 2b are to be referred to the oppressed in 2.9 (cf. Hillers,
42, who finds the reference for the suffixes in 'Jacob' and the 'House of
Israel).

Ehrlich's treatment (5, 278) of v. 2b has more far-reaching consequences, since it has the effect of changing the significance of the
imagery in vv. 2b–3a. According to Ehrlich, it is v. 3 as far as הפשיטו
which should be deleted and he explains the language in v. 2b and the
remaining part of v. 3 in terms of the expression 'bone of my bone and
flesh of my flesh' (Gen. 2.23: עצם מעצמי ובשר מבשרי). The third
person plural suffixes in v. 2b refer to the rulers themselves and it is they
who strip off their own skin and pare the flesh from their own bones.
The rulers are not being depicted as cannibals. Rather the concept of
community is that of an association of kin—a large family—and the
rulers are represented as eating the bone of their bone and the flesh of

their flesh. By their oppression of the people they are devouring themselves. The interpretation is ingenious but unlikely.

Another account of the imagery is given by Rudolph (70; also Wolff, 69) who finds the model in the slaughter and butchery of cattle and in the preparation of the cuts of meat for the pot. The assumption of the cannibalistic interpretation is that the third person plural suffixes in v. 2b anticipate עמי in v. 3. H. Graetz emends עורם in v. 2b to עור עמי and this is how v. 2b is taken by REB ('You flay the skin of my people and tear the flesh from their bones'). That v. 2b assumes the presence of עמי in v. 3 would be a further indication that it is secondary in the context of vv. 1– 4. Smith (73) supposes that the figure in v. 3 is that of watch-dogs savaging a flock of sheep which they should protect.

That the language is not literal but metaphorical is noticed by Kimchi and Ibn Ezra (also Robinson, 137), who describe the piece as a משל and Targ. brings this out clearly. The *Bild* is already explicated as a simile at v. 3b: the rulers misuse the people as if they were pieces of meat for the pot (Duhm, 86). Targ. interprets the imagery in terms of theft (גזל) caused by malicious greed—the snatching of the possessions of the people from their hands and the acquisition of the wealth which they have accumulated, the product of their hard work (יגיעה). Targ. elucidates the metaphor: 'In that they despoil the possessions of my people and take their accumulated wealth they consume their flesh continually and cut them up as joints for the pot and pieces for the cauldron.' Kimchi remarks that the evil-doing of the rulers is expressed as a משל: 'I have a complaint to make against you, heads and rulers, for it is your duty to know what is just and to rescue the oppressed from the oppressor.' As if it were not enough that they did not benefit the poor, they do them injury: they plunder their goods and their food, that is, their skin and their flesh and their bones—a hyperbole.

The separating of flesh from the bones and the chopping of it into pieces for the pot are clearly connected with the preparation of food, but it is not so evident that crushed bones (ואת עצמתיהם פצחו) would make a contribution to an appetizing meal. Targ. does not mention the crushed bones and for ועורם מעליהם הפשיטו (v. 3) it has 'and they consume their flesh continually' (both Sperber and *Miqrâoth Gedoloth*). פצחו is rendered as 'shatter' or 'crush' by Sept. (συνέθλασαν), Vulg. (*confregerunt*), Pesh. (*tbrw*) and Kimchi (שבר). Rashi makes this reference more understandable by glossing פצחו as פתחו and taking it as an allusion to the process of opening the bones in order to extract marrow from them (Hillers, 43). Wellhausen (137) remarks that Sept. ἐμέλισαν 'cut up' is an indication that פרש has been equated with פרס 'break bread' (Isa. 58.7; Jer. 16.7). He queries whether this sense can be extended to embrace 'cut up flesh', but Vulg. (*conciderunt*) and Targ. (מפלגין) have so taken it and have evidently regarded פרש as a variant form of פרס (so Rudolph, 74; Hillers, 42). Also Kimchi who glosses ופרשו with התיכה 'slice'. Pesh., on the other hand, renders ופרשו as *wʾrmyw* 'and they toss'—the flesh and meat which they have butchered is tossed into the pot (cf. Schmidt [137 n. 1] who renders ופרשו with *ausanderlegen* 'set out').

Another matter which should be noted in connection with the elucidation of the imagery is the reading of Sept. (ὡς σάρκας) for MT כאשר. MT is supported by Vulg., Pesh. and Targ., but the corruption of כשאר (Sept.) to כאשר is likely in view of the subsequent וכבשר which matches כשאר, 'like flesh for the pot and meat for the cauldron' (so Wellhausen, 137; Duhm, 86; Ehrlich, 278; Smith, 71; Schmidt, 137 n. 1; Weiser, 253; Robinson, 136; Rudolph, 67; Wolff, 61; Hillers, 42). ואשר (v. 3) is deleted by Ehrlich (278) and Wolff (60). It is represented by Sept. (ὃν τρόπον), Vulg. (*qui*), Pesh. (*d*) and Targ. (וד). ταῦτα (Sept.) and *hlyn* (Pesh.) are added to MT (v. 1) as an object for שמעו as in MT v. 9. Rudolph (67) holds that ואשר (v. 3) connects with v. 4 rather than v. 2: 'Those who eat the flesh of my people ... then call out to Yahweh' (cf. Sept. ὃν τρόπον ... οὕτως). The function of ואשר is to underline the bare-faced inconsistency between the scandalous behaviour of v. 3 and the pose of piety in v. 4. בעת ההיא (v. 4) is deleted as an addition by many scholars (Duhm, 86; Ehrlich, 278; Smith, 74; Schmidt, 137; Weiser, 253; Robinson, 136; Rudolph, 67; Wolff, 61). Duhm associates the addition with the eschatological interpretation which was given to the verse and Wolff (66) holds that it is a deuteronomistic reinterpretation which makes the verse into a predic-tion of the fall of Jerusalem. Hillers (42) argues that בעת ההיא 'serves to make אז more explicit', whereas Rudolph (71) holds that it gives a wrong, distant, temporal sense to אז whose function is rather to underline that an appeal to Yahweh will go unheeded ('if then').

The terminology (קציני בית ישראל/ראשי (בית) יעקב) occurs only at Micah 3.1, 9 and the question has to be raised whether this is a case of synonymous parallelism. so that one class instead of two classes with

different functions are mentioned (Rudolph, 69). לראש וקצין (Jud.
11.11), used of Jepthah by the elders of Gilead in connection with the
waging of war against the Ammonites, is equally troublesome, since one
can establish no more than that it refers to a kind of leadership. קצין has
elsewhere special reference to a military command (Jos. 10.24; Jud.
11.6) and Wolff (67) has supposed that קצין is related to Jephthah's
success in war against the Ammonites (Jud. 11.6), while ראש is
indicative of how this success was rewarded by the conferring on him of
permanent leadership by the elders of Gilead.

   ראש is so general a word ('head', 'leader') that it gives no clue as to
what the specific functions of the office may have been, whereas Arabic
qḍy has been called into service to define the office of קצין as that of a
'judge' and to establish that the קצין discharged a narrow juridical role.
It is unlikely that the קצינים mentioned in Mic. 3.1, 9 were so
employed. They were not 'judges' who sat on the bench and handed
down sentences, though they may not have been entirely divorced from
the machinery of the judiciary and may have exercised an influence on
legal decisions, directly or indirectly. But the pattern of use displayed by
קצין in biblical Hebrew does not support the view that a קצין held a
legal office (Rudolph, 69). The indications given by the distribution of
occurrences (*BDB*, 392) are that קצין is used of a 'military commander'
or a 'ruler', though Isa. 3.6f. needs special treatment. The evidence
supplied by the versions at Mic. 3.1, 9 is not clear-cut, but it tends to
support the view that ראשי and קציני are in synonymous parallelism and
that they are alternative titles of the same office rather than names for
two separate offices. Thus Pesh. renders ראשי in both places as rš' and
קציני as šlyṭn', 'heads' and 'rulers' (similarly Targ. רישי and שלטני). Vulg.
agrees with this in v. 1 (*principes* and *duces*), but unaccountably renders
קציני as *iudices* 'judges' at v. 9. Sept has the aberrant καὶ οἱ κατάλοιποι
at v. 1 and v. 9 and does not make a serious contribution to the
question whether ראש and קצין refer to one office or two.

   The tendency to dwell too much on the administration of justice by
judges in law courts in connection with the Micah verses is present in
Wolff (68f.) and is especially noticeable in Hillers (41) who translates
קציני (Mic. 3.1, 9) as 'judges', who renders טוב and רעה (רע) as 'right'
and 'wrong' (3.2) and interprets them as a reference to unjust verdicts
passed down by a judge. What can have been meant precisely by ראשי
and קציני in eighth century Jerusalem is a difficult question to answer. It

is acknowledged that ראש is an office which has to be correlated with the tribal character of Old Testament society in pre-monarchic times (Bartlett, 1969, 1–10; Wolff, 67) before the appearance of the bureaucracy which created royal officials, but קצין in Isa. 3.6f. seems to have the same *Sitz im Leben* as ראש. A man is button-holed by his brother in the house of their father, 'You have a cloak and you will be our קצין.' He is asked to assume responsibity for the well-being of the family (the extended family) in a situation where the fabric of the community has collapsed (המכשלה הזאת). 'You have a cloak' is presumably an idiom for 'You are a man of substance'—you can afford assuming financial responsibilty for the welfare of the family and dispense your liberality to its members. He refuses the offer and denies that he has the material resources to discharge the office: 'There is neither bread nor cloak in my house and you shall not make me head of the clan' (NEB, Hebrew חבש).

If ראש and קצין are both clan offices, the mystery deepens. Wolff (68) notices that Micah does not use the new terminology (שרים) which designates the cadre of royal statesmen installed by the monarchy in Jerusalem. Is his language (ראש and קצין) then deliberately archaic? Is he expressing contempt for the new breed of functionaries by comparing them unfavourably with the old regime? This train of thought may be taken further, but, for the time being, it may be concluded that Micah is inveighing against wicked and cruel government rather than the corruption of the judiciary, though this may be an aspect of the total corruption. Wolff does not distinguish adequately between the abuse of power by an iniquitous government, which destroys a society, and legal decisions made by those who sit on the bench. Not that it is necessary to deny that ראשי and קציני may have exerted an influence on the conduct of the law courts and on the verdicts passed by judges. Micah's quarrel, however, is not principally with those who interpret laws but with those who make them (government). It is those who maliciously produce degeneration in the texture of the community (משפט) which they should cherish whom Micah attacks. They destroy their society rather than exercising care for its well-being. They lack generosity of spirit; they are obsessed with power and greed; their motivation as rulers is perverted, and they substitute malevolence (רעה or רע) for benevolence (טוב). They abuse the society which they should nurture and they impose a selfish and a cruel tyranny instead of respecting constitutional

rule and customary law. Their thoughts towards the community which
they rule are those of evil and not of good and it is in this wider context
that משפט (v. 1) should be appraised (Rudolph, 69).

Isaiah was a contemporary of Micah whose controversy in a Jerusalem setting was carried on not with ראשים and קצינים but with שרים,
with the bureaucrats who had emerged in Jerusalem in connection with
the monarchy and who were the king's men, statesmen and officials
(McKane, 1965, 65–78). The circumstance that the subject of Isaiah's
concern was different, in this respect, from that of Micah has to be
taken into account. He was concerned with international relations, with
how national security could be best achieved; with how conflicts with
other nations were to be resolved and how the national peril arising
from them should be faced, whether by the diplomacy on which the
outside world relied or through trust in Yahweh.

Micah, on the other hand, concentrates on the internal social
structures of Judah and Isaiah shares this concern. Micah lays the blame
for the failures of government in that sphere at the door of admin-
istrators whose motives are malevolent and whose methods are cruel,
who seek to maximize their own gain at the expense of the well-being of
the community for which they are responsible. I return to the question
whether Jerusalem, the king's city, dominated by the king's men had
any room for ראשים and קצינים, the titles of offices which belong to a
pre-monarchic society with a different social structure. Are ראשים and
קצינים code-names for שרים which betray Micah's sympathy with a
kind of leadership, belonging to an earlier age, which perhaps survived
in the rural areas of Judah (Moresheth) from which Micah came? There
may be irony or an implication of disapproval in Micah's addressing of
שרים as ראשים and קצינים. They are unrecognizable as rulers of the old
stamp and quality. They are consumed with a base self-interest; they are
corrupted with power; they are obsessed with a greed for gain and they
inflict terrible suffering on their community.

It may be argued that we should question whether the public
assembly which Micah addressed was located in Jerusalem, but there is a
firm indication in vv. 10, 12 that this was its *locus* and scholars have
assumed (Rudolph, 68; Wolff, 67) that the setting of Micah's harangue
was the temple court and that the opportunity was given by a crowd
which had assembled for a cultic celebration in the Jerusalem temple. A
way of avoiding the conclusion which I have canvassed would be to urge

that שׂרים had different functions to discharge and that there was room
for ראשים and קצינים even in the king's city and among the king's men.
The ראשים and קצינים ought to have exercised a responsibility
comparable to that of their namesakes in pre-monarchic times in Judah
and Micah's point would be that their interpretation of these responsi-
bilities bore no resemblance to the benevolent concern for the people
whom they governed which had characterized the regime of their
forerunners. It is a puzzle, however, what functions ראשים and קצינים
could have performed in the royal city of Jerusalem, in the shadow of
the king's bureaucracy.

So I return to my hunch and I suggest that those who were addressed
by Micah in Jerusalem as ראשים and קצינים are שׂרים, officials of the
king's secretariat (cf. Schmidt, 136, who describes the ראשים and קצינים
as *Beamten des Königs*, 'royal officials'). Micah's intention in so naming
them is to underline the gulf between the old style of government and
the new. ראשים and קצינים were once informed with a discerning and
benevolent sense of responsibility and shepherded the community, but
the new governors are a different breed: they interpret their rule in such
a way that they are destroyers rather than conservers of society. They are
addressed satirically as ראשים and קצינים because of the entirely
negative and malevolent character of their rule which is in stark
contradiction with that of their predecessors.

It might be pleaded in defence of the שׂרים that the unleashing of new
economic forces had created pressures which the old social structures
could not withstand and under the weight of which they collapsed, but
Micah would not have been interested in this kind of explanation and
he would have been unimpressed by it. The mayhem is perhaps
connected with the combining of small-holdings into large farms and
the ruthless use of wealth to achieve this end, the burden of debt which
engulfed the small farmers and their being uprooted from their land and
becoming displaced persons. This kind of *exposé*, one in terms of
economic change and consequent social upheaval, would have left
Micah unmoved. It would have served only to confirm him in his
conviction that the combination of wealth and greed and its irresponsi-
ble and inhumane employment had destroyed the foundations of
Judaean society.

1. Listen[1] you leaders of Jacob,
    you rulers of the House of Israel.
    Is it not your duty
    to know what is right?
2. You hate good and love evil;
    you flay the skin from off my people;
    you tear the flesh from their bones.
3. They[2] eat the flesh of my people
    [they strip off their skin][3]
    and crush their bones.
    They cut them up like flesh[4] for the pot,
    like meat for the cauldron.
4. Then they call out to Yahweh
    and he does not answer them;
    he hides his face from them [at that time][5],
    for their deeds are evil.

vv. 5–8 FALSE PROPHETS

The formlessness of vv. 5–8 is striking. The messenger formula
(כה אמר יהוה) is not followed by 'word of God, but by indirect speech.
It may be that the whole of v. 5a should be regarded as the
superscription (כה ... עמי), but this would not remove the formal
oddness of vv. 5–8. Verses 5b and v. 6 continue in indirect speech, v. 6a
changes from third person to second person and v. 6b back to third
person. Verse 7 is third person in form and v. 8 first person—Micah is
speaking comparing the quality of his utterance with that of the נביאים
(false prophets; cf. Targ. נביי שקרא). Rudolph (67) supposes that
המתעים ... שלום is an epexegesis of על הנביאים and that v. 6a resumes
כה אמר יהוה—Yahweh is the speaker (also Hillers, 44) The *locus*,
according to Wolff (66), was the court of the Jerusalem temple. Micah's
audience included district elders to whose ranks he himself belonged
and the date was between 733 and 722 B.C.

The deletion of כה אמר יהוה (Smith, 74; Robinson, 137; Wolff, 66)

---

[1] Deleting ואמר as redactional.
[2] Delete ואשר.
[3] Delete, cf. v. 2bα.
[4] Reading כשאר.
[5] Delete as secondary.

eases the indirect speech after the messenger formula and reduces the superscription to על הנביאים or על הנביאים המתעים את עמי. This does not remove the formal irregularities which have been noticed, though, in view of v. 8, v. 6a should perhaps be taken as word of Micah and the remainder an indirect reference by Micah to נביאים of whom חזים and קסמים (including 'dreamers', according to Kimchi) are sub-classes. Sept. (οἱ ὁρῶντες ἐνύπνια) identifies חזים with 'dreamers'. Wolff (66) also traces כה אמר יהוה (v. 5) to later redactional activity and suggests that the same deuteronomistic circles who were responsible for the insertion of the formula at Jer. 26.18 (cf. Mic. 3.12) made the addition at 3.5. Rudolph (71) further analyses 'false prophets' (קסמים; חזים; נביאים). They are false prophets not in the sense that they do not receive a divine communication, but in the sense that they do not faithfully transmit the message which they have received. This is an improbable exegesis. Wolff (71, 74) similarly urges that the נביאים had a legitimate institutional function (also Hillers, 46), but the elaboration of 'falsehood' which this involves lacks economy and there is a need to use Occam's razor. Micah did not make so fine a distinction and he did not admit that these נביאים received communications from Yahweh: he condemned them as *poseurs* and mountebanks.

The conjecture of BHS (v. 5) that עמי is an abbreviation of עם יהוה (י = יהוה) is not supported by Sept. (τὸν λάον μου; Vulg. *populum meum*; Pesh. *l'my*; Targ. ית עמי) and it falls if כה אמר יהוה is secondary. The general charge made against the נביאים is 'they lead my people astray'. הנשכים בשניהם is more figurative and different senses are offered: 1. NEB, REB, 'who pronounce a favourable oracle in return for food'—if they are well fed, they issue a favourable oracle. 2. 'who gnash their teeth when they promise prosperity'—their favourable oracle is insincere and behind the prediction of prosperity there lurks a deep malevolence. Wolff (72) accepts the first exegesis, but his remark that נשך is used chiefly of a snake-bite (*BDB*, 675) might be thought to reinforce Ibn Ezra's interpretation: the bite is poisonous or lethal and this is indicative of malignity (cf. Hillers, 45, who associates נשך with 'animal ferocity').

Sept., Vulg. and Pesh. render MT literally and do not help us to discriminate between these two meanings. Sept. ἐπ'αὐτόν = אליו (Targ. להון) after וקראו is an addition to MT. Targ, represents the first exegesis

('Whoever gives them pieces of flesh to eat they prophesy to him prosperity and whoever does not give them food they condemn') and Ibn Ezra the second ('They bite with their teeth in that they lead Israel astray and so they bite them.' Rashi ('When they are fed, they prophesy peace') and Kimchi ('Their tongue speaks smooth words [שלום] to them as long as food is offered, but blandishment gives way to threat when it is withheld') agree with Targ. (also Wellhausen, 138; Schmidt, 134; Smith, 74; Weiser, 256; Robinson; Rudolph, 66; Wolff, 59; Hillers, 44). For וקדשו Sept. has ἤγειραν 'stirred up' which Rudolph (67) explains as a lapse for ἡγίασαν (Sept.^Qmg.). His alternative explanation is that קדש, a technical term for 'holy war', is thought inappropriate in relation to a private feud. Soggin's translation (1960, 79–83) 'and they declare war' is not a sufficiently idiomatic reduction of 'and they will declare holy war'. The phrase rather signifies a malign attitude to an individual, the resolve to pursue a vendetta (so Wolff, 73).

Kimchi's special contribution is his observation that whether the oracle is favourable or unfavourable in both cases it is false ('who lead my people astray'). There is no intrinsic difference between the 'good' and the 'evil' which is predicted: 'Do not be afraid of the message of these false prophets when it is unfavourable and do not rely on it when it is favourable.' Hence though Kimchi agrees with the first interpretation in respect of הנשכים בשניהם, he approaches the second in his emphasis on falsehood and malevolence and he has another exegesis of הנשכים בשניהם which points to the evil intent of the oracle, even if its content is שלום and which cites Prov. 27.6: it is the kiss of an enemy. The disadvantage of Ibn Ezra's exegesis is that it damages the antithetic parallelism of v. 5 by retaining a reference to the kind of oracle which is given if food is withheld and by removing the complementary reference to the oracle which corresponds to the case when food is offered. It may be, however, that this exact parallelism has been falsely discerned in the text and that what is being said is that a promise of שלום is not made in good faith, does not betoken good-will and conceals ill-will. This is complemented with the statement that the false prophet will turn nasty and utter a hostile oracle if he is refused food. The implication of this would be that such prophets expected to be fed for their work, but that whether they were fed or unfed, whether they prophesied שלום or מלחמה the oracle was false.

A less serious ambiguity has been noticed in the word-string נתן על פה,
but whether it means 'put (food) into their mouth' or 'give what they
demand' (Van Der Woude, 110; Wolff, 73), the sense is not altered
greatly and the antithetic parallelism is maintained, since 'what they
demand' must be food. Wolff notices that נתן ב is used (Deut. 18.18; Jer.
1.9; 5.14) for putting words (דברים) into the mouth, but he urges that
נתן על פה does not have this sense and cites Gen. 45.21 ('as Pharaoh had
demanded'), Num. 3.51 ('as Yahweh had demanded') and 2 Kgs 23.35
('as Pharaoh had demanded'). That there is no ambiguity in these three
instances is due to the combination of על פה with Pharaoh (twice) and
Yahweh. The suffix with על פה (על פיהם) does not preclude ambiguity,
unless one enforces a rigid distinction between נתן ב and נתן על. Sept.,
Vulg., and Pesh. have taken פיהם as 'their mouth'. Targ's paraphrase
of v. 5, an antithesis of tidings of שלום and מלחמה which matches
(ואשר לא יתן על פיהם) with ודלא מוכיל (הנשכים בשניהם) דמוכיל is too
general to throw light on the Hebrew text. The comments of Kimchi
('who does not give him the food and drink which they ask from him')
and Ibn Ezra ('what they eat and seek') are more helpful. A long line of
exegesis favours 'put nothing into their mouth' (KJV, RSV, NEB, REB;
Wellhausen, 23; Smith, 70; Weiser, 255; Robinson, 136; Rudolph, 66;
Hillers, 44).

The two occurrences of מן (v. 6a) have been variously interpreted and
MT חָשְׁכָה ('it is dark') has been emended to חֲשֵׁכָה 'darkness' which
gives a better parallel to לילה 'night' than חשכה (a verb, 3rd person
feminine; so Pesh. wthšk) Sept. (σκοτία) and Vulg. (tenebrae) represent
'darkness' (also Wellhausen, 138; Duhm, 86; Smith 72; Ehrlich, 5, 279;
Weiser, 255; Robinson, 136; BHS; Rudolph, 67; Wolff, 61; Hillers,
44). For a similar reason קסם (infinitive construct) is emended to קֶסֶם
as a match for חזון (Sept.; Vulg.; Pesh.; Duhm, 86; Ehrlich, 5, 279).
Sept. and Pesh translate מן literally (ἐξ ὁράσεως and ἐξ μαντείας; mn
ḥzw and mn qṣmʾ) and are not much help. Vulg. pro visione and pro
divinatione is perhaps 'instead of vision' and 'instead of divination'.
'Night' and 'darkness' signify unfavourable conditions for vision and
divination—a black-out. Kimchi (also Ibn Ezra) supposes that מן = 'as
a result of', 'because of': לילה and חשכה are references to the coming of
the enemy and this is the judgement which will result from the resort to
vision and divination. מן in both these occurrences is the מן which
precludes (GK 119w) and this is how it is rendered by Targ.,

Wellhausen (23), Duhm (87); Smith (70); Weiser (255); Robinson (136); Rudolph (66); Wolff (60, 61) and Hillers (44).

The straightforward interpretation of v. 6b is that the second stich is an intensification of the first. The setting of the sun over the prophets is an indication that the bright day of their influence and acclaim will pass into obscurity and loss of reputation so complete, a public neglect so utter, that not only will night fall on them but day will be darkened into night. Kimchi remarks that the going down of the sun is a figure of צרה 'distress': a realization that their influence has faded and their reign is over, perhaps also an awareness that they have been engulfed in judgement (Kimchi, Ibn Ezra).

Robinson (138) links v. 6b with a reference to false (Yahweh) prophets (נביאים) whom he distinguishes from חזים and קסמים (v. 6a), those who do not prophesy in the name of Yahweh. The contrast is that the חזים and קסמים practise their arts by night (v. 6a), whereas the נביאים predict by day. Not only will the setting of the sun overtake daylight, but the day will be preternaturally darkened and no daylight will be left for the predictions of the false prophets. This is an over-elaborate exegesis which should be ignored.

The seers and diviners will be discomfited and demoralized (v. 7), the elaborate sham of their pose destroyed by the relentlessness of truth. This exposure will produce signs of mourning, a mourning that the cosiness of a well-rehearsed fraud has given place to a comfortless reality. Targ. paraphrases, 'Therefore they will be confounded so that they cannot prophesy and humiliated so that they cannot teach.' שפם is properly the 'moustache' (BDB, 741; Wellhausen, 23, Schmidt, 134, Rudolph, 67, Wolff, 74, Lippenbart or Oberlippenbart or Schnurrbart, Weiser, 255; Robinson, 136, Rudolph, 66, Wolff, 60, Bart, 'covering the beard' is a sign of mourning). Wolff (74) suggests that here it may be a sign that the נביאים have been reduced to speechlessness. At 2 Sam. 19.25 Sept has τὸν μύστακα αὐτοῦ for שפמו. The word has not been understood by Sept. at Mic. 3.7 and the subject of עטו is taken as those who deride the חזים and קסמים: 'and they will all slander them (so Wolff, 61). Rudolph (67) equates κατ' αὐτῶν with καθ' ἑαυτῶν and proposes the improbable rendering, 'and they (the seers and diviners) will cry out against themselves'. Vulg., et operient omnes vultus suos, 'and they will all cover their countenance', apparently understands the mem of שפם as a suffix. Pesh. śpwthwn has rendered שפם as שפתם 'their lips' (cf. Symm. ἐπὶ τῶν χειλέων αὐτῶν). Targ. expands MT ('and they will all cover the beard as mourners').

Kimchi comments on כי אין מענה אלהים 'for they do not have the word of God' and Ibn Ezra, similarly, 'for the word of God is not in them'. Both use 'God' is a general title for Yahweh and this is the case with Vulg. (*Quia non est responsum Dei*) and Pesh. (*mṭl dl' 'n̄ lhwn 'lh̄*). Rudolph (72) suggests that אלהים is a play on the title 'man of God' to which these נביאים laid claim, 'God-forsaken men of God'. Targ. paraphrases 'for there is not in them the spirit of prophecy from Yahweh'. Sept. has read אלהים as אֲלֵיהֶם (διότι οὐκ ἔσται ὁ εἰσακαύων αὐτῶν ('for no one will listen to them') and has taken מענה as a Hiphil participle. The trend of Robinson's exegesis (138) in v. 6 is continued in v. 7 and it is shared by Ehrlich (279). אלהים is not a general title for Yahweh (so Wellhausen, 24; Smith, 71; Weiser, 255; Rudolph, 72; Wolff, 60; Hillers, 44). It is a reference to those who consult spirits, especially the spirits of the dead (1 Sam. 28). Ehrlich deletes את רוח יהוה (v. 8) as a gloss, but Robinson retains it as an antithesis of אלהים (v. 7). Whereas the false prophets dabble in spirits, Micah, as a true prophet, has the spirit of Yahweh. This further instalment of Robinson's exegesis is no more acceptable than the first and the judgement of Vulg., Pesh., Targ., Kimchi and Ibn Ezra contradicts it: the discomfiture of the נביאים is a consequence of their receiving no answer from God. The techniques which they employ do not result in a divine communication. When they are put to the test, they are manifestly fraudulent, perhaps at the moment when their prediction of שלום consequent on Yahweh's favourable intervention is falsified by the onset of judgement.

ואולם (v. 8) introduces a contrast between Micah and the נביאים (קסמים; חזים), not enhanced by his claim to possess the spirit of Yahweh (את רוח יהוה) which many scholars delete (Wellhausen, 138; Duhm, 87; Ehrlich, 279; Schmidt, 134; Smith, 76; Rudolph, 68), though it is attested by Sept. (ἐν πνεύματι κυρίου), Vulg. (*spiritus Domini*; Pesh. (*rwḥḥ dmry'*). Targ. has רוח נבואה מן קדם יוי, the same paraphrase as was employed for אלהים (v. 7). את רוח יהוה is retained by Robinson (138) in connection with his special exegesis and also by Weiser (256) and Hillers (45). Ehrlich explains את רוח יהוה as an expansion of כח and Smith (76) remarks that it is a prosaic gloss by an editor dotting the i's and crossing the t's so as to establish the source of Micah's power.

Rudolph supposes that את רוח יהוה is a marginal gloss which has entered the text and renders it as 'with (the help of) the Spirit of God' (cf. Sept.): את is taken as the preposition 'with', not as a mark of the object. The other versions have found את awkward. Vulg. (*fortitudine Spiritus Domini*, 'with the strength of the Spirit of the Lord') is similar to Pesh. *ḥyl' drwḥḥ dmry*, Targ. בתקוף רוח נבואה מן קדם יוי and Theod. ἰσχυς πνεύματος κυρίου (Ziegler, 213). The expression את רוח יהוה is suspicious in the mouth of Micah, since it is associated too clearly with the claims of the false prophets whom he excoriates and the terminology they used (Mowinckel, 1934, 199–227; Wolff, 61, 66). Wolff has associated את רוח יהוה with כה אמר יהוה (v. 5) as an early sixth century Deuteronomistic redaction.

Ibn Ezra has supposed that Micah's claim to exercise כח and גבורה has reference to his conflict with the ראשים and קצינימ rather than with his polemic against the נביאים, 'And I do not fear the heads (ראשים) and rulers (קצינים), for my words are true and I shall not have to eat them' (literally, 'and I shall not be put to shame'). Wolff (71) tends to this view by emphasising the connection between vv. 1–4 and 5–8: Yahweh's silence in v. 4a and v. 7b. Moreover, (so Wolff) Micah is addressing the rulers as well as the false prophets in vv. 5–8. He is telling the ראשים and קצינים that the hope held out to them by the נביאים will turn to darkness.

The topic of v. 8, however, should not be so disengaged from that of vv. 5–7 and there is no reason to suppose that Micah had the heads and rulers in mind rather than the false prophets. Their speech has the emptiness of falsehood and the lightness of confetti, while his has the power of truth and the force of authenticity. They are prophetic words which voice his deep and benevolent concern for the well-being of his society (משפט) and this quality of discerning moral earnestness marks him off from the prophets who peddle sweetmeats to the people with a calculated and base opportunism and a disregard for truth. Such prophetic confidence, such a grasp of truth, does not need the reminder that it proceeds from God and Micah makes it without an explicit avowal that it has divine authority. He will tell the community plainly where it has gone wrong , how deeply the rot has penetrated.

5.   These are the words of Yahweh concerning the prophets who lead my people astray, who prophesy prosperity for a bite of food and doom for whoever does not put bread into their mouths.

6.   Therefore you will have night and not vision,
     darkness and not divination.[1]
     The sun will set on the prophets
     and the day will be black over them.
7.   Seers will be shamed
     and diviners disconcerted.
     All of them will be at a loss,
     for there will be no answer from God.
8.   But I am full of strength[2]
     full of justice and power,
     to declare to Jacob his transgression,
     and to Israel his sin.

vv. 9–12 AGAINST RULERS, PROPHETS AND PRIESTS

The form of 3.9–12 is not consistent in view of the change from second person to third, from direct address to indirect reference at v. 11. Verses 9b and 10 may be regarded as an epexegesis of ראשים and קצינים in the direct address of v. 9a. Thus:

v. 9a   Hear this, will you not, heads of the House of Jacob and rulers of the House of Israel.
v. 9b   Who hate what is right and twist all that is straight,
v. 10   Who build Zion with blood and Jerusalem with iniquity.

Verse 11 continues in the 3rd person:

Her heads [that is Jerusalem's] rule with bribes and her priests give rulings
     for payment;
her prophets predict for money, yet claim Yahweh's authority.

Verse 11 is spoken by Micah to a third party concerning rulers, priests and prophets and v. 12 resumes vv. 9–10 by returning to the second person (לכן בגללבם)—direct speech:

Therefore because of you Zion will become a ploughed field, Jerusalem a
     heap of ruins and the temple hill wooded heights.

Ehrlich (279f.) has removed this unevenness by treating ראשים and קצינים as vocatives and במחיר יורו, בשחד ישפטו and בכסף יקסמו as relative clauses, but this is an improbable expedient:

---

[1]Reading וַחֲשֵׁכָה and מִקְּסָם.
[2]Deleting את רוח יהוה.

You, her heads, who rule with bribes, you, her priests, who give rulings for
     payment;
you, her prophets, who predict for money, yet claim Yahweh's authority.

In the absence of any evidence that the piece is 'word of God', it
should be concluded that Micah is the speaker and that he issues the
threat on his own account (לכן בגללכם), though v. 12 is repeated,
without לכן בגללכם and prefaced with כה אמר יהוה צבאות at Jer.
26.18.

Robinson (138) supposes that the passage consists originally of vv.
9–11 and that v. 12 is a fragment which constituted the beginning of a
separate passage (cf. Rudolph, 75) which, in view of Jer. 26.18, is also to
be assigned to Micah. Robinson attributes v. 12, in the context of
Micah 3.9–12, to a redactor and לכן בגללבם is his addition. A further
adjustment which is perhaps to be credited to him is the change in v. 9a
from an original הוי ראשי בית יעקב to שמעו נא זאת ראשי בית יעקב. The
implication of this may be that the extant form of the beginning of v. 9a
is, in Robinson's view, more appropriate to a 'word of God' than to a
speech of Micah. Rudolph (75) supposes that those responsible for Jer.
26.15 regarded the saying of Micah 3.12 as so ominous, of such
enduring perspicacity, that they concluded it must have been a 'word of
Yahweh'.

Verse 9a repeats v. 1a with slight alterations (זאת and בית are added;
Pesh. has both at v. 1a). Rudolph (68) deletes בית before יעקב at v. 9a
for metrical reasons. The identity of ראשים and קצינים has been gone
into at v. 1a. It has been urged there that the ראשים and קצינים in 3.1–4
are charged with iniquitous government, not with unjust and corrupt
legal decisions which they give as judges sitting on the bench (cf. Smith,
78, 80, v. 9, משפט 'justice'; v. 11, ישפטו 'judge'; Robinson, 138, v. 11,
sprechen recht, 'give verdicts'?). It will be enough here to reiterate that
hating משפט (v. 9b) similarly refers to their abuse of the community
over which they hold rule. When it is said that they govern with bribes,
what is indicated is corrupt government rather than legal verdicts given
by judges who are not even-handed in court. It is with crooked rulers,
with evidences that power has corrupted those who exercise it that v. 9b
is concerned: 'who hate all that is right and twist all that is straight' (so
Rudolph, 74).

The versions do not make this clear: they relate משפט and ישפטו to
legal decisions. Sept. has κρίμα for משפט and ἔκρινον for ישפטו. Vulg.

has *iudicium* for משפט and *iudicabant* for ישפטו. It renders קצינים as *duces* at v. 1 and *iuduces* at v. 9a. Pesh. is similarly oriented: *dyn* for משפט and *dynyn* for ישפטו (Targ. has the same renderings דינא and דינין). In connection with כל הישר יעקשו Kimchi introduces the figure of the straight road (Prov. 2.12–15). He glosses יעקשו with יעותו and comments 'they twist the straight road; all their ways and deeds are violence and robbery' (cf. McKane 1970, 284).

At v. 10 Sept. (οἱ οἰκοδομοῦντες), Vulg. (*aedificatis*), Pesh. (*dbnyn*) and Targ. (דבנן) all show בנה as בני, but they may be representing MT בנה (cf. Rudolph, 68). בני is preferred by Wellhausen (138), Duhm (87), Smith (79), Schmidt (136), Weiser (258), Robinson (138), Wolff (61—בני or בנים). Ehrlich (5, 279), also Rudolph (68) vocalizes בנה as an infinitive absolute (*bānôh*) and parses v. 10 as a circumstantial clause continuing v. 9, 'having built Zion with blood and Jerusalem with iniquity'.

בדמים is translated literally by Sept. (ἐν αἵμασιν) and by Vulg. (*in sanguinibus*). Pesh. translates בדמים as a singular (*bdm*) to which Targ. adds אשד (בדם אשד 'bloodshed'). Kimchi comments on בדמים, 'that is, with robbery which they practise against the poor (also Ibn Ezra), since they have the power to coerce them. בדמים signifies a bloody oppression, a lust for ill-gotten gain at the cost of the poor. Kimchi adds: 'They take a כופר "ransom" from those who shed blood and build their houses with the money.' That is to say, they connive with oppressors who do not stop short of murder.

Weiser (259f.) remarks that it is these palatial, private houses which Micah has in mind (also Robinson, 139) rather than the public works attributed to Hezekiah (2 Kgs 20.20). Rudolph's comment (73f.) is similar: Micah did not spell out 'they build Zion with blood'. There was no need; his hearers understood the reference. He does not have in mind building operations which were careless of the human cost and treated fatal accidents to workers lightly. Rather it is the megalomania of those who build or acquire property ruthlessly without regard to the social damage which they inflict and the trail of human suffering which they leave in their wake. The possession of power, access to wealth, the thirst for prestige and self-advertisement, has changed them into monsters emptied of moral sense.

Verse 11 resumes with allegations of corrupt rule against the ראשים, but it then turns to accuse the כהנים and נביאים of malpractices (cf.

3.5): the priests give rulings for a fee and the prophets predict for money. This does not necessarily mean that they too are corrupt and are influenced by bribes, but it does, at least, indicate that they sell their wares like merchants. It is likely, however, that it goes beyond this and that there is an implication that the priests give favourable rulings when there is a sufficient financial incentive and that prophets tailor their predictions to the amount of gain which they make. Priests and prophets are not just stipendiary or mercenary; they are corrupt, shoddy mountebanks. Kimchi says of the priests, 'Whoever gave them money, they pronounced for him a favourable ruling.' That the נביאים mentioned are 'false prophets' is a conclusion which Kimchi draws from the use of קסם which he supposes is pejorative.

'Yahweh is in our midst; disaster will not overtake us.' This has special reference to the arrogant and unfounded confidence of the נביאים and their summary dismissal of prophecies of doom (Smith, 80). It is correlated by Wellhausen (138; also Weiser, 260) with all three leading classes, rulers, priests and prophets, as an egotism associated with the discharge of their offices, the assurance that, despite the gloom spread by prophets such as Micah, the community was secure under their control. This brash and groundless confidence also has a special connection with the Jerusalem temple, as the threat of v. 12 shows: 'Therefore because of you Zion will be ploughed as a field, Jerusalem will become a heap of ruins and the temple hill will become wooded heights.' 'Yahweh is in our midst' is an expression of this unshakeable confidence that Jerusalem is inviolable because the temple is Yahweh's dwelling-place (so Weiser, 260; Rudolph, 74) and v 12. aims to demolish this illusion. Wellhausen (138) comments, 'The temple in Jerusalem would become one of the ruinous high-places in a waste-land—a feature of Palestine after the fall of the Northern Kingdom.' Hence he assumes that במות (or במת, as he emends) refers to a cultic site (*contra* Ehrlich, 1912: 279; see further below).

עיין (v. 12) has an Aramaic *nun* and the normal Hebrew form (עיים) appears at Jer. 26.18. Wolff (61) suggests that עיין is a play on ציון. Wellhausen (138) emends עיין to עיים at Micah 3.12 (also Duhm, 87; Schmidt, 136; Robinson, 138). Vulg. renders עיין as *acervus lapidum* 'heap of stones', Pesh. as *ḥrbt* 'a waste' and Targ. as יגרין 'a heap of stones'. Sept. has the odd rendering ὀπωροφυλάκιον 'a garden-watcher's hut'. ὀπωροφυλάκιον appears in Sept. as a translation

of מלונה 'lodging-place' at Isa. 1.8 and 24.20. The choice of
ὀπωροφυλάκιον to render מלונה at Isa. 1.8 is explained by the
synonymous parallelism in the verse (כסבה בכרם 'like a booth in a
vineyard'). כמלונה במקשה is interpreted by Sept. at Isa. 1.8 as 'like a
garden-watcher's hut in a field of cucumbers'. The matter is not so clear
at Isa. 24.20 where מלונה is not set in the context of field-watching. It
may be explained by the assumption that an ὀπωροφυλάκιον was a
ramshackle construction and that it was a *mot juste* in relation to the
imagery of the verse: 'The earth lurches as a drunkard and sways like a
garden-watcher's shed.'

ὀπωροφυλάκιον translates עי 'ruin' in four places (Mic. 1.6; 3.12;
Jer. 26[33]. 18; Ps. 78.1). At Jer. 33.18 Sept. ^AQ has ὀπωροφυλάκιον
and Sept.^B εἰς ἄβατον 'into what is inaccessible'. Ps. 78.1 reads, 'They
have reduced Jerusalem to ruins' (לעיים). עיים are here the ruins of a
city, the rubble of stones to which it is reduced, and it is difficult to
discover why Sept. has translated the Hebrew as ἔθεντο Ἰερουσαλὴμ εἰς
ὀπωροφυλάκιον. At Mic. 1.6 the association of השדה with עי (השדה)
לעי may have triggered the rendering εἰς ὀπωροφυλάκιον ἀγροῦ and
this would be reinforced by the parallelism, למטעי כרם, 'as a place for
planting vines'. In this context עי was identified with the ramshackle
hut of a field-watchman. Similarly at Mic. 3.12 the imagery set up by
שדה תחרש 'a ploughed field' in relation to Zion may have suggested
that וירושלם עיין תהיה was corresponding rural imagery, 'and Jerusalem
will become the ramshackle hut of a field-watchman' (καὶ Ἰερουσαλὴμ
ὡς ὀπωροφυλάκιον ἔσται). It is improbable that this is the correct
exegesis of the Hebrew; almost certainly עיין refers to the ruinous rubble
of a city.

לבמות יער (v. 12) is an awkward phrase, literally 'into the heights or
[(cultic) high-places'] of a wood'. Since הר is singular, scholars have
tended to emend במות to במת (Wellhausen, 138; Duhm, 87; Smith,
79; Schmidt, 136; Weiser, 258; Robinson, 138). Only Vulg. *in excelsa
silvarum* unambiguously reproduces MT. Sept. has a singular (ἄλσος
'grove'; cf. Symm. ὕψος 'height'; Theod. βουνόν 'hill') which may
represent במת as a cultic-place (so Wolff, 61f.), but 'grove of a coppice'
is a strange combination. Vulg. 'wooded heights' does not take במות as
a reference to cultic high-places. Pesh. *wṭwr byt' lbyt 'b*, 'and the temple
hill will become a temple in a wood', is an indication that במת has been
read and that the sense given to it is influenced by the preceding

הר הבית. So Pesh. like Sept. has identified במת as a reference to a cultic
place and as a play on הר הבית. Targ לחושת חרשא 'as an overgrown
thicket'? cannot be reconciled with לבמות יער but במות or במת is not
given a cultic nuance. Only those scholars who suppose that it has a
cultic sense (Wellhausen, 139; Duhm, 87; Smith, 79) have good reason
for emending במות to במת (cf. Ehrlich 5, 280). If לבמות יער is allowed
to stand, Vulg. 'wooded heights' is a correct translation (cf. NEB, 'a
rough heath'; REB, 'a rough moorland'). Ehrlich (5, 280; also Rudolph,
68; Wolff) emends לבמות יער to לבהמות יער, 'and the temple-hill will
belong to animals of the forest' (cf. Lam. 5.18).

According to Jer. 7.4 (היכל יהוה היכל יהיה היכל יהוה המה) Jeremiah's
contemporaries supposed that with the Jerusalem temple they possessed
an unfailing talisman which was proof against the onset of any disaster.
The Hebrew is not without its difficulties and המה has been explained
as an abbreviation for המקום הזה 'this place' (Torczyner, 1925, 276;
Driver, 1960, 122, *hēmmā* 'those' a false pointing for המקום הזה;
Brockington, 1973, 201). Sutcliffe (1955, 313f.) has elucidated the
verse by adopting the two-fold formula of Sept. (ναὸς κυρίου ναὸς
κυρίου ἐστίν) and explaining היכל יהוה המה as an explanatory marginal
note on דברי השקר, 'These (words) are "the temple of Yahweh, the
temple of Yahweh".'

Mic. 3.12 has been thought by Robinson (139) to be redactional in
the context of 3.9–12, though it is admitted to be a genuine saying of
Micah. In that case it is evidence that about a century before Jeremiah
Micah was plagued with the same powerful and crass illusion of security
as was still abroad in the Jerusalem of Jeremiah's day: 'Is not Yahweh in
our midst; no disaster can overtake us' (3.11). The Jerusalem temple
was Yahweh's property, he lived there and would not permit any
encroachment on his own home and city. It may be that this cosy and
insidious doctrine had been revitalized by the deliverance of Jerusalem
from the siege of Sennacherib in 701. In both periods it is likely that we
have to reckon with a lonely prophetic voice raised against a uniform
and overwhelming popular piety, not a prophet who speaks for a
significant opposition party (*pace* Vincent 1986: 182).

It is reported in Jer. 26 that when Jeremiah threatened the Jerusalem
temple with destruction (v. 6), he was arraigned on a capital charge (v.
11) and was defended by a group of district elders (זקני הארץ, v. 17)
who cited a legal precedent in his defence (v. 18). Micah had threatened

the temple with destruction and Hezekiah had not put him to death. They cite Mic. 3.12 as evidence of this: 'Zion will become a ploughed field, Jerusalem a heap of stones and the temple-hill wooded heights.'

Jeremiah's prophetic activity was centred in Jerusalem and, according to Wolff (66), the three sayings in Micah chapter 3 have a Jerusalem *locus*, vv. 11 and 12 expressly so. Hence the same conflict between prophet and institution, in relation to a dogma of Yahwism advertised by the Jerusalem temple, obtained in the eighth century and endured into the seventh and the early sixth centuries. Micah and Jeremiah had to contend with the same falsehood, one whose virulence was increased by the circumstance that it had acquired the status and rigidity of theology, the aura of incontestable dogma.

> 9. Listen to this, you leaders of the house of Jacob,
>   you rulers of the house of Israel,
>   who abhor what is right,
>   and make crooked what is straight;
> 10. who build Zion with blood
>   and Jerusalem with iniquity.
> 11. Her leaders govern corruptly for a bribe,
>   her priests give rulings for money,
>   her prophets prophesy for silver.
>   Yet they claim Yahweh's support and say,
>   'Is not Yahweh in our midst?
>   Disaster will not overtake us!'
> 12. Therefore, because of you, Zion will be ploughed up like a field,
>   Jerusalem will be a heap of ruins
>   and the temple mount will be hilly scrub.

CHAPTER 4

MICAH 4.1–5 AND ISAIAH 2.2–5

Jerusalem the light of the Gentiles

Wellhausen (1892, 39f.) holds that Mic 4.1–5 is very odd in the environment of the book of Micah and that it does not fit the Messianism of first Isaiah which concerns itself only with Judah and Jerusalem and does not embrace the nations in a Kingdom of God. This appears only at Isa 40–66, Zech. 8 and, perhaps, in a few Psalms. Mic. 4.1–5 is a plaster applied to the wound inflicted by 3.12 and is the work of a redactor or interpolator. It seems to have been known to the prophet Zechariah (3.10; 8.20) but whether priority is to be attached to Micah/Isaiah or Zechariah is not known.

Duhm (1897, 87) introduces further complications. Chapters 4–5 of Micah are to be dated in the second century B.C. and vv. 1–4 are among the many additions which chapter 4 has received. These verses are out of place in chapter 4, in general, and, in particular, they interrupt an original continuity between 2.12f. and 4.6–8. They describe a state of affairs which could not have existed before the events of 4.6–5.14. The first examples of this kind of 'weal' prophecy in the book of Micah are 2.12f. and 4.6–8.

Smith (1912, 84) locates Mic. 4.1–3 (Isa 2.2–4) in the post-exilic period and notices that the conversion of the nations is not found elsewhere in the book of Micah, but that it is found in the writings of the exilic and post-exilic periods. The pilgrimage of the nations to Zion is a post-exilic idea (Zech. 14.16–19). The conversion of the nations (86) is a common thought in Deutero–Isaiah, but it could not have found expression until monotheism was firmly fixed in the religious consciousness of Israel through the discipline of the exile. Eighth century prophecy shows no trace of this thought and its appearances in the book at Isaiah (11.10; 18.7; 19.16, 25) are of late origin (Canna-wurf, 1963, 63, holds that the author of Mic. 4.1–4 is post-exilic).

The new element which emerges with Ehrlich's criticism (5, 280) is that Mic. 4.1–3 (Isa. 2.2–4) are described as 'the old oracle' and are distinguished from the remainder of chapter 4. The latter belongs to a collection of smaller pieces which gaze into the future and it differs from 4.1–3 both in content and vocabulary. Ehrlich does not explain further 'the old oracle', but the term itself and the way in which he contrasts chapters 4–5 (post-Deuteronomist) with 'the old oracle' suggests that his intention may be to connect Mic. 4.1–3 (Isa. 2.2–4) with the use of a common source by the prophets Micah and Isaiah.

That the Messianism of first Isaiah is restricted to Judah and Jerusalem is disputed by Wildberger (78–80) and Rudolph (78) and they offer an elucidation of Ehrlich's 'old oracle'. Micah does not display any interest in the conversion of the nations to Yahwism, but this is not true of the Messianism of first Isaiah. The source of his universalism is the Jerusalem temple and the Zion tradition associated with it, according to which Zion is the glory of the whole earth (Ps. 48.3) and the praise of Yahweh's name is heard at the ends of the earth (Ps. 48.11). Zion is the foundation-stone of the community (Isa. 28.16f.) and the temple will never fall into enemy hands. The call of Isaiah is set in the temple (chapter 6) and the location of his prophetic ministry was Jerusalem. The trickle of Israelites making the pilgrimage to Zion (Ps. 122) is to be overtaken by the mass pilgrimage of the nations, like a river in spate (נהרו; Isa. 2.2/Mic. 4.1). Isaiah's prophetic ministry was Jerusalem-centred and it had cultic connections. The source of his eschatological and universalist Messianism was the Zion tradition and we do not have to look far for the author of Isa. 2.2–4/Mic. 4.1–3. Isaiah of Jerusalem is a prime candidate and a redactor was responsible for its insertion at Mic 4.1–3. The concern of Hillers (51–53) is not to establish the authorship of Isaiah for Isa. 2.2–4/Mic. 4.1–3, but to leave open the possibility that Mic. 4.1–3 may have been the work of Micah.

That the 'Zion tradition' as it is proclaimed by first Isaiah in Isa. 14.28–32 and 28.14–18 contains all the threads of Mic. 4.1–3 and Isa. 2.2–4 is denied by Wolff (88f.). The three elements contained in these verses do not appear until Trito–Isaiah (56.3–7; 66.18–23) and Zech. (8.20–22.3). They are (a) Zion is the goal of the pilgrimage and the place where Yahweh issues his word (b) There is a streaming of the nations to Zion (c) The outcome is an era of universal peace. He therefore dissents from the opinion of Wildberger and Rudolph that Isaiah of Jerusalem is the author of Isa. 2.2–4/Mic. 4.1–3 and he assigns these verses to a redactor who appropriated prophetic traditions

which were abroad in post-exilic times after the Jerusalem temple had
been rebuilt (87) but before the period of Haggai and Ezra with which
he associates the response of Mic. 4.5 (89). These traditions set up an
antithesis between the Jerusalem which lay in ruins and the Jerusalem
which would be restored and glorified at 'the end of days' (97). They
answered the question whether the destruction portrayed by Micah in
1–3.12 was the last word and they added to this 'ancient Micah
tradition' (87) a prediction that Jerusalem would undergo a glorious
renaissance.

Wellhausen (139f.; Smith 84) notice that from 3.12 to 4.1 there is a
sudden change of subject which comes about without the building of
any bridge and which requires of the reader a leap from woe to weal,
and they take this as a mark of literary discontinuity. Rudolph (77)
offers a literary explanation in terms of the pattern imposed on the book
of Micah by a redactor, alternate groups of chapters featuring woe and
weal respectively, and Hillers (p. 50) declares that the relationship is
'deliberate'. Weiser (262) builds a theological bridge: judgement and
salvation are complementary and together they constitute a profound
synthesis. They comprise the totality of Yahweh's governance of the
world: the destruction of Jerusalem and the temple is not the last word
and the vision of faith descries the weal of the end-time. This
eschatological perspective reveals the final sense of the divine judgement
proclaimed by the prophets. That the literary discontinuity is not
overcome by building a theological bridge is acknowledged by Weiser,
since he assigns 4.1–4 to a circle of ideas associated with post-exilic
eschatology which has probably been inserted by a later hand. It is
related neither to Isaiah's hope of the future nor to Micah's and neither
should be thought of as the author. The promise is of anonymous
origin: it is a liturgical confession of the post-exilic community which
confessed both Micah's word of judgement as well as the hope of
salvation which passed beyond judgement to Yahweh's kingdom of
peace. Robinson (139–141) similarly holds that Mic. 4.1–4 and Isa.
2.2–4 do not originate with either Micah or Isaiah. They were
incorporated in these books by collectors of prophetic sayings and they
reflect the hopes and ideals of a believer living in the exile who had a
vision of the New Jerusalem.

A first task is to compare the Massoretic text of Mic. 4.1–3 with that
of Isa. 2.2–4. These texts have a close verbal similarity, with small

variations, but they diverge from each other in their final verses and
Mic. 4.4 is a minus in Isa. 2.2–5. There are scholars who define the
original poem as Mic. 4.1–3 (Isa. 2.2–4) and who hold that Mic. 4.4–5
are secondary additions (Smith, 83; Robinson, 140). Weiser, on the
other hand, includes Mic. 4.4 in the poem (264), but he acknowledges
with Wellhausen (140) and Smith (87f.) that the picture is that of a
peasant in the peaceful countryside of Palestine (1 Kgs 5.5; 2 Kgs 18.31;
Zech. 3.10). There is more unanimity that Mic. 4.5 has to be
disengaged from Mic. 4.1–3 (Smith 88; Ehrlich, 5, 280; Weiser, 264f.;
Robinson, 141). Mic. 4.5 reads, 'For the nations each walk in the name
of their gods, but we shall walk in the name of Yahweh, our God, for
ever' (REB, 'Other people may be loyal to their own deities, but our
loyalty will be for ever to the Lord, our God'). Isa. 2.5 is a verse which
raises fewer problems and which has a better connection with the
preceding verses than Mic. 4.5: 'House of Yahweh, come and let us
walk in the light of Yahweh.' Wildberger (77) has, however, noticed
that this address to the 'house of Yahweh' is not a fitting conclusion to
vv. 2–4 which describes a pilgrimage of the nations to Zion.

Rudolph (80) wrongly claims the support of Wildberger for his
statement that Mic. 4.4 is a logical consequence and a fitting conclusion
of Mic. 4.1–3 (also Hillers, 51) and Isa. 2.2–4 (where it is a minus). He
acknowledges that it is a 'traditional metaphor' and that in other
contexts it portrays the peaceful life of a Palestinian peasant, but he
urges that it is idle to question the unity of Mic. 4.1–4 for this reason
and that its adaption to a context of universal peace presents no
difficulty. Wildberger (77f.) holds that the original context of Mic. 4.4
disqualifies it from being a conclusion to Mic. 4.1–3/Isa. 2.2–4. It
relates to the serene and secure life of the Palestinian peasant, safe from
interruptions to the even tenor of his life by invading armies: it is the
king's peace (also Wolff, 83f.). Hence Wildberger (78; also Wolff)
concludes that Mic. 4.4a is secondary and that Mic. 4.4b has fallen out
of Isa. 2.2–4 and is the original conclusion of both passages.

Rudolph (81) takes Mic. 4.5 as a later insertion which contradicts vv.
1–4. It is a rejoinder to these verses: the heathen nations will not receive
instruction in Zion, but will adhere to their own gods. The division
between Israel and the nations, between idolatry and true religion, is
eternal. Verse 5 is not an admonition but the statement of a hard fact.
עד רחוק (v. 3) is a kind of 'tell it to the marines', but v. 5 is a disavowal:

the chasm between idolatry and true religion will last for ever—the heathen world is not Yahweh's affair. Wolff (85, 89, 94) does not discern so outright a rejection of vv. 1–3 in v. 5 ('a redactional addition'). It is a later cautious, liturgical interpretation of vv. 1–3 for difficult times (כי is 'though' not 'for'). It is not a direct negative in relation to vv. 1–3, but its vision of a glorious future is tempered by a cool appreciation of the nature of the present. Hillers (51), similarly, describes v. 5 as a liturgical addition, a congregational response, which is not intended as a contradiction to vv. 1–4 (also Weiser, below, p. 126).

The variants in Mic. 4.1–3 and Isa. 2.2–4 are as follows: (a) הוא is a minus in Isa. 2.2 (b) Mic. 4. 1, ונהרו אליו כל הגוים/Isa. 2.2, ונהרו עליו עמים (c) Mic. 4.2, והלכו גוים רבים/Isa. 2.3, והלכו עמים רבים (d) Mic. 4.3, לעמים רבים/Isa. 2.4, עמים רבים (e) Mic. 4.3, לגוים עצמים/Isa. 2.4, הגוים (f) עד רחוק (Mic. 4.3) is a minus in Isa. 2.4 (g) Mic. 4.3, ישאו/Isa 2.4, ישא. Wolff (85) connects these variants with a stage of oral tradition when the text was fluid and with the reflection of that fluidity in the texts of Micah and Isaiah when they were fixed in writing. Special notice should be taken of the different word-order of נכון in Mic. 4.1 and Isa. 2.2: in Micah it precedes בראש and in Isaiah it comes at an earlier point in the verse, before יהיה, but the syntax of the verse is not affected and in either position it is connected with הר בית יהוה, of whose location further information is given by בראש ההרים. The differing word-order of Micah and Isaiah is preserved by Vulg. and Targ., but Pesh. shows the word-order of Micah in both passages. That the position of נכון does not result in a difference of sense can be seen by inspecting the translations of the passages in REB: Mic. 4.1, 'In days to come the mountain of the Lord's house will be established (נכון) higher than all other mountains'; Isa. 2.2, 'In days to come the mountain of the Lord's house will be set over (נכון) all other mountains.'

The matter is not so simple with the Sept. of Micah which represents נכון twice (ἐμφανές; ἕτοιμον), once in the position which it occupies in Micah (ἕτοιμον) and once in the position which it occupies in Isaiah (ἐμφανές). This conclusion is reinforced by the circumstance that the Sept. of Isaiah shows ἔμφανές for נכון with a word-order which corresponds with that of the MT of Isa. 2.2 (ἐμφανὲς τὸ ὄρος κυρίου). בית is a minus at both Mic. 4.1 and Isa. 2.2 (Sept.). Hence that ἐμφανές and ἕτοιμον are doublets in Micah (so Hillers, 49) is corroborated by the appearance of ἐμφανές in a position corresponding to MT נכון at Isa. 2.2. The puzzle is not quite solved, because neither ἐμφανές 'visible', 'manifest' nor ἕτοιμον 'ready', 'prepared', are accurate translations of נכון, though Vulg. has produced a synonym of ἕτοιμον (*praeparatus*) and the sense 'prepared' can be transformed into that of 'established'. The question has been raised, however, whether ἐμφανές is a rendering of נכון at Isa. 2.2 and the Hebrew equivalent has been given as יחזה (Meek, 1929, 162f.) and יראה (Robinson, 141) 'are visible' (Niphal). In that case נכון is a minus in Isa. 2.2 (Sept). On the other hand Rudolph (75f.) holds that ἐμφανές has been added secondarily to the text of Mic. 4.1 from Isa. 2.2 and that it was not inserted as a doublet (cf. Wolff, 83). It is a contamination of the Micah text by an expander who made no judgement as to the Hebrew which underlay ἐμφανές in Isa. 2.2 (Sept.).

It may be too speculative to raise the question of the intention of the Greek translator of Mic. 4.1. Was he attempting to take account of the differing positions of נכון at Mic. 4.1 and Isa. 2.2? At any rate the effect of the adjustment which he made was to change the sense of Mic. 2.4, because he has associated ἐμφανές with הר יהוה, as Isa. 2.2 does, and his additional ἕτοιμον with בראש ההרים: 'And at the end of days the mountain of the Lord will be manifest, prepared on the peaks of the mountains.' 'On the peaks of the mountains' is to be preferred (cf. Hilliers, 49) to 'as the head of the mountains' (*beth essentiae*: Wildberger, 63; Rudolph, 76).

נהרו is perhaps a denominative of נהר 'river' (I נהר) which is used figuratively for nations 'streaming' (Mic. 4.1; Isa. 2.2) or not 'streaming' (Jer. 51.44) to a destination (Wellhausen, 24, *strömen*: also Weiser, 261; Robinson, 138; Rudolph, 75; Wolff, 82; Smith, 86, 'flow; Hillers, 49, 'stream'). Wiklander's suggestion (1978, 40–64) that נהר in these three passages is to be derived from II נהר, 'shine', 'rejoice at', 'look with joy at', finds support in the rendering of Pesh. at Isa. 2.2 (*nskwn* 'look in expectation') and has been proposed by Ehrlich (4, 1912, 10; cf. Hillers, 49). Sept. renders ונהרו עליו עמים at Mic. 4.1 as καὶ σπεύσουσιν πρὸς αὐτὸ λαοί 'and peoples will hasten to it'. At Isa. 2.2 the rendering of virtually the same Hebrew (ונהרו אליו כל הגוים) is καὶ ἥξουσιν ἐπ᾿ αὐτὸ πάντα τὰ ἔθνη, 'and all the nations will head for it.' These different renderings of ונהרו make it unlikely that וימהרו is the *Vorlage* of καὶ σπεύσουσιν (*pace* Wolff, 83).

Mic. 4.2 and Isa. 2.3 differ in respect of ויורנו (וירנו). Isaiah reproduces the grammar of MT (χαὶ ἀναγγελεῖ ἡμῖν) with 'announce' or 'proclaim' for MT 'teach'. Micah (Sept.) substitutes a third plural verb for a third singular and also translates ירה 'teach' freely: χαὶ δείξουσιν ἡμῖν, 'and they will show us'. It is difficult to explain this translation which assumes that ויורנו is pointed וְיוֹרֻנוּ. 1QIsaᵃ (1950, i, plate 2) throws some light on this: MT at Isa. 2.3 reads the singular *defectiva* (וירנו) and 1QIsaᵃ has converted the *plene* into a *defectiva* plural with the metathesis of ר and ו (Hillers, 50). This is the text which the Greek translator has read at Mic. 4.4. Since the nations streaming to Jerusalem are the speakers, the intention of the translator is presumably to represent that the inhabitants of Zion are envisaged as the teachers rather than Yahweh (Smith, 87; Wolff, 93; Hillers, 51) or the Messiah (Kimchi and Ibn Ezra). Wolff's assumption that the 'mountain' and 'temple' are the grammatical subjects of δείξουσιν (Mic. 2.2) is another possibility. The singular ויורנו (וירנו) in MT should be read; its subject is the same as that of ושפט (Mic. 4.3; Isa. 2.4). At both Mic. 4.2 and Isa. 2.3 מדרכיו 'of his ways' is given as τὴν ὅδον αὐτοῦ which Rudolph (76) describes as a dogmatic alteration made to remove the possibility that MT should be understood as a recognition of other gods. The מן of מדרכיו is explained by Rudolph (76) as a partitive מן and this should be compared with Wellhausen's exegesis (140): מדרכיו signifies the provisional character of the teaching, what the nations needed to know and what answered the questions which were in their mind (cf. Hillers, 51). Wolff (92) says much the same thing as Wellhausen, but he makes a point of denying that מן is partitive. ונהרו is rendered by Vulg. at Mic. 4.1 and Isa. 2.2 as *et fluent*, the nations 'flow' to Zion's hill. This is a derivation from I נהר. *et docebit nos* 'and he will teach us' is an exact translation of ויורנו which is repeated in Pesh. (*wnlpn*) and Targ. (דילפיננא) at both passages.

There is evidence in Pesh. of an equalization of the variant texts in MT of Micah and Isaiah. בין עמים רבים (Mic. 4.3) and בין הגוים (Isa. 2.4) are both represented by *byt ʿmmʾ* and the word-order of נכון (*mtqn*) in both Mic. 4.1 and Isa. 2.2 is that of Mic. 4.1 (MT). At Mic. 4.3 ושפט and והוכיח are rendered by Pesh. as second person singular verbs (*wtdwn; wtks*). If the speech of the nations ends at v. 2a, as seems likely (so Kimchi; Wellhausen, 140; Weiser, 263; Wolff, 84, 92; Hillers, 51; pace Smith, 87), the subjects of ושפט and והוכיח are Yahweh (or the Messiah) and vv. 2b–4 are spoken by the prophets as 'word of Yahweh' (cf, v. 4, דבר ... כי) With the second person verbs of Mic. 4.3 (Pesh.) Yahweh is presumably assigning responsibility for the world judgement to the inhabitants of Jerusalem. Isa. 2.4 (Pesh.) represents the verbs as third person singulars (*wndwn; wnks*) in agreement with MT. Where Mic. 4.1 (Pesh.) renders ונהרו as *wntknšwn* 'be collected' (cf. Sept. at Jer. 51.44, συναχθῶσιν), Isa. 2.2 translates ונהרו as *wnskwn* 'look in expectation', perhaps *ex* II נהר.

The variant texts of Mic. 4.1 (ונהרו עליו עמים) and Isa. 2.2 (ונהרו אליו כל הגוים) are paraphrased identically by Targ.: 'And all the kingdoms are turned to offer worship to him.' עד רחוק (Mic. 4.3) is a minus in Isa. 2.4 and it is rendered variously by the versions at Micah. Smith (87) supposes that it is an editorial addition in MT at 4.3. Targ. עד עלמא refers it to endurance in time not a geographical remoteness, an enduring dominion rather than a sway over distant nations. Sept εἰς μαχράν and Vulg. *usque in longinquum* can be taken in either sense (cf. Weiser, 261, *weithin*; Rudolph, 76), but Pesh. *dbrwḥq* points to 'distant nations' (NEB, 'among mighty nations afar'; REB, 'among great and distant nations'; Wellhausen, 24, *weit und breit*; Wolff, 82, *bis in die Ferne*) rather than 'enduring dominion'. Rudolph (76) supposes that עד רחוק is a sceptical marginal comment on v. 3b which has found its way into the text, a query whether it may not be the description of a never-never land (cf. Wolff, 84). Hillers (50) suggests that עד רחוק may be a conflation of variants: גוים עצמים and גוים עד רחוק.

Mic. 4.3b (Isa. 2.4b) describes a process which is the reverse of that described in Joel 4.10. In the one the weapons of war become agricultural implements (וכתתו חרבתיהם לאתים וחניתתיהם למזמרות) and in the other agricultural implements become weapons of war (כתו אתיכם לחרבות ומזמרתיכם לרמחים). Joel 4.10 is part of a declaration of war, a call to arms and rearmament, to a switch of production and the refashioning of ploughshares into swords and pruning-hooks into spears: 'Beat your ploughshares into swords and your pruning-hooks into spears.' It is likely that the author of Mic. 4.3 (Isa. 2.4) had this in mind and that it triggered his description of the reverse process of disarmament as a prelude to universal peace.

Mic. 4.5 is not easily integrated with vv. 1–4: 'For all nations will walk in the name of its gods, but we shall walk in the name of Yahweh, our God, for ever.' Targ's interpretation of this makes the nations into dyed-in-the-wool idolaters and appears to consign vv. 1–4 to the status of idle dreams. It replaces a universal acclamation that Yahweh is the only true God with an insuperable division into sheep and goats: 'For all the nations sin because they worship idols, but we trust in Yahweh, our God, for all time coming.' Rashi notices Targ. and comments: 'They will go to destruction, because they serve idols.' Sept. renders ילכו איש בשם אלהיו with πορεύσονται ἕκαστος τὴν ὁδὸν αὐτοῦ and ואנחנו נלך בשם יהוה אלהינו with ἡμεῖς δὲ πορευσόμεθα ἐν ὀνόματι κυρίου θεοῦ ἡμῶν. This reinforces the divide between idolatry and true religion: the nations go their own ways, while Israel remains steadfastly loyal to Yahweh. Kimchi's comment on v. 5 is not easy to disentangle. It establishes a hiatus between Israel and the nations which will obtain until the Messianic age, whereas vv. 1–4 predict a reconciliation which the Messiah will effect. Until that time is reached each nation will walk in the way of its god and then they will return to the 'good way' after the war of Gog and Magog. Hence Kimchi agrees with Sept., Targ. and Rashi that v. 5 formulates an antithesis of idolatry and true religion, but he establishes compatibility between v. 5 and vv. 1–4 by assigning them to different periods. But does באחרית הימים (Mic. 4.1; Isa. 2.2) signify the Messianic Age? Smith (85f.) equates the phrase with the dawn of the Messianic era and so agrees with Kimchi's exegesis, as do Robinson (140f.) and Weiser (262f.), who conclude that its sense is eschatological and that it is to be associated with the end of history (also Cannawurf, 1963, p. 33). Wolff (83) has noticed that support is gathered for this from the renderings of באחרית הימים (Mic. 4.1) in Sept. (ἐπ᾽ ἐσχάτων τῶν ἡμερῶν), Vulg. (*in novissimo dierum*) and Targ. (בסוף יומיא). Ehrlich (4, 1912, 10), who holds that באחרית הימים means no more than the distant future and does not have an eschatological sense, takes another view. Also Hillers (49) who is influenced by his tendency to cling to a pre-exilic date for Mic. 4.1–4 and Isa. 2.2–4. Smith (88), Robinson (141) and Weiser (264f.) agree with Ehrlich (5, 1912, 280) that v. 5 is a kind of rejoinder to vv. 1–3 and so they reject Kimchi's formula of compatibility.

According to Smith v. 5 is the utterance of a practical man who assesses vv. 1–3 as a dream-like vision of the future and who returns doggedly to things as they are. Irrespective of whether the future will be so blessed, and even if the idolatry of the nations proves to be inveterate, Israel must remain loyal to Yahweh for all time coming. Robinson (141) concentrates rather on the lack of monotheistic belief in v. 5. The author was still at the stage where he thought it proper that the nations should worship their own gods, the reality of whose existence he did not question. Israel, for its part, should adhere exclusively to Yahweh who was their God. Robinson supposes that this may have been a protest against syncretism. Weiser (264f.) describes v. 5 as a sober return to the realities of the present which does not amount to a disavowal of a glorious future when all nations will worship Yahweh. The difference between Smith and Weiser is between a 'meanwhile' and a 'nevertheless'. According to Smith v. 5 douses vv. 1–3 with cold water and returns to the realities of the present. According to Weiser it confronts these realities but holds to the future hope to which vv. 1–3 give expression notwithstanding.

The conclusion to be drawn from all this is that the scope of the description of the nations streaming to Zion is Mic. 4.1–3/Isa. 2.2–4, that neither Micah nor Isaiah is the author of the passage and that it is post-exilic; that v. 4a is not part of it, since that verse assumes a different state of affairs, namely, the blessing conferred by the king's peace on Palestinian peasants, though a threat still exists that the even tenor of their lives will be disturbed by invading enemies. The nations are not yet streaming to Zion with peaceful intentions to learn Yahweh's ways. they would create havoc if they could and the peasants would have to crowd into fortified cities for refuge, but the strong defences installed by the king is their guarantee of security and of a placid existence. Verse 5, despite the apologetic of Kimchi and Weiser, is a rejoinder to Mic. 4.1–4 by someone who was sceptical about the description of the ideal future which it contained, or even viewed it with hostility, and who contrasted the Utopian portrayal with the realities of the present which contradicted it.

1. In days to come
    the mountain of Yahweh's house
    will be higher than all other mountains,
    lifted above the hills,
    and peoples will stream to it.
2. And many nations will come and say:
    Let us go up to the mountain of Yahweh,
    to the house of the God of Jacob,
    that he may teach us his ways
    and we may walk in his paths,

for instruction issues from Zion
and the word of Yahweh from Jerusalem.

3. He will govern many peoples
    and rule over mighty nations;
    they will beat their swords into ploughshares
    and their spears into pruning-hooks;
    nation will not lift up sword against nation
    nor ever again be practised in war.

4. Each man will dwell under his vine
    and under his fig tree, free from threat,
    for Yahweh Sebaoth has declared it.

5. All peoples will submit to the authority of their own gods
    and we shall bow to the authority of our God for ever and ever.

vv. 6–8 THE DISPERSED ASSEMBLED AND THE KINGDOM RESTORED

הצלעה (v. 6) means 'those who were lame' (Vulg. *claudicantem*;
Kimchi הצולעים; Wellhausen, 24; Smith, 89; Weiser, 215; Robinson,
140; Rudolph, 82; Wolff, 83; Mendecki, 1983, 219; Hillers, 54).
Kimchi generalizes the sense of הצלעה: חולים 'sick', כואבים 'distressed'.
הצלעה, הנדחה and הנהלאה are feminine singular participles which
function as collectives (Wolff, 84). Ibn Ezra comments on הצלעה,
'Referring to those Israelites who were unable to keep up the pace and
who were left behind' (הנדחה). That the returning exiles are being
likened to a herd of sheep is an unnecessary assumption (Weiser, 266;
Robinson, 141; Rudolph, 83; Wolff, 84, 94f.; Mendecki, 1983, 219,
221; Hillers, 54f.) which has influenced the translation of הנהלאה
('lost' [sheep], NEB, REB) and הנדחה ('strayed', Hillers, 54). Mendecki
(1983, 221) has appealed to Ezek. 34 for support. It should be noticed,
however that G. R. Driver (1946, 161f.) has produced lexicographical
support for the sense 'lost' by postulating II צלע in biblical Hebrew
(Arabic ḏlʿ 'deviate', 'go astray'). He reinforces this with a dubious
appeal to synonymous parallelism (הנדחה/הצלעה; Mic. 4.6, Zeph.
3.19): 'astray' is not a synonym of 'scattered'. Rudolph's decision (82)
to retain 'lame' is the right one.

Wolff concedes that the metaphor of the flock is not so fully
developed in vv. 6–7a as it is in 2.12, but he does not doubt its presence
and he connects the third sing. fem. collectives with an implicit צון

(fem. sing.). So precise an explanation of the 3rd sing. fem. collectives should not be sought. It is more probable that vv. 6–7a refer to the gathering of the dispersed of Israel directly rather than by means of a metaphor. The suggestion that מגדל עדר (v. 8) is a deliberate echo of the 'sheep' metaphor in vv. 6–7a (Kimchi; Robinson, 141; Wolff, 96; Hillers, 56) should be discounted.

Kimchi supposes that באחרית הימים = (v. 6) ביום ההוא points to the end of the exile (also Smith, 93; Weiser, 266; Robinson, 141; Wolff, 87; Mendecki, 1983, 218) and that what is described is the march home of the returning exiles (cf. ἐκ βαβυλῶνος, a plus in Sept at v. 8, *ex* v. 10, according to Rudolph [82]). Hillers (56) may be right in identifying ἐκ βαβυλῶνος as an exilic or post-exilic gloss, but it is, at any rate, a correct gloss and it does not serve to bolster his unconvincing argument that vv. 6–8 belong to the age of Micah (54, 56).

Sept renders הצלעה with τὴν συντετριμμένην, 'those who have broken limbs', a free translation of הצלעה, 'the lame who have fallen behind', perhaps a reference to those who have broken off from the main company and have disintegrated into ones and twos (cf. Wolff, 84, *zusammengeschlagenen*). Their separation from the main company and their consequent isolation is possibly indicated by Pesh. *rḥyq* 'remote'. Targ. attaches the sense 'detached'? (מטלטליא) to הצלעה. Rashi favours 'heal' for אספה with reference to 2 Kgs 5.3 אז יאסף אתו מצרעתו and so he interprets הצלעה as an indication of a physical handicap, a permanent disability rather than sore feet as a consequence of a long march ('I shall cure the lame'). However, the emphasis is on gathering the dispersed of Israel in both clauses and separate statements are not being made: 'I shall cure the lame and gather the dispersed.' אשר הרעתי is filled out by Pesh. ('and those with whom I have dealt severely') and paraphrased by Targ. ('and those among the guilty of my people with whom I have dealt severely'). According to Ibn Ezra אשר הרעתי is not a third category separate from הצלעה and הנדחה. It is rather a general reference to the afflictions of Israelites in exile ('those whom I set in disgrace among the Gentiles'). Wolff (95) similarly detects a reference to *Gericht* (3.12) and Smith (93) notices that ואשר הרעתי is a minus at Zeph. 3.19. NEB 'and I will strengthen the weaklings' is founded on an emendation (Brockington, 256): וְאֲשֶׁר הָרֵעוֹת. Formations from שרר appear in biblical Hebrew, but not the verb (*BDB*, 1057). Wellhausen (141) and Smith (94) assume that there is a relation of synonymous parallelism between

שארית and גוי עצום (v. 7a) and that this requires a more enriched sense for שארית than it had in the eighth century. Wolff (95) likewise observes that שארית has a negative ring (*negativen Klang*), but that it is being used positively rather than negatively: not of the remnant which survives a disastrous judgement, but of the enduring posterity which will grow into a mighty nation (Weiser, 267, the cell of a new community; cf. Rudolph, 83).

The degree of divergence among the versions in the renderings of identical words in vv. 6 and 7 is notable, but this process has its beginnings in MT, where the parallelism of הצלעה and הנדחה is not retained at v. 7 (הנהלאה /הצלעה). At v. 6 Sept. has τὴν συντετριμμένην for הצלעה and τὴν ἐξωσμένην for הנדחה. At v. 7 it has τὴν συντετριμμένην for הצלעה and τὴν ἀπωσμένην for הנהלאה. τὴν ἐξωσμένην and τὴν ἀπωσμένην are indistinguishable in meaning and both render הנדחה. Vulg. represents הצלעה by *claudicantem* 'those who are lame' at both v. 6 and v. 7. It renders הנדחה by *et eam quam eieceram* 'and those whom I had cast out' at v. 6 and הנהלאה by *et eam quae laboraverat* 'and those who had been in the toils' at v. 7. The first person *eieceram* perhaps occurs under the influence of *afflixeram* (הרעתי) and *laboraverat* suggests a derivation of הנהלאה from לאה (so Robinson 140, הנלאה 'those who are exhausted'; also Rudolph, 82; cf. Wolff, 84) rather than a denominative Niphal from הלא (Kimchi, Ibn Ezra; *BDB*, 229; Ehrlich, 5, 281; Weiser, 265; KB³, 235; Wolff, 84; Mendecki, 1983, 219; Hillers, 54), 'removed far off'. Kimchi comments that הלא denotes distance in space (רחק) or time (זמן) and he connects this use with the oily smell which a flock of sheep sends into the distance (cf. *BDB*, 229). Wellhausen (24) emends והנהלאה to ונחלה 'those who are sick' (also Duhm, 88; Smith, 90).

Pesh. has *rḥq* for הצלעה and *wmbdr* for והנדחה. At v. 7 הצלעה is given as *mbdr* and והנהלאה as *wrḥq*, agreeing with the lexicography of Kimchi, Ibn Ezra and *BDB*. Pesh. is inconsistent in rendering הצלעה by *rḥq* at v. 6 and by *mbdr* at v. 7. Targ achieves greater consistency between v. 6 and v. 7, but at the cost of using מבדריא to render both והנדחה (v. 6) and והנהלאה (v. 7). מטלטליא serves for הצלעה in both verses.

The cohesiveness of vv. 6–8 does not extend beyond vv. 6–7a, and v. 7b and v. 8 are separate supplementations which have an element of incompatibility with each other: kingship of Yahweh and Davidic kingship (Wolff, 86, *in einer gewissen Spannung*; Rudolph, 83). Verses 6–7a contain a promise that Yahweh will gather the dispersed of Israel at the end of the exile and rebuild them as a nation, but the issues which are explored in v. 7b and v. 8—how Yahweh's kingship would be exercised in a Jerusalem context, whether directly or through a Davidic king—presuppose that the returning exiles have arrived in Jerusalem and have begun to ask these kind of questions (Wolff, 89f.). Moreover there are evidences of a formal inconcinnity between vv 6–7a and v. 7b: a change from an oracular (first person) to a third person style and from feminine singular collectives to a third plural suffix (עליהם; Wolff, 86; cf. Rudolph, 84). On the other hand, עליהם is an indication of an intention to link v. 7b to v. 7a.

Weiser (265) agrees with Wolff that v. 7b is not a continuation of vv. 6–7a and he describes it as a liturgical response, a confession of Yahweh's kingship in a cultic setting (cf. Wolff, 96). His remark that it functions as a bridge between v. 7a and v. 8 is puzzling, since the incompatibility which has to be eased is between v. 7b and v. 8, kingship of Yahweh and kingship of David. What he has in mind is perhaps the transition which is made in v. 7b from the gathering of the exiles and the promise which is made to them (vv. 6–7a) to the general affirmation that Yahweh will be king in Jerusalem (v. 7b) which leads to v. 8: this will be achieved by a restoration of Davidic kingship (this idea is also expressed by Hillers [56] whose unit is vv. 5–7 and who deals with v. 8 separately). Robinson (141) acknowledges that v. 8 is 'another thought' in relation to v. 7b, but he does not suppose that either v. 7b or v. 8 disrupt the cohesiveness of the unit vv. 6–8 and there is something of this in Hillers' treatment of the passage. Rudolph (83) approaches the position of Hillers (56f.) in urging that there is nothing in vv. 6–7 which could not have been written by Micah. The discontinuity appears at v. 8, according to Rudolph (83), because 'from then and for all time coming' is a closure (*Fermate*) at v. 7b (also Mendecki 1983, 218: v. 8 stands alone as a fragment). מעתה, in the context of a prediction (v. 6, ביום ההוא) is 'from then' rather than 'from now' (Ehrilich, 5, 1912, 281).

Wolff (86f., 96) advances further considerations in connection with v. 8. From the circumstance that the seat of Davidic kingship (הממשלה הראשנה) in v. 8 is Jerusalem and not Bethlehem (5.1; מושל) he draws two conclusions, that v. 8 is a later modification of 5.1 and that the

modification was a consequence of Jerusalem being the destination of
the returning exiles. Rudolph remarks that v. 8 presupposes that
Jerusalem has been laid waste and that the Davidic dynasty has been
overthrown. Hence, unlike vv. 5–7 it does not come from Micah.

Verse 7b ('And Yahweh will be king over them on mount Zion from
then and for all time coming') is interpreted by Targ. so as to take away
the incompatibility between v. 7b and v. 8: 'And the kingdom of David
will be revealed to them on mount Zion from then and for all time
coming.' Ibn Ezra remains closer to MT: 'And Yahweh alone will reign
over them.' Kimchi comments on v. 7: 'For the exile will not be the
end. I shall gather from them a remnant which will dwell in the land at
that time' (cf. Sept v. 8, plus ἐκ βαβυλῶνος).

Ehrlich's approach to v. 7b and v. 8 (281) is a different one. His
emphasis is not on the incompatibility of the kingship of Yahweh and
the kingship of David so much as on the greater glory of the kingship of
Yahweh as compared with the earlier kingship of David, but his
translation of v. 8 should not be accepted: מגדל עדר and בת ציון are
descriptions of David's kingdom surpassed by the glory of Yahweh's
kingdom and v. 7b and v. 8 are cohesive: 'And to you, tower of the flock
and hill of the daughter of Zion, the first kingdom will be compared'
(Ehrlich). ממלכת לבת ירושלם is then a tautological equivalent of הראשנה
הממשלה. Ehrlich justifies his rendering by citing 2 Sam. 23.23, 'he did
not rival (לא בא) the three', but the uncertainty of the sense of v. 8 is
compounded by תאתה ובאה, for which Hillers offers a stylistic
justification (56). If it is a doublet (Duhm, 88, תאתה is primary) it is
evidence that באה was taken as 'come' not 'rival or 'match'. According
to Elliger (BHS) תאתה is primary, and Rudolph (82) gives באה as the
original, either a prophetic perfect or a participle. תאתה was written in
the margin as a gloss on באה and entered the text joined with באה by
means of waw. Verse 8 is a promise that the kingdom of David will be
restored, not a disparaging contrast of that kingdom with the sovereignty of Yahweh: 'And to you, tower of the flock, hill of the daughter
of Zion, will return the first kingdom.'

For מגדל עדר (v. 8) Sept (πύργος ποιμνίου), Vulg. (*turris gregis*) and
Pesh. (*mgdl r̊y*) reproduce MT, whereas Targ. paraphrases מגדל עדר as
'And you, Messiah of Israel' (noticed by Rashi). According to Targ., the
Messiah is about to bring sovereignty to the congregation of Zion
(בת ציון = כנשתא דציון) and the first dominion will come again. Rashi

glosses מגדל with מעוז 'a strong point' and עפל with מגדל עוז 'a hill fortress', citing Isa. 32.14 עפל ובחן, 'citadel and watch-tower' (also Kimchi and Ibn Ezra). On מגדל עדר Kimchi comments: 'That is, the tower of David which was named the tower of the flock, for Israel is likened to a flock of sheep, as they often are. Jerusalem is mentioned as the chief city, where Israel assembled three times a year (cf. Rashi מגדל עדר = בית מקדש) and were a flock in the midst of the pasture.'

It will be noticed that Kimchi associated מגדל עדר ('tower of David') with the promised restoration of the Davidic kingdom, but how precisely does עפל בת ציון and מגדל עדר discharge this function? How does the imagery work? Wellhausen (141) does not discern a reference to Jerusalem, but rather a 'tower of a flock' on a 'hill' in a wasteland which represents Jerusalem as a desolate and ruined city (*contra* Smith, 94). Ehrlich (281) identifies מגדל עדר with a place in the neighbour-hood of Jerusalem (cf. *Shekalim* 7.4; also Gen. 35.21) and supposes that עפל בת ציון is in apposition to מגדל עדר and is identical with it. Hillers (56) accepts this account, but concludes that both מגדל עדר and עפל בת ציון refer to the old city of David and are a synecdoche for Jerusalem. Robinson (140) has equated עפל with the hill where the old Jebusite city was sited and Smith (95) and Weiser (267) have located it in the same area.

Smith's remark (94) that מגדל עדר is a tower overlooking a sheepfold, where a shepherd keeps watch over his flock by night is further elucidated by Wolff (96f.) who gives a fuller account of the appropriateness of the imagery. He agrees with Smith and Weiser as to the location of עפל and holds that this was an area of Jerusalem which had become dilapidated and ruinous. מגדל עדר was in the same area; it had once been a defensive position, but in new circumstances, set in pasture, it had become a watch-tower for shepherds. Wolff's intention, however, is not to follow the negative sense which Wellhausen attaches to the imagery. Its function is not to contrast the desolation of Jerusalem with what it will become when David's kingship is restored. Rather the imagery is part of the vision of Jerusalem restored to its former glory: those parts which once had noble buildings and a bustling life will participate in its renaissance. Rudolph (84) agrees with Wolff's siting of מגדל עדר and עפל. He is aware of the reference in the Mishnah which establishes that מגדל עדר was a place in the vicinity of Jerusalem, but, like the others, he associates both מגדל עדר and עפל

with the area south east of the temple complex, 'with the old city of Solomon'. The dilapidation and ruin of that area will be reversed and its material grandeur restored when David's sway is revived. מגדל עדר was perhaps a residue of palace fortifications which had become a watch-tower for shepherds (so Wolff). In addition Rudolph uses מגדל עדר and עפל as evidences that Jerusalem was in ruins when v. 8 was written.

Sept. (αὐχμώδης), Vulg. (*nebulosa*) and Pesh. ('*mwṭ*') are renderings of עפל which follow from its identification with (or confusion with) אפל 'darkness'. αὐχμώδης derives less obviously from עפל (אפל) than does *nebulosa* and '*mwṭ*'. Vulg. and Pesh. are to be translated, 'And, you, dark tower of the flock of the daughter of Zion.' Sept. reads, 'And, you, dusty tower of the flock, daughter of Zion'. This can be brought nearer to Vulg. and Pesh. and to a derivation from אפל, if 'squalid' is substituted for 'dusty' (cf. Rudolph, 82). Rashi comments on עפל that Targ. has read it as if it were synonymous with אפל and were an epithet of מגדל עדר. מגדל עדר אפל is then indicative of the decline which had overtaken Zion and this is expressed more explicitly by Targ. which renders עפל (אפל) by חובי 'sins' (dark deeds). Moreover, Targ. develops the contrast between decline and restoration more than the other versions: 'To you the sovereignty is about to come and the former dominion will return to the kingdom of the congregation of Jerusalem.'

Rashi and Kimchi differ in their interpretation of Targ.: Rashi asso-ciates עפל (אפל) with חובי and Kimchi associates עפל with טמיר 'hidden' on the basis of Targ. at 2 Kgs 5.24 which renders ויבא אל העפל as ועל לאתר כסי 'and he climbed to a concealed place'. Hence 'conceal-ment' is the sense of עפל and this is represented by טמיר in Targ's paraphrase: 'And, you, Messiah of Israel, hidden because of the sins of the congregation of Zion etc.'. Rashi is to be followed in his opinion that Targ.'s חובי is the equivalent of עפל or אפל.

According to Rudolph (83), the thread which runs through vv. 6–8 is the transition from *Unheil* to *Heil* and the connection between vv. 1–4 and vv. 6–7 is achieved by stitch-words: 'at the end of days' (v. 1) and 'in that day' (v. 6); 'Zion' (vv. 2, 7; also Mendecki, 1983, 218).

6.   On that day (this is Yahweh's word),
       I shall gather[1] those who have fallen lame[2];

[1]Above, p. 128.
[2]Above, p. 128.

I shall assemble the scattered and those I have afflicted[3].

7. I shall make a remnant[4] of the lame
and a mighty nation of those who are worn out[5].
Yahweh will reign over them on Mount Zion
from then[6] and for all time coming.

8. And you, watch-tower[7] of the flock,
hill[8] of Zion's daughter,
to you will come again[9] the sovereignty you once had,
the dominion of the daughter of Jerusalem[10].

vv. 9–13 EXILE, CONTUMELY AND VINDICATION

Wellhausen (141) comments on the lack of connection between v. 8 and vv. 9–10. He supposes that מגדל עדר and עפל (v. 8) are indicative of Jerusalem in ruins and uninhabited and he contrasts this with the different setting of vv. 9–10: the inhabitants of Jerusalem are about to be expelled. Rudolph (86) remarks that v. 9 is stitched to v. 8 by means of מלך (ממלכת) and v. 10 to v. 8 by means of בת ציון. Hillers (59, 60) holds that vv. 9–10 and vv. 12–13 are self-contained units and he does not discern any problem with the cohesiveness of vv. 9–10. Similarly Smith (93) supposes that vv. 9–10 could have been spoken by a prophet who was active in the later years of Jeremiah's ministry. Weiser (268, 269) accepts that vv. 12–13 are not continuous with vv. 9–10. They may be by different authors or they may both be assigned to Micah. Weiser halts between two opinions.

REB, 'Why are you crying out in distress?' (v. 9, למה תריעי רע) is perhaps influenced by the subsequent reference to birth-pangs (vv. 9–10), but even these do not establish that the show of anguish is to be taken seriously and the intention may be to indicate that these are histrionics, that the display of extreme suffering is exaggerated (cf. Smith, 91). Hence NEB translates למה תריעו רע as 'Why are you now filled with alarm?' which suggests that those who behave as if they were

---

[3]Above, p. 128.
[4]Above, p. 129.
[5]Above, p. 129, reading הנלאה.
[6]Above, p. 130.
[7]Above, pp. 131–133.
[8]Above, pp. 131–133.
[9]Above, p. 131, deleting ובאה.
[10]Above, p. 131.

distraught in the grip of desperate pain have been overtaken by panic and its consequences. Vulg., *quare maerore contraheris,* 'Why do you collect in grief?' may be derived *ex* II רעה (*BDB*, 945) 'associate with' (Smith, p. 91). The correct derivation is from רוע (Weiser, 267; Robinson, 140; Rudolph, 85; Wolff, 110; Hillers, 58). So the question is: 'What are you making such a noise about (Wellhausen, 25, 'Why are you bawling?') as if you were a woman suffering birth pangs?' and this conclusion is supported by Vulg.'s rendering of חולי וגחי (v. 10): 'Writhe in pain and take your fill' (*dole et satage*) = 'Writhe in pain and make a meal of it.'

Sept. represents למה תריעי רע (v. 9) as ἵνα τί ἔγνως κακά, 'Why are you acquainted with evil?': ד and ר have been confused (תדעי instead of תריעי; so Wolff, 102) and רע has been vocalized as רֹע or רַע *ex* I רעע (*BDB*, 947). Alternatively Sept. represents למה תריעי רע (MT) and תריעי has been derived from II רעה (*BDB*, 945) instead of רוע (*BDB*, 929). Wolff has noticed that Aq. and Symm. ἐκακώσας have derived הריעי from רעע, but the variant renderings of Sept. and Aq. are not to be explained (*pace* Wolff) by postulating that they read different Hebrew texts. The matter rather turns on the different ways in which they have derived תריעי. Pesh. has for למה תריעי רע 'Why do you commit evil' (*lmn̆ 'bdty byšt*). רוע has been taken as an equivalent of רעע and רע vocalized as רֹע or רַע. Ehrlich (5, 281) arrives at the same result by emending למה תרועי רע to למה תרועי רע (*ex* רעע). Targ. has treated תריעי as if it were derived from II רעה (*BDB*, 945) and has vocalized רע as רֵע: כען למא את מתחברא לעממיא, 'Now why do you make friends with the nations?'

Both Kimchi and Ibn Ezra identify מלך and יעץ with Yahweh (v. 9; also Rudolph, 85, 86; Wolff, 111), whereas Pesh., with a plural form (*mlwkyky*) and a corresponding *'bdw* (MT אבד), supposes a reference to counsellors (שׂריך?; also Targ. מלכי מלכך, 'counsellors of your king'). Sept. ἡ βουλή represents יועצך with עצתך 'your counsel'. The sense of the second question is, 'Do you not still have a God to rely on?'. The message is that exile is imminent, but that Yahweh has not finally forsaken his people; that He will rule over them and give them counsel in exile; that, at this critical and excruciating juncture, they should not be too full of woe or be overcome with despair: 'Remember the consolation (which will come) and do not reckon that your hope has perished' (Kimchi). 'Do not cry out, for, if you writhe like a woman in labour, if you are ejected and go to Babylon, there you will be delivered, there your king and counsellor will redeem you' (Kimchi). Targ. renders חיל as עקא וזיע, 'distress and writhing'.

Wolff (111) raises the question whether המלך אין בך may not be an ironical query (so Smith, 89), a reference to the flight of Zedekiah out of Jerusalem, but he rejects the thought. Smith (91), however equates מלך and יועץ with an earthly king, as does Weiser (268). Hillers (59), in search for support that the verse is to be assigned to Micah, suggests that המלך ... אבד may be an attack on Hezekiah. Weiser's treatment of the question, 'Have you no king or has your counsellor perished?' assumes that it is not in any respect a critical query. It takes the show of anguish with the utmost seriousness and is not an observation that they protest too much. Its intention is to allow a glimpse of the desperate despair of the people to break through.

There is something odd about this minimizing of the disaster of exile. The equation of exile with the threat of doom is replaced by counsel not to magnify the extent of the disaster: 'You that are close to exile why do you mourn and weep? Remember the day of consolation and deliverance' (Kimchi). The note is a different one from that which is normally heard: 'Lament for the sins which have brought this ultimate disaster on you and which have exposed you to inconsolable suffering and anguish.' The impression is that the exile has already been overtaken by deliverance and restoration and that this minimizing of the destruction of Jerusalem by Nebuchadrezzar (according to Ibn Ezra this is the reference) and the overthrow of Judah are evidence of the post-exilic period. The matter looks different if vv. 9–10 are thought to be a prediction of the siege of Jerusalem by Sennacherib (701) and ובאת עד בבל (v. 10) is excised as a later and erroneous gloss (Wellhausen, 141; cf. Weiser, 269). Verse 10 is then compared with Hos. 2.16f: Israel will go out into the desert and there she will be saved and renewed by Yahweh. Wellhausen's other proposal that MT should be retained and that the prediction is a post-exilic *vaticinium post eventum* is to be preferred.

Robinson (141f.) retains MT but proposes a historical setting in 597 or 588 B.C., in connection with the siege of Jerusalem by Nebuchadrezzar and so allocates vv. 9–10 to the time of Jeremiah. The interpretation of vv. 9–10 on which this rests is dubious. If the background is the siege of Jerusalem and if the 'gasping in anguish' (he emends וגחי to והתיפחי after Jer. 4.31) of the daughter of Zion is to be taken seriously, my exegesis that it is being dismissed as a case of protesting too much falls to the ground. Robinson's conclusion depends on his assumption that the coupling of מלך and יועץ points to an earthly king, either Jehoiachin or Zedekiah, rather than Yahweh and that the intention of the questions ('Do you not have a king? Has your counsellor perished?') is not to administer a mixture of reproof and consolation but to indicate that the earthly king is a broken reed. Neither of these two pieces of exegesis is acceptable. Moreover, Robinson (142f.) expresses doubt whether he can accommodate אביך ... ובאת in his interpretation of v 10. MT is not altogether satisfactory and יועצך (v. 9) should be emended to יועציך 'your counsellors' (with Pesh. and Targ.: 'Do you not have a king (Yahweh) or have your counsellors (יועציך = שריך?) perished?' (אבדו with Pesh. and Targ.).

Wolff (107–110) shares with Robinson the view that the historical background of vv. 9–10 is the siege of Jerusalem by Nebuchadrezzar, but he extends this context to vv. 11–13, assumes vv. 9–13 are a cohesive unit and, in general, argues his case differently from Robinson. These verses are spoken by a prophet who is a disciple of Jeremiah, who maintains the emphasis on doom in Micah's proclamation, but who sees light at the end of the tunnel, rescue and restoration after exile (vv. 9–10). Further, there is an eschatological element: on another occasion in the future the nations will mass against Zion, but, this time, they will be the prey rather than the predators (vv. 11–13).

Wolff's endeavour (110–114; 120–121) to make an intrinsic unity out of vv. 9–13, spoken by the same prophet in the shadow of the fall of Jerusalem and the imminence of exile, is a desperate enterprise. The unity after which he laboriously strives is broken at v. 10 and shattered at vv. 11–13. Is it conceivable that the same prophet should have addressed people crying out in anguish in the presence of a great disaster (v. 9), have told them that they would be driven out of their city as a consequence of defeat and, in the same breath, have asked them to swallow the good news that they would be delivered from the power of their enemies in Babylon (v. 10)? The view that there is an element of hope in the command to show anguish (v. 10: 'Writhe and bear a child') is fanciful (cf. Weiser, 269). חולי וגחי (v. 10) is linked directly with כי ... בשדה, 'for you will have to evacuate the city and live in the open country'. חולי וגחי in the context, encompasses only severe, unendurable pain, not the joy that a child has been born or a hope for the future which the birth signals. It is even less conceivable that while they were being organized for exile outside the city, miserable and hopeless, a prophet should have offered them the consolation of an eschatological prophecy (vv. 11–13), have advised that, in the future, the nations would again mass against Zion and would suffer a devastating defeat. If his intention had been to exacerbate their anguish, he could not have hit on a better expedient.

Compared with v. 9, the first half of v. 10 ('Writhe and give birth, daughter of Zion, like a woman bringing forth a child, for you will go out of the city and live in the open country; you will go to Babylon') emphasizes the negative aspects of the exile, the extent of the loss which will be suffered, and it acknowledges that the disaster merits manifestations of lamentation. The verse then takes a turn which justifies the exegesis offered for v. 9: 'There (Babylon) you will be delivered; there Yahweh will redeem you from the grasp of your enemy.' In the last analysis v. 10 thus confirms the post-exilic setting of the piece.

A different explanation of the relation of v. 9 to v. 10 and of their historical setting is offered by Rudolph (86f.). Verse 9 is to be allocated to the *Heil* prophets (van der Woude, 1969, 249f.) and v. 10 is Micah's rejoinder. The occasion is the siege of Jerusalem by Sennacherib in 701 which Micah experienced. The *Heil* prophets dismiss the daughter of Zion's show of extreme distress as histrionic exaggeration and ask her whether her king has perished (מלך and יועץ = יהוה). The implication of the question is that she need not fear the siege conditions which obtain in Jerusalem and that Yahweh will guarantee her security.

The rejoinder of Micah (v. 10) is that the daughter of Zion writhes and cries out like a woman in labour with good reason, for the inhabitants of Jerusalem are about to be driven from their city into the open country, and arranged in companies for exile. Micah (so Rudolph), unlike Isaiah, does not prophesy that Jerusalem will be delivered from the threat of Sennacherib, but he predicts that Yahweh will rescue them in Babylon and that he will save them from the grasp of their enemies.

The obvious objection to this interpretation of vv. 9–10 is ובאת עד בבל which indicates the exile brought about by Nebuchadrezzar rather than the threat to Jerusalem by Sennacherib. Rudolph wrestles with this problem and remarks that his solution may be thought far-fetched. It is certainly special pleading of an elaborate kind: ובאת עד בבל identifies the destination of the exiled Judaeans, but it does not state by whom they were exiled. Since the Assyrians ruled Babylon at the beginning of the eighth century and since the exchange of populations was a feature of their policy (2 Kgs 17.24), it is understandable that Sennacherib might have settled the Judaean exiles in Babylon. Neither this ἀπολογία nor its alternative should be accepted: the text was originally ובאת עד אשור and was changed to ובאת עד בבל, because the exile presided over by Nebuchadrezzar became the normative exile (cf. Hillers, 59). Hillers' concern, unlike that of Rudolph, is to attribute both v. 9 and v. 10 to Micah; also vv. 11–13 on the assumption that Micah was appropriating a 'Zion tradition' (60). Smith's conclusion that Micah cannot be the author, if ובאת עד בבל is retained, is correct.

גחי is the only lexicographical matter that needs to be investigated in v. 10 Vulg. *et satage* for וגחי has been noted, but 'and have your fill' or 'and make a meal of it' is not a rendering of וגחי. Sept. ὤδινε καὶ ἀνδρίζου καὶ ἔγγιζε for חולי וגחי is a puzzle. ὤδινε represents חולי 'writhe', but 'behave like a man and draw near' has the appearance of a marginal comment on חולי rather than an attempt to render וגחי. ὁ θεός σου is a plus after יהוה. Attempts at a text-critical elucidation of the Greek text have been made: ἀνδρίζου is taken as a doublet of ὤδινε (חולי is connected by the Greek translator with חיל 'strength'—Ryssel: Smith, 91; Wolff, 102) or ἀνδρίζου is a rendering of גחי *ex* גיח 'break open the womb', with the sense 'make a man-child' cf. Gen. 4.1) not 'be a man' (Schleusner, Rudolph, 86). καὶ ἔγγιζε is explained as a rendering of וגעי which the Greek translator erroneously derived from נגע instead of from געה 'cry out' (*BDB*, 171; proposed as an emendation of גחי by KB³, 181). In Pesh. (*ḥbly wḥsny*) *ḥbly* ('suffer birth-pangs') and *ḥsny* are synonyms (= חולי). Smith (91) takes *ḥsny* 'be strong as a rendering of ἀνδρίζου. Targ. has מרעי וזועי, 'become ill and writhe' for חולי וגחי.

BDB (161, גוח, גיח) associates גחי with the breaking open of the womb at the birth of a child. In this respect it follows Ibn Ezra and, perhaps, Kimchi (הוצאה, 'issuing'), though Kimchi also gives the sense 'groan' (אנחה) which Duhm (88) achieves by emending גחי to הגי or פעי. Wellhausen (141) notices that Hitzig favours 'Writhe and give birth' for חולי וגחי (also, Smith, 90), but he dismisses this as not giving an appropriate sense. If, however, the point is that בת ציון is exaggerating her anguish, behaving like a woman with birth-pangs, the sense is not poor. Wolff (100, 111) so translates, but his conclusion that גחי is *ex* גחה (cf. *BDB*, 161), with an appeal to the obscure Ps. 22.10 ('deliver from the womb'), is not an improvement on a derivation from גיח ('break open the womb', 'give birth'). Wolff's rendering indicates that a midwife assists at the birth. Wellhausen is inclined to conclude that גחי is a synonym (Pesh.) of חולי, but he remarks that it is lexicographically obscure.

NEB ('Lie writhing on the ground' for חולי וגחי) has, perhaps, been influenced by Rashi's association of גחי with גחון 'belly': גחי 'crawl on the belly'. Gen. 3.14, which is cited by Rashi (על גחונך תלך 'On your belly you will crawl'), does not directly support the sense 'crawl on the belly' for גחי. Rudolph (85) retains MT and claims support from post-biblical Hebrew and Aramaic for the sense 'cry out' (*ex* גיח or גוח; cf. Weiser, 267, 'Break out in cries of anguish' for חולי וגחי). Rudolph supposes that גחני is the best of the emendations which have been proposed, 'Writhe and twist'. NEB's translation may have the same lexicographical justification as that adduced by Ehrlich (5, 282): גחי is derived from גחה, Arabic *jḫḫ*, 'lie on the ground'. Robinson (140) emends וגחי to והתיפחי ('and gasp'; Jer. 4.31).

A question about the sense of חולי וגחי is also raised by Duhm (88). Because he interprets v. 10 as an earnest injunction to the people by a prophet to raise a lament in view of imminent expulsion, he establishes the incoherence of v. 9 and v. 10. In v. 9 the prophet asks, 'Why are you so full of anguish, since Yahweh is still your defence?', while in v. 10 he earnestly demands a show of anguish. But is חולי וגחי an earnest demand? Is it not rather a continuation in the ironical vein of v. 9, a chiding of an extravagant display of anguish. The disadvantage of my exegesis, as I have noted, is that the exile is then taken with unusual lightness, but I have supposed that the post-exilic date of vv. 9–10 explains this.

Verses 11–13 do not cohere with vv. 9–10, but, presumably, they are to be set in a time after the exile and return and they seem to have an eschatological character: they are the vision of a seer 'at the end of days' (so Smith, 98). Rashi comments that the events described take place at the end of time. Wellhausen remarks (142) that the assembling of the nations against Jerusalem and their subsequent destruction is a fixed characteristic of eschatological predictions from Ezekiel onwards (cf. Robinson, 143). Verses 11–13 have, however been stitched to vv. 9–10 and there is some evidence of skilful needlework: עתה (v. 9) and ועתה (v. 11); חולי וגחי (v. 10) matched by קומי ודושי (v. 13). But עתה at v. 9 is a prelude to expulsion and ועתה at v. 11, while it has the initial appearance of a threat, issues in the slaughter of those nations massed against Jerusalem (cf. Wellhausen, 142). Wolff (105–110), however, holds that the significance of עתה at v. 9 and ועתה at v. 11 is deeper, that there is an intrinsic connection between vv. 9–10 and vv. 11–13 and that vv. 9–13 are a unit spoken by the same person. 'Threshing' is a metaphor for a final war in the valley of Jehoshaphat fought against nations who have massed (v. 11) to destroy Israel. The war is against Gog and Magog (Rashi). Kimchi remarks that גוים (v. 11) are Gog and Magog and their allies and he discerns a reference to the Messianic age, Ibn Ezra notices this interpretation, but contents himself with saying that the war described lies in the future: it is a הנה יום בא kind of prediction.

Rudolph (92) sets vv. 11–13 against the background of the siege of Sennacherib and they are comfortable words spoken by the *Heil* prophets. The גוים רבים are Sennacherib and his allies and political and military events are interpreted in terms of Zion theology, as a war waged by the nations against Jerusalem and Zion (Isa. 8.9f.; 17.12ff.; 29.7). Weiser (269) and Hillers (60) share Rudolph's view that the eschatological character of vv. 11–13 does not necessitate the conclusion that they are post-exilic and hold that their intention is to make Micah the speaker.

The coalition massed against Israel is represented as saying: 'Let her be defiled and let our eyes (singular 'eye', Vulg., Pesh., Targ.) gloat over Zion' (v. 11; ראה ב = חזה ב). Rudolph (89) notices the singular verb (ותחז) and the dual subject עינינו which he tolerates (GK 145n; also Wolff, 102). Weiser (267) prefers עינינו 'eye'. Rudolph (89) remarks that the versions have repaired the grammar in different ways: Sept. has made the verb (ἐπόψονται) plural and Vulg., Pesh. and Targ. have made the subject singular. NEB (REB) translate 'Let her suffer outrage, let us gloat over Zion' and this is founded on the vocalization of תחנף as תֶּחֱנַף (Brockington, 256). Sept. has a first person plural ἐπιχαρούμεθα, 'we shall rejoice' for תחנף (adopted by Robinson, 142: נשׂמחה), that is, rejoice in the sense of 'gloat' which Pesh. attaches with

more reason to ותחז (*wtḥdy*; Wellhausen, 25, *weiden* 'pasture'; also
Wolff, 101; Weiser, *weide*). Rudolph (88) describes ἐπιχαρούμεθα as a
free translation. Vulg.'s rendering is *lapidetur*, 'let it be stoned', perhaps
'it will be a reduced to a heap of stones', 'it will be a ruin' (cf. Targ., 'let
our eyes look on the downfall [מפלת] of Zion'). Wellhausen (142)
emends תחנף to תחסף (Niphal; 'razed') and Ehrlich (5, 282) secures a
similar effect by emending תחנף to תחרב 'destroyed'.

קרנך (v. 13) is rendered as a plural by Sept. (τὰ κέρατά σου) which
matches τὰς ὁπλάς σου (MT פרסתיך). Pesh. apparently has two
singulars (*qrntky; prstky*) or perhaps two plurals. החרמתי is rendered by
Sept. as ἀναθήσεις 'dedicate' (cf. Vulg., *interficies Domino*, 'Destroy for
the Lord', that is, put under the ban; also Pesh., *wtḥrmyn lmry*). Kimchi
paraphrases תחנף (v. 11), 'Because of its iniquities it will be destroyed as
it was previously (by Nebuchadrezzar)' and Targ. also connects תחנף
with sin and guilt (תחוב). The nations state that they will feast their eyes
(Kimchi, מה שקוינו, 'what we had eagerly anticipated') on the sack of
Jerusalem, but they take no account of Yahweh's plans; they do not
discern his policy (v. 12; עצתו; Pesh. *trʿyth*, 'what is in his mind') which
is to encompass their destruction. Ehrlich (5, 282) holds that כי (12)
means 'that' or 'namely that' (*dass*): the intention of the final clause of v.
12 is to spell out the sense of עצתו. They will be 'threshed' (Ibn Ezra,
דרך משל) as sheaves are on a threshing-floor.

This metaphor is still maintained in v. 13, where the threshing of the
sheaves is done by iron horns (tearing at them; *pace* Hillers, 61) and
bronze hooves (stamping on them). Rudolph's opinion (93) that the
'threshing' metaphor is represented by 'hooves' but not by 'horn' (he
reads the singular with MT) is unlikely. He holds that 'horn' is a figure
for irresistible strength; also Wolff, 102, 114, Hillers, 61). Smith (99)
also reads קרנך (singular) which he describes as a 'new metaphorical
element'—a figure of the angry ox goring its foe. קרניך 'horns' should
be read (Weiser, 268). Israel will 'pound' many nations whose spoil and
wealth they will devote (החרמתי second feminine singular; cf. *Jeremiah*
i, 20; 1986) to Yahweh. Vulg. is the only version which takes בצעם as
'their spoil' (*rapinas eorum*). For וחילם Sept. (χαί τὴν ἰσχὺν αὐτῶν)
and Vulg. (*et fortitudinem eorum*) have 'and their strength' or 'and
their power'. Pesh. 'and their possessions' (*wnksyhwn*) and Targ.
(וממון יקרהון), 'and the wealth of their treasure', indicate the sense
'wealth' for חיל. Targ. interprets the metaphorical language in v. 13:

דושי becomes קטלי 'slay', קרנך becomes עמא דביך, 'the people within
you'; ברזל is rendered as תקיפין כברזלא, 'strong as iron', ופרסתיך as
ושארהון, 'and their remnant', נחושה as חסנין כנחשא, 'powerful as bronze'
and והדקות as ותקטלין, 'and you will slay'.

9. Now what have you to shout about[1]?
    Have you no king[2], have your counsellors[3] perished
    that birth-pangs have seized you like a woman in labour?
10. Writhe and give birth[4], daughter of Zion,
    like a woman bringing forth a child,
    for now you are to be expelled from the city
    and are to live in the open country;
    you will go to Babylon[5]; there you will be rescued,
    there Yahweh will redeem you from the hand of your enemies.
11. And now nations are massed against you;
    they say: Let her be defiled
    and let our eyes[6] gloat over Zion.
12. But they do not know Yahweh's plans
    and they do not discern what he has in mind,
    that he has gathered them as sheaves to the threshing-floor.
13. Set to and thresh, daughter of Zion,
    for I shall make your horns[7] iron
    and your hooves bronze.
    You will pound many peoples
    and devote their spoil to Yahweh,
    their wealth[8] to the Lord of all the earth.

v. 14 JERUSALEM BESIEGED AND HUMILIATED

Mic. 4.14 is a fragment which bears no relationship either to the
preceding verses, 11–13, or to what follows in 5.1ff. Duhm (88) and
Ehrlich (5, 283) delete it. Wellhausen (142), Smith (100), Robinson
(143), Weiser (270) and Hillers (62) describe it as an isolated fragment,
added to vv. 11–13, according to Robinson, whereas Weiser discerns its

[1]Above, pp. 134f.
[2]Above, pp. 135f.
[3]Reading יעציך and אבדו, above, p. 136.
[4]Above, pp. 136–139.
[5]Above, p. 136.
[6]Above, p. 140.
[7]Reading קרניך, above, p. 141.
[8]Above, p. 141.

redactional function as a background of distress provided as a preliminary to the hope of *Heil* in 5.1ff. Smith suggests that its original place
may have been after v. 9 or after v. 10 as a marginal note. He also
notices that עתה without the *waw* shows that the redactional intention
to connect v. 14 with v. 13 was absent. Rudolph (87) sets out 4.11–5.5
as a unit and Wolff, similarly, 4.9–5.5. Wolff relies on the presence of
עתה in v. 9 and v. 14 and of ועתה in v. 11. He postulates a series of עתה
sayings, redactionally contrived and originating with a prophet who, in
the wake of the fall of Jerusalem, combined Micah's and Jeremiah's
predictions of doom with a consoling prophecy of hope. But עתה
appears at 5.1 and this must presumably signal for Wolff the beginning
of another עתה saying, so that v. 14 is reduced to a fragment of an עתה
saying out of context.

Verse 14a is translated by KJV, 'Now gather thyself in troops, O
daughter of troops: he hath laid siege against us.' Two questions are
raised: (a) What is the sense to be attached to תתגדדי בת גדוד? (b) Who
is being addressed? In deriving תתגדדי from גדוד 'band' KJV is
following Rashi, Kimchi and Ibn Ezra. The last-mentioned glosses
תתגדדי with קהלת הגדוד 'the massed force'. Pesh. ('Now you will go
out in a troop, daughter of a troop') and Targ. ('Now mobilize in
camps') agree with the Jewish mediaeval commentators in connecting
תתגדדי with גדוד. Vulg. *vastaberis* 'you will be devastated' is a puzzle,
but Rudolph (89) notices that Jerome in his commentary has stated that
vastaberis is intended as a rendering of MT, that its sense is 'gash' and
that Vulg. supports the derivation of תתגדדי from גדד. Certainly
Vulg.'s translation of בת גדוד (*filia latronis* 'daughter of a mercenary') is
an indication that תתגדדי has not been connected with גדוד.

Sept. gives ἐμφραχθήσεται θυγάτηρ ἐμφραγμῷ 'a daughter is
enclosed with a wall' for תתגדדי בת גדוד. Why תתגדדי, second feminine
singular, is rendered by a third singular remains obscure, but otherwise
a different Hebrew text from MT has been read, namely,
תתגדרי בת גדור. Rudolph (89) suggests that גדור has been vocalized as
an infinitive absolute (גָּדוֹר) which Sept. has represented as a noun
(ἐμφραγμῷ) cognate with the verb, 'A daughter is enclosed with a
barrier.' NEB (Brockington, 256; also RSV) has been influenced by the
Greek text and has adopted the emendation תתגדרי בת גדר, 'Get you
behind your walls, you people of a walled city.' Robinson's emendation
(142), 'You are enclosed in a fence' follows van Hoonacker (1908) and

substitutes בגדר for בת גדוד. However, Robinson's exegetical intention is different from that of NEB (REB) and he translates the remainder of v. 14a as 'a siege-wall has been erected against us'. The emphasis is that of being under siege, whereas the emphasis in NEB is that of resisting siege in a fortified city: 'Get you behind your walls, you people of a walled city.' Robinson conveys the meaning 'You are besieged' rather than 'You have the protection of a walled city.'

Another emendation based on גדד 'gash' rather than גדר 'enclosed' involves the alteration of בת גדוד to התגודד, an infinitive absolute, 'You are to keep gashing yourselves' or 'Keep gashing yourselves' (Wellhausen, 25; Duhm, 88; Smith, 100). The tendency of more recent scholarship is to derive תתגדדי from גדד (Ehrlich, 5, 282; Weiser, 270; Rudolph, 88; Wolff, 101; Hillers, 62).

(b) The second matter is to ascertain who is being addressed in v. 14a and there has been a difference of opinion about this since mediaeval times. Rashi appears to equate בת גדוד with בת כשדים and so it is the force besieging Jerusalem which is being addressed in v. 14a, 'Now, invading army, arrange your dispositions; it has laid a siege against us.' Ibn Ezra also explains בת גדוד as the force (קהלת הגדוד) which was besieging Jerusalem. Kimchi, on the other hand, concludes that בת גדוד is an address to the besieged and not the besieger and he comments on תתגדדי בת גדוד 'You are surrounded by bands, for bands of invaders are come against you, so that you are called בת גדוד.' Kimchi's supposition that בת גדוד is an address to the besieged and not the besieger is the same as that of KJV ('Now gather thyself troops, O daughter of troops'; so Pesh. 'Go out with a troop, O daughter of troops'; cf. Targ.), that is, make preparations to defend the city. Rashi and Ibn Ezra take v. 14a differently: 'Make your dispositions to assault the city, O invading army.' When תתגדי is derived from גדד the assumption, for the most part, is that the besieged are being addressed and that בת גדוד refers to them (Wellhausen, Duhm, Smith, Weiser, Wolff), but Ehrlich (5, 282) disturbs this consensus. His exegesis of v. 14a has to be taken along with his speculative treatment of v. 14b. We may notice, for the present, that, according to Ehrlich, it is the besiegers (בת גדוד) who are urged to gash themselves, to engage in mourning rites (תתגדדי), since the enterprise which they have undertaken of besieging Jerusalem is utterly futile.

Hillers (62) dispenses with the vocative בת גדוד in his somewhat free translation, thought there is no doubt that it is the besieged who are being addressed ('Now you are gashing yourself with gashes'). Rudolph (88) spells out the sense of בת גדוד, 'you that have to deal with besiegers'—there is word-play, תתגדדי *ex* גדד 'gash' and גדוד 'band', 'force'. Rudolph also holds that מצור שם עלינו is a relative clause with אשר implicit. The antecedent is then גדוד and so Rudolph stands apart from the consensus: he agrees that the besieged are being addressed (תתגדדי), but, according to his grammar, גדוד refers to besiegers. Wolff (115) conjectures that בת גדוד, addressed to the besieged, may be an allusion to the גדוד which accompanied Zedekiah on his ill-fated sortie from Jerusalem (Jer. 39.4–7). Sept,[B] ἐφ' ὑμᾶς 'against you' (MT עלינו 'against us') does not have the support of Vulg. (*super nos*) nor of Pesh. (*ʿlyn*) and Ziegler (217) prefers ἡμᾶς in his text with Sept.[VQ].

The Hebrew text of v. 14b is straightforward: 'With a rod they strike on the cheek the judge of Israel.' Presumably the subject of יכו, though it is plural, is identified with the subject of שם which is singular and the plurals of Vulg. (*posuerunt*), Pesh. (*qmw*) and Targ. (אשׁדין) are probably a repair of this incongruence rather than evidence that the versions read a different Hebrew text from MT. Striking the cheek of a person is a ritual which demeans and offers a deadly insult to his rank and status. It is an affront to his self-respect and the calculation is that he will not regain it, but will live in the shadow of the moment of humiliation for ever afterwards. In addition to this the idiom may refer to the administration of physical abuse and torture.

Ibn Ezra identifies the שפט with the Messiah or with Zerubbabel. Smith (101) detects a reference to the insults heaped on Hezekiah by Sennacherib's generals (Isa. 36.4–20). He explains the choice of שפט over against מלך or משל for 'king' in terms of the word-play on שבט and שפט (also Weiser, 271; Rudolph, 94; Wolff, 115). Rudolph (94) assigns the verse to Micah and supposes that the allusion to the king's cheek being struck is not to be taken literally or attached to a particular occasion when his royal dignity was debunked. It is not the carrying out of a ritual; it is rather a metaphor for the loss of dignity and the despite to kingly rank which Hezekiah suffered at the hands of the Assyrians (cf. Smith): the imposition of tribute and the seizure of his daughters and the palace concubines (*ANET*[2], 1955, 288). Wolff (115) also takes 'striking the cheek with a rod' as an idiomatic expression and he connects v. 14b with the treatment meted out to Zedekiah after his attempt to escape with a body of men from Jerusalem: the slaying of his sons in his presence, the putting out of his eyes and the chains in which he was conveyed to Babylon (Jer. 39.4–7).

Vulg. renders שפט exactly (*iudicis*), Pesh. 'shepherd' (*rʿy*) and Targ. 'judges' (דייני) more freely. דייני may be an indication that Targ. has taken שפט as a collective and Pesh. 'shepherd' that it was equated with 'king'. The main interest lies with the translation of שפט in Sept., τὰς πύλας in Sept.[B] and τὰς φυλάς in Sept.[AQ]. Zeigler (217) prefers φυλάς with good reason, since שבט 'tribe' is graphically close to שפט, whereas שערים (πύλας) 'gates' is not. The latter is used by Ehrlich (282) in a speculative reconstruction of MT. There can be little doubt that πύλας is a copyist's error, that φυλάς represents correctly that text of Sept. and that the Greek translator was reading MT. It may be that he identified שפט and שבט as variant spellings of the same word, 'rod' or 'tribe': ב and פ are phonetically close. The only deviation from MT in Sept. is the plural φυλάς 'tribes'. שפט (שבט) is perhaps taken as a collective (cf. Targ; Hillers, 62).

14. Now keep gashing yourself[1];
     siege has been laid against us;
     the enemy strikes the ruler of Israel on the cheek.

[1]Emending בת גדוד to התגודד, above p. 145.

CHAPTER 5

vv. 1–5 THE REIGN OF THE MESSIAH VERSUS SELF-HELP

Sept. (v. 2) follows MT (v. 1) closely, but represents MT אפרתה as
בית אפרתה (οἶκος Ἐφράθα) and Wellhausen (142), followed by Duhm
(89), Smith (102) and Weiser (272), explains בית לחם (MT) as a correct
gloss. בית לחם is also read by Sept. It renders צעיר as a superlative
(ὀλιγοστός) and makes it into a statement (as it is in Vulg., Pesh. and
Targ.) rather than an item in the opening address: 'You are the smallest.'
Sept. reproduces להיות[1] (τοῦ εἶναι) in addition to εἶ, whereas Vulg.,
Pesh. and Targ. convert להיות[1] of MT into *es, 'nty dthwyn* and הויתא
respectively. With להיות[1] deleted as dittography of להיות[2] (Wellhausen,
142; Ehrlich, 5, 283; Smith, 102; Weiser, 271; Rudolph, 90; Wolff, 103;
Hillers, 64) צעיר is more evidently part of the opening address. Wellhausen (142), following Hitzig, has redivided אפרתה צעיר as
אפרת הצעיר (also Duhm, 89; Smith, 102; Weiser, 271).

Ehrlich (5, 283) has held that מהיות is required to give the sense 'too
small to be', but Fitzmeyer (1956, 10–13) has urged that this can be
had from להיות. It has been held (Lescow, 1967, 195) that a copyist
would have been more likely to miss the second occurrence of להיות
than the first (also Ehrlich, 283) and he retains להיות[1], 'small for a tribe
in Judah'. Ehrlich holds that צעיר has a temporal nuance: 'Only
recently were you counted among the regions of Judah which supply a
thousand men.' באלפי יהודה is translated as ἐν χιλιάσιν Ἰούδα by Sept.,
'among the thousands of Judah (also Vulg.). ממך is represented by ἐξ οὗ
'from where' and לי by μοι. Fitzmeyer has emended לי יצא to ליצא (ל
an emphatic particle).

The grammatical subject of יתנם (v. 2; Sept. v. 3) is not explicit and
MT is repeated in Sept. (δώσει αὐτούς) and Vulg. (*dabit eos*), while
Pesh. (*nšlm*) and Targ. (יתמסרון) bring out the sense 'give them up' and
'be given up' more clearly. Sept. (ἕως καιροῦ), Vulg. (*usque ad tempus*)
and Pesh. (*lzbn'*) are all straightforward renderings of עד עת and do not
relieve the ambiguity of MT which can be translated either 'Until a
woman who is pregnant gives birth' or 'Until a woman who is now

pregnant gives birth'. The second translation indicates that the period of affliction will be short, while the first does not give any indication.

Rashi and Kimchi are aware of a Rabbinic tradition that the anguish will last nine months. Another exegesis which they prefer is that the sufferings of Zion are likened to the birth–pangs of a woman (so Lescow, 1967, 198–205). Sept. represents אחיו 'his brothers' as τῶν ἀδελφῶν 'their brothers' (also Targ.) and על is taken as an equivalent of אל (ἐπί; also Vulg. (*ad*) and Pesh. (*lwt*). All the versions render יתר as remnant. Vulg. (*convertentur*), Pesh. (*ntpnwn*) and Targ. (יסתמכון) render ישובן as a passive tense and Vulg. and Pesh. indicate 'are repentant towards' or 'are turned towards' rather than 'return from exile to'. Sept. ἐπιστρέψουσιν is active, 'will turn towards', while Targ. has the meaning 'be supported by'.

Sept. (v. 4; MT v. 3) has a plus (καὶ ὄψεται) which Smith (102) describes as a doublet, a doublet of στήσεται, according to Rudolph (91) and caused by the misreading of רעה as ראה according to Wolff (103). Sept. has spelled out ורעה as καὶ ποιμανεῖ τὸ ποίμνιον αὐτοῦ, 'and he will feed his flock'. Targ. interprets ורעה as וישלוט 'and he will rule'. After θεοῦ αὐτῶν 'their God' (MT אלהיו 'his God') Sept. replaces וישבו with ὑπάρξουσιν 'they will live' and this has the effect of altering the syntax of MT, since ὑπάρξουσιν connects with what has preceded it, 'and in the majesty of the name of the Lord, their God, they will live'. Sept. has followed the vocalization of MT (וְיָשְׁבוּ), but Vulg. and Pesh. have offered the same rendering of וישבו as they did for ישובן in the previous verse and have pointed it as וְיָשֻׁבוּ. Targ. has done likewise with the paraphrase, 'and there will be a gathering from those among their exile'.

Wellhausen (143), Weiser (271) and Rudolph (91) do not discern any difficulty in taking וישבו as וישבו בטח 'and they will dwell in security', while Ehrlich (5, 283) and Smith (102) assert that a bare וישבו cannot have this sense and Hillers (65) has expressed doubt. Ehrlich describes וישבו as a variant of ישובן (cf. Vulg., Pesh. and Targ.) and Smith as a gloss or doublet of the same word. Duhm (89) had also connected it with ישובן as a stitch between v. 2b and v. 3b. Wolff (119) also holds that וישבו is secondary, an insertion from 4.4a (וישבו) intended as a comment on the peace which the Messiah would bring. Unlike Duhm, Ehrlich and Smith he does not relate it to ישובן (v. 2) and translates it 'and they will dwell in security'.

והיה זה שלום (MT v. 4; Sept. v. 5) is either 'And this state of affairs will be peace' or 'And this man (the Messiah) will be peace.' The versions do not enable us to discriminate between these two choices: Sept. (καὶ ἔσται αὕτη εἰρήνη); Vulg. (*Et erit iste pax*); Pesh. (*wnhw šlmʾ*); Targ. (ויהי מבכין שלמא). Sept., Vulg. and Targ. render זה differently, 'This itself will be peace' (Sept.), 'this man' (Vulg.) and 'from then on' (Targ.). זה is a minus in Pesh. Sept. renders בארמנתינו 'in our palaces' as ἐπὶ τὴν χώραν ὑμῶν 'on your territory' and Vulg., Pesh. and Targ. represent MT. בארמנתינו has been emended to באדמתנו after Sept. (Ehrlich, 5, 284; Robinson, 142; Rudolph, 91; Hillers, 68). Sept. has converted והקמנו 'and we shall raise' to καὶ ἐπεγερθήσονται 'and they will be raised', Pesh. to *nqym*, and Targ. to וימני לנא 'and he will appoint for us'. The variations do not rest on text-critical foundations. They are concerned to save the integrity of vv. 1–5 as a unit by establishing that the continued activity of the Messiah is described. Sept. does this by means of a passive verb, 'and seven or eight shepherds, leaders of men, will be raised against it' (Assyria), while Pesh. and Targ. substitute a third person active verb which resumes ורעה ועמד (v. 2b) and is further resumed by והציל at v. 5b. Vulg. (*suscitabimus*) retains MT.

Sept., however, goes further than this by replacing the first person plural suffixes by second person plurals in vv. 4b and 5b. (Sept. vv. 5b. and 6b), whereas Pesh. and Targ. follow MT in respect of these suffixes. The consideration which moved Sept. was that vv. 1–5 were oracular, that Yahweh was the speaker and that the suffixes desiderated at vv. 4b and 5b were second person and not first person. Hence Ziegler (218) is mistaken in supposing that this is a text-critical matter and in representing that a Greek text which agrees with MT and has no support from Greek manuscripts is a critical text.

Vulg. translates נסיכי אדם (v. 4) as *primates homines* 'leaders of men' and Pesh. (*rwrbnʾ dʾnšʾ*) and Targ. (רברבי אנשא) as 'notables'. Sept. δήγματα ἀνθρώπων 'stings of men' is a misreading of נסיכי אדם as נשיכי אדם (Rudolph, 91; Wolff, 104; Hillers, 68). Targ. (וידינון) 'and they will rule' interprets ורעו (v. 5) as it did at v. 3. ארץ¹ is a minus in Sept. whose text is adopted by Weiser (272) and Robinson (142). בפתחיה is explained by *BDB* (836) as entrances to a country, but a parallel to בחרב is desiderated. Sept. (ἐν τῇ τάφρῳ αὐτῆς 'in its pit' is perhaps (Rudolph, 91) a translation of בפחתה which may betray the

influence of the reference to Nimrod as a mighty hunter (Gen. 10.8f.):
he will be caught in the trap which he has laid for his prey (cf. Rudolph,
'in his (own) pit'. Pesh. (*brwgzh*) 'in his anger' and Targ.
(בתקוף כרכהא) 'in its strongholds' have no contribution to make, but
Vulg. *in lanceis eius* 'with its spears' may reflect a vocalization of בפתחיה
as בְּפִתְחֶיהָ (Ps. 55.22). NEB 'with bare blades' and REB 'with drawn
blades' indicate בפתחות (not בפתחיה, Brockington, 256). בְּפִתְחָה is
preferred by Weiser, 272; Robinson, 142; Wolff, 104; Hillers, 68f.).
Ehrlich (5, 284) בפתחיה 'with their (own) swords' sticks closer to MT:
their shame is increased by the circumstance that they fall on their own
weapons. Pesh. (*wnpṣn*) and Targ. (וישיזבינא) attach the suffix ('us') to
והציל (Wellhausen, 143; Weiser, 272).

Rashi associates בית לחם and ממך (v. 1) with the circumstance that
the Messiah promised will be a 'son of David' and on יתנם he
comments, 'he (Yahweh) will give them to their enemies, until the time
comes that Zion is in labour and bears her child.' Thus, as noticed
above (p. 2) Rashi and Kimchi suppose that יולדה ילדה (v. 2) is a
metaphor for the travail of Zion which does not refer directly to the
birth-pangs of a woman and does not give an indication of the duration
of the period when Zion will be given up to her enemies. Its function is
rather to establish that there will be an intensification of the time of
anguish before it gives place to the coming of the Messiah. The suffix of
אחיו refers to the king of Judah, the remnant of whose people will be
joined (יתחברו; cf. Targ. and Ibn Ezra) to the other tribes (those of the
former Northern Kingdom?). They will become one kingdom again
and will no longer be divided. ורעה (v. 3) is glossed by ופרנס 'feed',
'sustain' and וישבו read as וְיָשְׁבוּ, 'and they will return' (so Vulg., Pesh.
and Targ.) receives the comment 'from the exile'. Rashi's comment on
והיהזה שלום (v. 4a) is 'A final and constant peace, never to be
interrupted again, unlike those periods of peace which were followed by
affliction.' This is compatible with either 'He (the Messiah) will be
peace' or 'This state of affairs will be peace. אשור כי יבוא בארצנו
(v. 4b) is explained as 'If Assyria invades our land as it does now' and
ורעו (v. 5) is derived from רעע = רצץ 'shatter'. He cites Ps. 2.8:
תרעם בשבט ברזל, 'You will shatter them with a rod of iron'. A sword,
however, cuts rather than shatters and the association of ורעו in this
sense with בחרב is infelicitous. בפתחיה is taken by Rashi as 'at the gates
of its (Nimrod's) cities'.

Kimchi adopts the same derivation of ורעו (also KB³, 1185, ורעעו telescoped to ורעו), while Ibn Ezra elucidates it as a משל *ex* רעה: the metaphorical sense is 'to shepherd' and the developed sense 'to rule' (so Hillers, 68). The question then is whether the metaphor should be preserved (Sept.; Vulg.; Pesh.; Weiser, 272; Robinson, 142; Rudolph, 88; Wolff, 101) or explained (Targ.; Hillers) in translation. Kimchi remarks that the function of אפרתה (v. 1) is to establish that the reference is to the Judaean Bethlehem, since there was another Bethlehem in Galilee. The one who will emerge (יצא) is the Messiah. להיות¹ = להיותך, 'though you are accounted small among the tribes of Judah'. He comments further, 'For the Messiah will be of the seed of David who was from Bethlehem.' On ומוצאתיו he remarks that there is a great historical distance between the Messiah and the first David described by the phrase מקדם מימי עולם. לכן יתנם (v. 2) receives the comment, 'God will give up Israel to affliction' and, like Rashi, he takes יולדה ילדה as a metaphor of the time of affliction: 'He will bring them to a time when a pregnant mother bears a child. That is to say, pangs will seize them like the birth-pangs of a woman.' Hence it is the intensity of Israel's affliction which is indicated by יולדה ילדה.

Kimchi differs from Rashi in taking the suffix of אחיו (v. 2) to refer to the Messiah (also Ehrlich, 5, 283), but agrees with him in identifying יתר with Judah and Benjamin. So the southern tribes are represented as returning to the northern tribes, but על (so Kimchi) is an equivalent of עם not of אל. Ehrlich (283) holds that the יתר אחיו refers either to the close relatives of the Messiah or to members of the tribe of Judah who returned to Jerusalem with Ezra. After the time of distress passes (Kimchi, v. 3) the Messiah will come (ועמד ורעה). יגדל denotes the extent of the Messiah's sway and its subject is not Yahweh. Unlike Vulg., Pesh., Targ. and Rashi. Kimchi derives וישבו from ישב not שוב: they will dwell in security and peace forever (also Ibn Ezra).

Kimchi has two interpretations of והיה זה שלום (v. 4a). The first goes with the translation 'and this state of affairs will be the peace', the other with 'and he (the Messiah) will be the peace'. The רעים and נסכי אדם are the same persons, officers of the Messianic king. 'Seven or eight' is an idiom for a large number and Kimchi cites Eccles. 11.2 (REB, 'Divide your merchandise among seven or eight ventures'). Kimchi glosses בפתחיה with בחרבותיה 'with its swords' and so he vocalizes it as בפתחיה with a reference to Ps. 55.22 (also Ibn Ezra).

According to Ibn Ezra אפרתה (v. 1) is an alternative name for
Bethlehem and the sense of v. 1 is that a Messiah descended from David
will come to Israel. ישובן (v. 2) is glossed as יתחברו (so Rashi) and the
suffix of אחיו is referred to the Messiah (so Kimchi), 'until the Messiah
and his relatives are joined to the people of Israel'. It is the reunion of
the tribes of Israel into a single kingdom rather than the return of a
remnant from exile which is the centre of Ibn Ezra's interest. His
comment on v. 3 is, 'He (the Messiah) will be the shepherd of Israel in
the power of God and they will dwell in security' (וישבו ex ישב). Ibn
Ezra, like Kimchi, relates והיה זה שלום to the removal of the Assyrian
threat: 'If the Assyrians come to our land, many generals of the ruler
(the Messiah) will arise.' שבעה ושמנה means seven or eight, רעים and
נסיכי אדם are the same persons and the total is not fifteen (so Ehrlich, 5,
284).

Wellhausen (25) translates אלפי (v. 1) as 'regions' (*Gauen*) and (142)
raises the question whether קדם מימי עולם can refer to the historical
David, whether Micah could have regarded him as a man of primaeval
times. He compares Mic. 5.1 with Isa. 11.1: the new David, according
to the Isaiah passage, will spring from a stump in Jerusalem, while,
according to Micah, he will come from a hidden root in Bethlehem.
עד עת יולדה ילדה (v. 2), 'until a certain pregnant woman gives birth' is
less than an indication how long the period of affliction will last. It
means no more than 'until the Messiah is born of a woman', without
specifying when the event will take place. Wellhausen discerns here (p.
143) an allusion to Isa. 7.14 and remarks that such dark hints with
literary connections are not in the vein of the older prophets. He also
detects in ישובן (v. 2) a development of the שאר ישוב of Isa. 7.3 and
supposes that יתנם (where Yahweh is the subject) and אחיו (where the
suffix refers to the Messiah) are further examples of dark allusions which
are associated with later prophecy. He remarks: 'Older prophecy was
not in love with a combination of darkness and light and did not create
the impression of knowing more about the future than it actually did'
(p. 143). Hence he is not disposed to assign 5.1–5 to Micah and he
remarks that the designation of Assyria as the hostile power is not
necessarily evidence of the Assyrian period.

At v. 3 Wellhausen (143) derives וישבו from ישב (so Kimchi and Ibn
Ezra) and fills out its sense with וישבו בטח, 'and they will live in
security'. והיה זה שלום (v. 4a) is rendered as 'and this state affairs will be

the peace' (25) and בגבולינו 'on our boundaries' (v. 4) is preferred to
בארמנתינו (143). A more important emendation is that of והקמנו to
והקים with Pesh. Wellhausen does not enlarge on this, but it is clear
that he has made the emendation in order to resume the third person
singulars of v. 3 (עמד ורעה) and to represent the Messiah as the
grammatical object at v. 4. He is followed by Weiser (272 n. 1).
Wellhausen's proposal that והציל (v. 5b) should be emended to
והצילנו is unhappy, because if the passage is an oracle and Yahweh
is the speaker, 'and he will deliver us' is inappropriate. He queries
whether בפתחיה may be a corruption and conjectures בפתחי חרב
'with the blades of the sword.' This produces synonymous parallelism
(143).

Duhm (89) holds that the original author of 5.1–5 is responsible for
vv. 1, 3a, 4a and 5b. The insertion (vv. 2, 3b) is an arcane apocalyptic
exegesis of Isa. 7.14 and v. 2b is an allusion to שאר ישוב (Isa. 7.3). Verse
3b grounds the return of the diaspora in the extension of Messianic
authority throughout the world. This statement implies that Duhm is
vocalizing וישבו as וְיָשְׁבוּ. According to the original text the Messiah's
rule is limited to Israel and a particular association with the removal of
the threat presented by Assyria is the consequence of the elaboration
present in v. 4b and v. 5a which are stitched to v. 5b (מאשור) by means
of אשור at vv. 4b and 5a. This addition furnishes a new exegesis of
והיה זה שלום (v. 4a), since it is now connected with the deliverance from
Assyria, 'And this is what the peace will consist of'. Originally
והיה זה שלום had been associated with vv. 1, 3a, 'and he (the Messiah)
will be the peace' and this is continued by v. 5b (והציל). The new
exegesis of v. 4a ('And this state of affairs will be the peace') substitutes a
policy of self-help for the work of the Messiah. When the Syrians
(אשור; the Seleucids) attack the citadels of Judas, these Maccabaean
heroes will respond by ruling Syria with the sword and by subduing
other Seleucid territories with the drawn blade (בפתחיה vocalized as
בפתחיה). The structure which Duhm has outlined for 5.1–5, though
not his critical position, has been influential (Rudolph, Wolff) as we
shall see.

Ehrlich (5, 283) holds that the setting of 5.1–5 is post-exilic and that
the Messianic 'Son of David' is Zerubbabel. Verse 2b is not a reference
to the reunion of the divided kingdoms of north and south, but to the
return of Judaeans with Ezra to Jerusalem. The most important textual

comment which Ehrlich made was developed by Smith (107) in the same year (1912) and we shall look at this presently. Ehrlich's conjecture is that שלום אשור is a construct relationship and that this disposes of the inexplicable word-order of v. 4b. The other consequence is that והיה זה שלום אשור is linked to what follows and not to what precedes. Ehrlich's translation is, 'And such is the peace which Assyria will give us.'

A more systematic account of the different approaches to the structure of 5.1–5 may now be set out and investigated in turn: (a) 5.1–5 is a unit whose integrity can be demonstrated (Weiser and van der Woude) (b) 5.1–5 consists of a core (vv. 1–3, 4a, 5b) and a secondary elaboration (vv. 4b, 5a). This is the view of Rudolph. (c) 5.1–5 consist of a core (vv. 1, 3*, 4a, 5b) and a secondary elaboration (vv. 4b, 5a—so Duhm and Wolff). (d) There are two units, vv. 1–3 and vv. 4–5 (Ehrlich, Smith and Robinson). Ehrlich and Smith adopt the vocalization שְׁלֹם אשור, whereas Robinson retains MT (שָׁלֹם אשור) (e) There are two units, vv. 1–4a and 4b–5 (Hillers). The implication of this is that the word–string is והיה זה שלום and not והיה זה שלום אשור and that והיה זה שלום goes with what precedes. A consequence of the division of vv. 1–5 into two units is that והציל (v. 5b) has to be emended to either והצילו or והצילנו (cf. Pesh. and Targ.).

Weiser (271) renders וישבו (v. 3) with the vocalization of MT as 'and they shall dwell in peace'. The translation of והיה זה שלום which he favours is 'and he (the Messiah) will be the Lord of peace'. He emends והקמנו (v. 4) to והקים with Pesh. and Wellhausen and vocalizes בפתחיה as בפתחוה. He follows Pesh. and Targ. in supplying a suffix for והציל (v. 5b), והצילנו, 'and he (the Messiah) will deliver us' (272).

Weiser (272), like Wellhausen, comments on the mysterious tone of 5.1–2. It supplies a dark hint concerning the Messiah of the end time, but it does not throw a full light on the event. מקדם מימי עולם is not simply a reference to the historical David (cf. Wellhausen, 142); it is a combination of the *Urmensch* with the Messiah, the construction of a bridge between the *Urzeit* and the *Endzeit*, between creation and eschatology. Yahweh (273) will give up Israel to her enemies, until the time when a woman gives birth to the Messiah and then the remnant of his brothers will return to the Israelite community. This, according to Weiser, is an eschatological prediction made by Micah in the eighth century B.C. When the Messiah comes at the end of time, this event will be accompanied by a regathering of the dispersed of Israel.

Micah, in Weiser's view, has not created the elements of this Messianic hope. He has taken over from 'tradition' the thought of the birth of a child and the return of a remnant whose model is perhaps found in Isa. 7.14 and 7.3. 'And he (the Messiah) will be the peace' is to be compared with שׂר שׁלום 'prince of peace' (Isa. 9.5). Weiser supposes that 5.1–5 is all of a piece, that v. 4b and v. 5a are integral to it and that the Messianic hope, though eschatological, is not distant and arises out of the urgency of the Assyrian threat to the integrity of Judah in the eighth century B.C. Hence the prominence which is given (vv. 4b, v. 5) to the Messiah's part in the removal of that threat. The 'seven or eight' (v. 5) derive from a mythological tradition and thse heroes have been transformed into helpers of the Messiah. The precise historical setting is Sennacherib's siege of Jerusalem and, in this attitude to the aggression of the Assyrians, Micah stood on the shoulders of Isaiah (9.1f.), though the security which he predicted (v. 2) was not identical.

Without becoming too involved with higher criticism at this juncture it may be remarked that this picture of an eschatological prophet in the eighth century B.C. raises eyebrows, but there is a more elementary objection which can be raised against the Weiser's presentation of 5.1–5 as an integral unit. Already the translator of the Septuagint was aware (above, p. 150) that it was not enough to change והקמנו (v. 4b) into a third person singular in order to achieve this, as both Pesh. and Targ. supposed. This produces a consistency in so far as it makes the Messiah the subject of גדל (v. 3) עמד ורעה, and והציל (v. 5b). If, however, 5.1–5 is oracular, if Yahweh is the speaker throughout, the first person plural suffixes in v. 4b and v. 5b (emended) cannot be tolerated. This was why the Greek translator changed them to second person suffixes. Yahweh cannot be thought to have said 'our land', 'our palaces' and 'our borders'. Weiser has proposed an emendation at v. 5b (והצילנו), 'and he will deliver us' which increases the confusion. The only way in which Weiser can escape from this criticism of the appearance of the suffix 'us' is for him to hold that 5.1– 5 is not an oracle, that Yahweh is not represented as the speaker, and that in these verses the prophet Micah speaks in his own person and identifies himself with the people. This assumption requires the deletion of לי

(v. 1), if לי refers to Yahweh, and the transition from עתה (v. 1) to יתנם (v. 2) remains perplexing.

Van der Woude (1969, 255) also sets 5.1–5 in the time of Micah and what has been said about the improbability of assigning an eschatological Messianic prophecy to an eighth century prophet also applies to his account. According to him 5.1–5 has the form of a dialogue and the participants are the prophet Micah, speaking with Yahweh's authority, and the false prophets. Micah's contribution is vv. 1–4a and והיה זה שלום means 'and he (the Messiah) will be a man of peace'. This is the conclusion and the climax of Micah's proclamation. The riposte of the false prophets is in vv. 4b–5 and והציל (v. 5b) is to be emended to והצילונו. The *Heil* prophets are recommending a policy of *Realpolitik* and the seven or eight shepherds and leaders of men are members of a coalition of nations which they propose to set up (והקמנו, v. 4b). 'They will save us from the Assyrians' the *Heil* prophets declare (v. 5b). It may be remarked that these are not normally the parameters of the conflict between doom and *Heil* prophets. The answer to threats of doom is usually that Yahweh will take care of his community. It is a false trust in Yahweh which the *Heil* prophets proclaim. The conflict between the diplomacy which seeks security in coalitions rather than in a reposing of trust in Yahweh is more characteristically between doom prophets and statesmen (McKane, 1965, 65–93).

Rudolph holds that 5.1–3, 4a, 5b constitute a unit and that vv. 4b and 5a are secondary expansion. He (89f.) notices Wellhausen's proposal (82) that οἶκος Ἐφραθα offers a clue to the original Hebrew text (בית אפרת הצעיר) and that בית לחם is a correct gloss. Rudolph objects to the supposition that בית לחם would be added to an original בית אפרתה and he holds that οἶκος is an addition whose function was to indicate that בית אפרתה (v. 1) is not the region but the members of the clan resident in the region (cf. Wolff, 101, בית is a dittography). להיות[1] is to be deleted (so Rudolph) and לי emended to ילד (Sellin). אחיו (v. 2) refers to the Messiah and light is thrown on its use by אחי (2 Sam 19.13), which is supplemented by עצמי ובשרי 'my bone and my flesh' (91), where David is speaking of his own family. David was chosen before his brothers as king of Israel and so אחיו refers to the promised Messiah who is also the 'preferred one' (יתר) among his brothers (cf. Gen. 49.3; Jer. 29.1) and is David *redivivus* (also, 96). This exegesis requires the emendation of ישובון to ישוב and the לכן at the beginning of v. 2 is justified by the logic that the time of affliction will be limited by the appearance of the Messiah (v. 1). With this exegesis of v. 2 (על = אל) an allusion to the reunion of north and south does not disappear, because בני ישראל is a reference to the restored united kingdom. MT ישובון is explained as a consequence of the mistaken lexicography applied to יתר ('remnant').

Sept. ὄψεται (v. 3), which appears to be a plus, is elucidated on the assumption that ועמד embraces the sense of 'standing on watch' and so ὄψεται is a suppplementation of עמד supplied by the Greek translator. והיה זה שלום (v. 4a) is translated (88) *Und er wird der Heilbringer sein* and this is followed by v. 5b which completes the original unit. Rudolph emends בפתחוה (v. 5a) to בִּפְתָחֶהָ 'with the drawn blade' and so restores the parallelism (בחרב). He suggests that Sept. ἐν τῇ τάφρῳ αὐτῆς 'in its pit' is an allusion to Nimrod the hunter (Gen. 10.9) who will fall into the pit which he has dug to trap animals.

Micah (Rudolph, 95f.) deliberately underlines that the first David had belonged to Bethlehem, had been a member of the tribe of Ephrathah and a youngest son. The promised Messiah is, in all these respects, David *redivivus*. Rudolph holds that the intention of ומוצאתיך מקדם מימי עולם (v. 1) was not simply to represent that the Messiah would continue the line of the Davidic dynasty. This would would have been a a truism, since that dynasty had long been established in Judah and it was taken for granted that the promised Messiah would be a Davidic king. Rudolph is influenced here by his assumption that 5.1–3, 4a, 5b is the work of Micah, that its historical setting is the siege of Sennacherib and that there was still a Davidic king on the throne of Judah when it was spoken. If the passage is post-exilic, and the Davidic dynasty lay in the distant past, the promise of a new Davidic king takes on a different significance.

Rudolph (96) does not find any difficulty in attaching the language used (מקדם מימי עולם) to the age of the historical David (Amos 9.11, כימי עולם), but he notices that it has been used to support the view that a supernatural, pre-existent Messiah is promised, in which case מקדם means 'from primaeval times' and ימי עולם 'the days of eternity'. Rudolph (97) does not suppose that a short, specific period of affliction is indicated by עד עת יולדה ילדה, the time between pregnancy and birth, though NEB ('only as long as a woman is in labour') and REB ('only until she who is pregnant has given birth') yield this sense.

עד עת יולדה ילדה (Rudolph) means no more than a woman will become pregnant and bear a child in the unspecified future and that this child will be the Messiah. Rudolph's paraphrase is, 'until a mother bears her child in her clan at Bethlehem'.

According to Rudolph (97) there is no literary connection between Mic. 5.1 and Isa. 7.14 which does not supply any information about the identity of the mother. Another exegesis with which he contends is that of Lescow (1967, 199f.) who argues that יולדה ילדה is metaphorical language and that it refers to the period of anguish which will precede the coming of the Messiah, not to the birth of a child. The Messiah's rule (Rudolph, 98), which will be universal, will display the care of a shepherd for his flock (v. 3) and will be a guarantee of security for Israel (וישבו), so that his title will be זה שלום 'the man of peace'. When the Assyrians attack Jerusalem (v. 5b) and encroach on its boundaries, he will deliver his people. Hence the Messiah of Micah is a political and military figure and his first task is to remove the Assyrian threat.

Verses 4b and 5a are a *vaticinium ex eventu* in which the heroes who act are human beings and the policy of self-help which is promulgated is antithetic to Messianic hope.. The situation in which they act is envisaged as an Assyrian invasion and so past history is recreated. Those who speak in tones of triumphalism are Judaeans and what the Messiah (vv. 1–4a, 5b) first achieved they would repeat. These heroes, who are the Maccabaeans (so Duhm) and who celebrate their victories against the Seleucids (אשור = Syria), do not need supernatural help. What then supplied the motive for combining vv. 4b and 5a with vv. 1–4a, 5b? and for supposing that a coherent unit could be made out of these elements? Rudolph's answer is that the 'we' of והקמנו (v. 4b) was taken as the 'we' of majesty (Gen. 1.26; 3.22) and was referred to God, so that the action of God in raising up 'seven or eight' heroes alternates with that of the Messiah in vv. 3, 4a and 5b. But רעים (v. 3) is re-used or abused at v. 4b (רעים) and v. 5a (ורעו) and it is evident that whoever composed vv. 4b and v. 5a had v. 3 as a source.

According to Wolff (101) the primary unit in 5.1–5 consists of vv. 1, 3, 4a, 5b and vv. 2, 4b, 5a are secondary elaborations (also Duhm, see above). להיות[1] (v. 1) and לי are retained (103). If לי is kept, it is established the Yahweh is the speaker. אשר (v. 2) is implicit after עת and יתר ('remnant') is a collective which requires a plural (ישובון). Sept. καὶ ὄψεται (v. 3) is a doublet of ורעה misread as וראה and ὑπάρξουσιν (without καί, cf. MT) combines with what precedes in v. 3a, 'and in the majesty of the name of the Lord, their God (MT, אלהיו) they will exist'. Hence Sept. destroys the parallelism of v. 3aα and v. 3aβ. Barthélemy (1960, 172) opts for וְיָשְׁבוּ (with Vulg., Pesh., Targ. and Rashi), but Wolff prefers MT, 'and they will dwell securely', though he indicates in his translation of v. 3 (101) that it is an addition to the text (also 106). והיה זה שלום (v. 4a) is rendered 'And he (the Messiah) will establish peace' and בפתחיה (v. 5a) is emended to בפתחה 'with the drawn blade'.

Wolff (106; cf. Smith, 102, 104) remarks on the oddness of v. 2: the suffix of יתנם cannot be the מושל of v. 1 and the suffix 'them' has no antecedent. He concludes that v. 2 interrupts the continuity of v. 1 with v. 3. וישבו (v. 3) belongs to the same redaction as v. 2 (106f.) and is an allusion to the conditions of life of the 'brothers' of the Messiah when they return from exile. Verse 3, minus וישבו connects with והיה זה שלום (v. 4a). Verses 4b, 5a are a larger addition and they create a tension between divine and human action so insupportable that their author cannot be the same person as the one responsible for vv. 1, 3* and 4a. Verse 5b received a secondary exegesis in vv. 4b, 5a, involving a re-use of vocabulary which appears in v. 3 (ורעה).

The historical setting of 5.1, 3, 4a, 5b is post-587 B.C. and these verses, containing the promise of a Messiah, issue from a prophet of consolation belonging to the school of Jeremiah (110). Verse 1 (115) is an address by Yahweh (לי) to Judah and all-Israel (מושל בישראל). Jesse (116), the father of David, came from Ephratha (1 Sam. 16.18; 17.58) which denotes the name of the clan and its location. The end of the Davidic dynasty is presupposed (Mic. 4.14) and the metaphor of Isa. 11.1 is taken up and developed: the tree has fallen (the dynasty), but from the root (Jesse) a new growth sprouts. There is an allusion to Isa 7.14 in v. 2 and עד עת יולדה ילדה is an indication that the time of affliction will be short. Wolff is not entirely clear about this, but *Solange die Gebärende in Wehen liegt und schreit* (118) can have no other meaning than 'until the time that a woman who is *now* pregnant bears her child', since only then does the Hebrew indicate that the period of affliction will be short and prescribes a time-limit for it. זה (v. 4a) is the Messiah and his most urgent task as the bringer of peace is set out in v. 5b, so that זה is related to v. 5b rather than vv. 1, 3: he will deliver his people from the Assyrian threat (119f.). Since his historical setting for

the oracle is later than the Assyrian period, Wolff remarks that foreign
invaders were not unusually called 'Assyrian' in the Babylonian and
Persian periods (119) and he connects the oracle with the affliction
caused by Babylonian incursions after the fall of Jerusalem in 587 B.C.

Verses 4b, 5a (120) were originally a marginal comment which took
אשור (v. 5b) to mean 'the land of Assyria' and so conjoined it in
synonymous parallelism with 'the land of Nimrod' (v. 5a). The new
elements in vv. 4b, 5a are: (a) The emphasis on self-help (b) The
plurality of shepherds over against the one shepherd of v. 3 (c) The
description of these shepherds as 'leaders of men' (d) The characterizing
of their shepherding as warfare against enemies. Wolff (120) conjectures
that the intention of vv. 4b, 5a may have been to give more information
about the interim period (v. 2) before the birth of the Messiah and that
its model may have been Mic. 4.13, the empowerment of the daughter
of Zion to 'thresh' many nations (עמים רבים). Wolff observes (120) that
no firm date can be assigned to vv. 4b, 5a, but the conclusion which he
produces to account for their presence is a lame one. The 'interim
period' which v. 2 allows is, according to his interpretation of
עד עת יולדה ילדה, a short one and, in any case, it is taken up entirely by
the affliction meted out by enemies.

Robinson and Hillers divide 5.1–5 into two units, Robinson vv. 1–3
and 4–5 and Hillers 1–4a and 4b–5. To facilitate this division והציל is
emended to והצילונו (v. 5b) by Robinson (142). Hillers translates 'they
will deliver us' (68), but he does not register his emendation (69)
precisely. The principal difference between them is in their translation
of והיה זה שלום (v. 4a). Hillers attaches it to vv. 1–3 and renders 'And
he will be the One of Peace' (64), while Robinson connects it with vv.
4b–5 and renders 'And this will be the peace' (142).

Robinson deletes לי (v. 1) and emends ליהות to לא היית (v. 1); he
emends אל = על (v. 2) and בערמנתינו (v. 4b) is emended to באדמתנו
with Sept. (also Smith, 109; Hillers, 68) The progression seven-eight is
illustrated by the numerical sayings (Prov. 30.15f.): 'seven and eight'/
'seven or eight' signifies an indefinite number (also Hillers, 68) of
'shepherds' and 'leaders of men' (who are the same persons). At v. 5a
בפתחיה should be emended to בפתחה 'with the blade' (also Hillers,
68).

Verses 1–3 (Robinson, 143) are post-exilic and presuppose that there
has been a return from exile but not a complete return (v. 2). A king of

the house of David will appear who will establish the security of Israel
and rule in the strength and majesty of Yahweh to the ends of the earth.
The passage is dependent on Isa. 7.14 and 11.1–10 (vv. 1–2) which are
exilic or later. Isa. 7.14, in particular, became a characteristic expression
of the Messianic hope which embraced the Northern Kingdom as well
as Judah and the poet looked forward to their reunion (v. 2).

Hillers (65) describes 5.1–4a as an eighth-century oracle which has
been reworked in the exilic period (v. 2). Either the author is describing
the emergence of a new Davidic king or his Messiah is David *redivivus*,
but, in any case, it is probable that his oracle is tantamount to the
rejection of the ruling Davidic king. Hillers comments on the ambiguity of the phrase עד עת יולדה ילדה: it means either 'until the time
that a woman who is *now* pregnant gives birth to a child' or 'until the
time when a particular, unspecified woman gives birth to a child'. Verse
2b predicts the union of the dispersed of Israel, both north and south.
יתר אחיו is obscure and Hillers (67) entertains the thought of Rudolph
that it may refer to the Messiah, 'he who is preferred before his
brothers'. Verse 4a goes with vv. 1–3 and should be rendered, 'And he
(the Messiah) will be the One of Peace.'

Those who speak in the first person plural (v. 4b) declare their
intention to take joint action (69) and unfold a programme of self-help
which is to be undertaken with the assistance of Aramaean states
(נסיכי ארם [emended] are 'Aramaean chiefs'). Hillers assumes that the
second unit (vv. 4b–5), like the first, comes from the period of Micah
and that he embraced the 'imperial dream', the heroic concept of
empire, along with his Messianic hope.

According to Smith (104) v. 2 is to be deleted as a marginal note
(104) which arose at a time when v. 1 was being given Messianic
significance. לכן is logically weak and the reasoning is that that since the
coming of the Messiah is predicted, the oppression will be transitory.
Moreover, the change from לי (v. 1) to the third person (יתנם) is
awkward, the lack of an explicit subject is notable and 'them' has no
antecedent. וישבו (v. 3) is deleted as a gloss or a doublet of ישובון (v. 2).
This assumes that v. 2 was part of the text when וישבו was added. יתר
(v. 2) may be an allusion to Isa. 7.3. The subject of the suffix of אחיו is
the Messiah, but the sense of 'the rest of his brothers' is obscure. Verse
2b refers either to the return of the exiles and their reunion with their
brothers already in Judah or to the regathering of Judah in the

Messianic age. יצא (v. 1) implies that the verse was written when there was no king in Judah and ומוצאתיו ... מימי עולם that the Messiah will be Davidic and that he belongs to one of the oldest families in the Bethlehem area. This makes the phrase easier than its identification as as a reference to the historical David.

I have left Smith to the last, because I am inclined to agree with his analysis of the two units in 5.1–5. His distinctive position is created by the circumstance that he does not include v. 4a and v. 5b in the first unit and so he expunges from it any reference to Assyria. This holds also for Robinson's analysis, but Smith goes beyond Robinson in his vocalizing of שלום אשור as שְׁלֹם אַשּׁוּר (also Ehrlich) and so disposes of the awkward word-order in v. 4b. The only emendation which is required in order to secure the integrity of his second unit (vv. 4–5) is the one which both Robinson and Hillers have made: והציל (v. 5b) to והצילו (NEB, REB; Brockington, 256; Robinson, והצילונו). והצילו then resumes ורעו (v. 5a). שְׁלֹם אַשּׁוּר connects v. 4a with vv. 4b and 5 and the translation of v. 4a which is desiderated is, 'And this will be our peace with Assyria' or 'And this will be our protection from Assyria.' The mention of Assyria does not show that Micah is the author (Smith, 107), since 'Assyria' was the symbol of the great world tyrant (108) and could have been used either of the Persians or the Seleucids. נמרוד is used in synonymous parallelism with אשור. Smith stops short of associating vv. 4–5 with the exploits of Maccabaean heroes—we do not know enough about the Maccabaean period to confirm this hypothesis.

The Messiah will reign to the ends of the earth 5.1–3

1. And you, Bethlehem Ephrathah, you who are small among the clans
       of Judah,
    from you will arise for me one who will be a ruler in Israel.
    His origins are from a primaeval time, from ancient days.
2. [Therefore Yahweh will give them up until the time comes
    when a woman is pregnant and bears a child;
    and the remnant of his brothers will return to[1] the sons of Israel.]
3. And he will rise up and shepherd them in Yahweh's strength,
    in the majesty of the name of Yahweh, his God.
    They will dwell securely, for now the Messiah's greatness
    will extend to the ends of the earth.

[1] אל = עלי.

Heroes will arise and defeat Assyria 5.4–5

4. This is the peace we shall have from Assyria:
When they come into our land and trample over our soil[1],
we shall raise against them
seven or eight shepherds, leaders among men.

5. They will rule the land of Assyria with the sword
and the land of Nimrod with the blade[2].
They will deliver[3] (us) from Assyria,
when it comes into our land,
when it tramples over our boundaries.

vv. 6–8 THE REMNANT OF JACOB AMONG THE NATIONS

Both Sept. ἐν τοῖς ἔθνεσιν) and Pesh. (*b'm'*) make v. 6 identical with v. 7, whereas Vulg. and Targ. reproduce MT at v. 6. It is unlikely that the text of Sept. and Pesh. at v. 6 has a text-critical basis and rests on a different Hebrew text from MT. In that case it is related to no more than the conviction that neatness is achieved by making v. 6 the same as v. 7, on the assumption that it is not obvious why the effect brought about by the reinforcement of v. 7 (בגוים) should not have been used in v. 6. The insertion of בגוים has been proposed by Wellhausen (25—in his translation), Smith (110), Robinson (144) and Hillers (70). Ehrlich (5, 285) deletes ברוב עמים רבים as superfluous and supposes that בגוים (v. 7) is an alternative of בקרב עמים רבים (v. 6). Duhm (89), Weiser (274) and Wolff (123f.) delete בגוים at v. 7 and so achieve identical opening lines at v. 6 and v. 7. Rudolph (100f.) retains MT as do the English versions (KJV, RV, RSV, NEB, REB). On balance the advantage lies with making v. 6aα and v. 7aα identical and metrical reasons have been given for this emendation.

Sept. πίπτουσα (v. 7; MT v. 6) is an expansion to help out with the sense of כטל מאת יהוה—it is Yahweh who causes the dew to fall. The difficulty presented by ὡς ἄρνες 'like lambs' for כרביבים 'like showers of rain' is more serious. Ziegler (219) notices a conjecture of Cappellus, ῥανίδες 'drops of rain' for which ἄρνες is thought to be a scribal error. His other proposal is too convoluted to gain assent: כרביבים is

[1]Reading באדמתנו.
[2]Reading בפתחה.
[3]Reading והצילו.

corrupted to כרבים by haplography of ב and further corrupted to ככרים 'like lambs'. On the one hand he posits an inner Greek scribal error and on the other a double corruption of the Hebrew text (cf. Rudolph, 101; Hillers, 70). Vulg. *stillae* 'showers of rain') and Pesh. (*rsys*) 'fine rain' translate MT correctly, while Targ. (כרסיסי מלקושא) 'like showers of fine rain' has a fuller translation. Sept. συναχθῇ 'is gathered' is a wrong derivation from II קוה (יִקְוֶה).

Smith's contention (112) that the antecedent of אשר is not the dew nor the rain but the grass (עשב) is mistaken and its point is difficult to grasp. It is the entire preceding simile which is interpreted by the relative clause in v. 6b and applied to the שארית: the dew and the showers of rain which cause the grass to grow are likened to the special provision which God and only God makes for the well-being of his people among the nations. The special providence which he exercises over them is not one which can be imitated by human devices or resources: it does not depend on the efforts of men nor does it await a human contribution.

I raise the question whether the attaching of different senses to אריה 'lion' and כפיר 'young lion' has the exegetical significance which is attached to it. The distinction is made by Sept. (λέων and σκύμνος), Vulg. (*leo* and *catulus leonis* 'a lion cub'), Pesh. (*'ry* and *gwry d'ry*). Targ. (אריא and ליתא) does not make this distinction, but most modern commentators show it in their translations (Weiser, 274; Robinson, 144; Rudolph, 101; Wolff, 123; Hillers, 70; also the English versions, KJV, RV, RSV, NEB, REB). Wellhausen (25, *Löwe* and *Leu*, like Targ., does not make the distinction of 'lion' and 'young lion' between אריה and כפיר and this may be connected with the circumstance that they treat them as cases of synonymous parallelism. On the other hand Kimchi (also Wolff, 129) makes an exegetical point out of the alternation of אריה and כפיר. The lion is the king of the forest and has more strength than all the other beasts, such as the leopard, the bear and the wolf. The כפיר by contrast does not have the strength to break the necks of the more powerful animals, but it can ravage flocks of sheep.

In Sept. and Pesh. the relative clause of v. 7b has puzzling features. Vulg. and Targ. reproduce MT, though Targ. substitutes the general ויקטול 'and kill' for וטרף 'and tear' (at the flesh). Sept. διέλθη 'penetrate' is perhaps the correct sense of עבר, that is penetrates into the forest or the sheepfold. ורמס 'and trample' (NEB and REB), which has been translated 'strike down' by some commentators (Wellhausen, 25; Weiser, 274; Rudolph, 101; Wolff, 123), is rendered by Sept. as an aorist participle and is joined to καὶ διαστείλας ἁρπάσῃ 'and having divided (it up) he tears at its flesh'. Pesh. appears to have been influenced by this rendering, but to have introduced confusion by swopping the word-order of עבר and רמס: dmʾ dprš wpsq tbr. wpsq 'cross over' is an equivalent of ועבר and prš has a similar sense to διαστείλας tbr represents 'break in pieces' rather than 'tear at its flesh' (טרף). Rashi associates רמס with the stamping of lions when they are hungry and their devouring of the prey on the spot. טרף he connects with the carrying away of what is left to their dens so as to feed the lion cubs and the lionesses.

MT has vocalized תרם (v. 8) as a jussive (תָּרֹם) and Sept. (ὑψωθήσεται) and Vulg. (exaltabitur) as an imperfect (תָּרֵם). Pesh. (ttrym) and Targ. (תתקף) are probably imperfects. It has been thought by some (Ehrlich, 5, 285) ; Smith, 112; Weiser, 275; Robinson, 244; Hillers, 71?) that v. 8 is secondary and is a comment on vv. 6–7 by a 'collector' (Robinson) or by a pious reader (Smith). The principal decision which has to be made is whether to retain תָּרֹם with MT (Ehrlich, 5, 285; Weiser, 274; Robinson, 144; Rudolph, 102; Wolff, 130) or to adopt תָּרֵם with Sept and Vulg. (Wellhausen, 143; Smith, 112; Hillers, 70).

With the jussive v. 8 has been described as 'the wish of a reader' (Ehrlich) or as a prayer to Yahweh (Weiser, 275; Rudolph, 102; Wolff, 130). If it is a wish, the second person singular suffixes refer to the שארית: 'May your hand be raised over your adversaries and all your enemies be cut off.' If it is a prayer, the second person suffixes refer to Yahweh: 'Let your hand be raised over your adversaries and let all your enemies be cut off.' The vocalization of תרם as תָּרֵם makes v. 8 into a confident affirmation and the reference of the suffixes is to the שארית: 'Your hand will be raised over your adversaries and all your enemies cut off.' If v. 8 is deemed to be a comment on v. 7, perhaps a secondary comment, there is a clear advantage in reading תָּרֵם. V. 8 is then a continuation and reinforcement of the note of dominance and triumphalism which is sounded in v. 7.

Rashi comments on אדם ... כטל (v. 6) 'which never comes by the agency of men and concerning which they (the שארית) do not seek the favour of men'. Kimchi, similarly, 'For the dew comes from heaven and the expectation is not that men will bring it but that God will bring it, for he is the one who ... bestows dew and rain on the earth. Israel, having this kind of security, has expectation only in God. He is the one who saves them and there is no saviour but him ... He brought down his salvation on them like dew on the ground and rain on the grass, that is, he gave them great prosperity.' On אדם ... כטל Ibn Ezra comments that the trust of the שארית was in God and not in the kings of the nations: 'The dew is not in the power of men, only in the power of God.' These three exegeses are broadly correct and have been followed, though other interpretations have been given and such an alternative has been offered by Ibn Ezra: 'Israel teaches the nations to call on the name of God, when they (the nations) were in their (Israel's) midst, as if to say, 'I am like the dew to Israel and no nation should trust in men'. The thought occurs here, and also in modern commentaries (Weiser, 275; Robinson, 144f.), that אדם ... כטל is not just concerned with the special providence which watches over the שארית but with a teaching or missionary activity of the שארית among the nations.

Kimchi and Ibn Ezra suppose that the שארית 'in the midst of great peoples' (v. 6) or 'among the nations' (v. 7) is not an indication of a location in the Gentile world, that is, of exile, but is rather a reference to the gathering of nations around Jerusalem. According to Kimchi the שארית is the residue of a process of refining and בקרב עמים רבים alludes to the siege of Jerusalem by Gog and Magog, when Israel will be among them like dew from Yahweh. That Ibn Ezra shares this exegesis of בקרב עמים רבים is shown by his comment, 'The kings of the nations who were in their (Israel's) land.' Hillers (70f.) revives this interpretation: he comments that בקרב עמים רבים and בגוים 'do not imply the scattering of Israel, but its gathering at a focal point, where it is surrounded by the nations'. The attitude of Kimchi to v. 7 is influenced by his assumption that the historical situation is the siege of Jerusalem by the nations. Israel was a small nation and the forces deployed against it were large. Yet Israel was like a lion among the beasts of the forest and this dominance is also thought of as the working of Yahweh's special providence (v. 6). In this way he demonstrates the unity of v. 6 and v. 7.

It is not obvious that v. 6 and v. 7 hang together and different accounts have been given of the nature of their coherence. It is tempting to conclude that v. 7 has been stitched to v. 6 by the device of an almost identical opening line. However that may be, it should be noted that the presence of יהוה (v. 6) seems to preclude the possibility that Yahweh is the speaker in vv. 6–7—that these verses are an oracle. In that case they are comfortable and reassuring words addressed to Israel in exile, a promise by an unknown person, perhaps setting himself up as a prophet. How v. 6 and v. 7 are related requires further consideration.

Smith (112) does not discern any distance between v. 6 and v. 7. Both contribute to the affirmation that the שארית will rise to power among the nations without human help. Weiser's account (275) of the coherence of these verses is essentially the same and Wolff's is not significantly different (130). According to Weiser v. 6 focuses on the apparent weakness of the small שארית in the environment of great nations, whereas v. 7 affirms that Yahweh's special care over it amounts not only to preservation (v. 6) but contributes to its dominance. Wolff (130), reacting to the antithesis which Rudolph (130) formulates, holds that the combination of a belief in a special providence (v. 6) and a programme of self-help whose objective is the domination of the nations (v. 7) are complementary attitudes: that the belief expressed in v. 6 does not imply that everything is to be left to Yahweh and that the שארית is to remain completely passive. They are not required to sit on their hands and exert no effort to exert power over the nations.

Rudolph's antithesis, however does not do justice to the opposition of v. 6 and v. 7. The verses are not a deliberate statement of two different responses which are made to the remnant's experience of being stranded on an island in a sea of nations, a quietist one and a militant one being set out as possible alternatives. Rather there is an unmistakeable incompatibility between the attitudes which are struck in v. 6 and v. 7. The emphasis in v. 6 is on Yahweh's mysterious preservation of a שארית which is surrounded by great nations and whose situation is manifestly weak and fragile. Verse 7, on the other hand, sound a warlike, imperialist, triumphalist note in connection with which one has the impression that there is a tilting at windmills. Thus Rudolph supposes that v. 8 is a reaction to v. 7 and that it arises out of a feeling that v. 7 has gone too far and that it brags too much. Verse 8 (so Rudolph) is a falling back on prayer for Yahweh's assistance. Wolff holds that the final prayer of v. 8 gives expression to a renewed realization that more than a conflict between Israel and the world (v. 7) is involved and that the deepest reason for the defeat of the nations is

that they are Yahweh's enemies. Verse 8 (reading (תָּרֹם) is rather a
secondary comment of a different kind by someone who is stirred by
the description of the rout of the nations in v. 7 and who eggs on the
שְׁאֵרִית: 'You hand will be raised over your adversaries and all your
enemies will be cut off.'

There is general agreement that 5.6–8 are post-exilic and Wellhausen
(143) comments: 'The desire of the Jews for world dominion and the
boasting in its portrayal are late.' Smith (110) locates these verses in the
middle or late Persian period (also Wolff, 127), adding that they are
certainly post-exilic (also Weiser, 274; Robinson, 144) and are later
than Deutero-Isaiah and the return of the Golah. Rudolph (100) is
satified that בקרב עמים רבים and בגוים settle the question, since they
can refer only to the situation of the diaspora in exile. Only Hillers
(70f.), who connects 5.6–8 with 4.1–3, is perhaps inclined to assign
5.6–8 to Micah. He does not do this explicitly, but he lays the
foundation for it by proposing that בקרב עמים רבים and בגוים reflect a
state of affairs where the nations surround Israel (in Jerusalem?) rather
than one where Israel in exile is surrounded by the nations.

6. The remnant of Jacob will be in the midst of many peoples,
   like dew from Yahweh, like showers of rain on the grass
   which do not depend on man
   nor rely on human effort.
7. The remnant of Jacob will be[1] in the midst of many peoples,
   like a lion among wild beasts,
   like a lion among flocks of sheep
   which attacks them, tramples them down, tears at them
   and no one can save them.
8. Your hand will be lifted up[2] over your foes
   and all your enemies will be cut off.

vv. 9–14 IDOLATRY WILL BE ROOTED OUT

At v. 11 (MT v. 10) Sept. (τὰς πόλεις τῆς γῆς σου), Vulg. (*civitates
terrae tuae*), Pesh. (*qwry' d'r'k*). render ערי ארצך 'cities of your land'
exactly. Targ. (קרוי עממיא מארעך) fills out the sense: it is cities within
Israel which are 'foreign' to it that are to be cut off. In view of the
synonyymous parallelism of MT at vv. 9, 11, 12 the match of ערי ארצך

[1]Deleting בגוים as a gloss on בקרב עמים רבים.
[2]Reading תָּרֹם.

with מבצריך 'your fortified cities' is puzzling, but Rashi regards them as synonymous and Kimchi and Ibn Ezra (also Targ.) elucidate ערי ארצך as cities surrounded by walls, 'walled cities'. עריך (v. 13) is a bigger problem. Here again Sept. (τὰς πόλεις σου), Vulg. (*civitates tuas*) translates it as 'your cities', as does Pesh, with a different word from v. 10 (*mdyntk*). Targ., on the other hand, has בעלי דבבך 'your enemies' and this has a lexicographical basis as Rashi, Kimchi and Ibn Ezra all notice, ערך 'your adversary' (NEB, REB) at 1 Sam. 28.16. ערך is an Aramaizing form of צרך. This does not clear up the problem, since the parallelism of 'your sacred poles' (אשיריך) and עריך 'your enemies' is defective, but more of this later.

At v. 12 (MT v. 11) Sept. gives τὰ φάρμακά σου 'your sorceries' ('magic potions'?) for כשפים and Vulg. *maleficia* 'evil deeds' is a general rendering. Pesh. (*ḥrš*) and Targ. (הרשין) 'sorceries' are more exact. For מעוננים 'soothsayers' Targ. reproduces MT (מעננין), Pesh. has *zkwrʾ* 'soothsayers', Vulg. *divinationes* 'diviners' and Sept. (ἀποφθεγγόμενοι), 'those who declare opinions plainly', perhaps 'wiseacres', or 'those who affect to make the unknown future as plain as a pikestaff', that is, 'soothsayers'. Ibn Ezra associates מעוננים with ענן 'cloud'. The מעוננים are those who inspect the clouds in order to foretell the future. Kimchi glosses מידך with מרשותך 'from your authority'. Presumably the parallelism is synonymous and מידך has approximately the same sense as לא יהיו לך. Kimchi's exegesis is influenced here, as we shall see, by the opinion (also that of Rashi and Ibn Ezra) that vv. 9–13 are a promise rather than a threat and describe a future when weapons of defence, fortifications, sorcery, soothsaying and idolatry will disappear.

Rashi on v. 9 explains that Egypt was the source of the horses and chariots which Israel had acquired for their defence. In the future they will have no need of armaments and fortified cities (v. 10). Kimchi comments that horses and chariots will be made redundant, for peace will be permanent after the war of Gog and Magog. Kimchi supposes that Micah is casting his prediction into the distant future and is describing the peace which will ensue after an eschatological war. when there will no longer be any need for walls and fortifications. Kimchi, however, is aware that there are elements of condemnation against sorcery, soothsaying and idolatry and he comments, 'That is to say, there will be no sorcerers in their cities nor soothsayers as there is now. The sense is that he will take away the heart of stone from the heart of flesh.' Nevertheless, this is to be accounted part of the promise for the future and Kimchi's position is that threat does not make its appearance until v. 14 and that then it is directed against the nations. Ibn Ezra's view of vv. 9–14 is broadly the same. The destruction of horses and chariots is a making of swords into ploughshares and spears into pruning-hooks. The need for armaments and walled cities will disappear, because the land will be at peace.

Wellhausen's remark (143) that vv. 9–13 may have been spoken by Micah is made on the assumption that these verses contain an oracle of doom and this is the view of Ehrlich (5, 285) whose unit is 5.9–14a. Thus its conclusion is 'And I shall wreak vengeance (against Israel) in my hot anger' and v. 14b arose as a consequence of a dittography of שמעו *ex* 6.1. A relative clause which redirected Yahweh's anger to the גוים was constructed and the sense of שמע changed from the one it has in 6.1: Yahweh is to take vengeance on the גוים because of their heedlessness.

I return to v. 13, where the fundamental difficulty is that עריך 'your cities' or 'your adversaries' does not match אשיריך 'your sacred poles'. Gaster's lexicography (1937, 163f.), founded on Ugaritic *'r* or *ġr*, produces a suitable parallelism, 'images', but this sense for the Ugaritic word has been discredited (Hillers, 72). G. R. Driver (1940, 169) proposes 'bloody stones' for ערים at Ezek. 6.6 and NEB (REB) has 'your blood–spattered altars' for עריך at Mic. 5.13. Driver's lexicography is perhaps related to Arabic *ġry*, which is given by Robertson Smith (1927, 201) as 'blood–bedaubed', rather than to Ugaritic. The suggestion of Fisher (1931, 4–41) that עיר means 'temple-quarter', does not meet the case of Mic. 5.13 (he does not deal with this verse in his article). 'Temple-quarter' is not a parallel for 'sacred poles' and Hillers, who mentions Fisher, has 'idols' in his translation, though it is not clear where he gets it, perhaps by adopting the emendation עצביך. NEB and REB have rendered עד עיר בית בעל as 'into the keep of the temple of Baal' at 2 Kgs 10.25, so the question is not whether עיר can have the sense 'temple-quarter' (as Nicholson supposes (1977, 114), but whether this sense is suitable in parallel with אשיריך at Mic. 5.3. The parallel should be another cultic object and Nicholson admits (1977, 116) that עיר is part of a temple and not a cultic object. Hence Van der Woude (1976), on whom he leans, does not solve the problem.

Wellhausen (27) leaves a blank and does not translate עריך (v. 13).

Ehrlich (5, 285) emends it to הָרֶיךָ 'your mountains' = בָּמוֹתֶיךָ 'your high places'. Smith (114) describes עָרֶיךָ (v. 13) as a weak repetition of עָרֵי (v. 10) and he supposes that v. 13 is a marginal note on v. 12. Duhm (90), Weiser (276) and Robinson (144) emend עָרֶיךָ to עֲצַבֶּיךָ, (Steiner), 'your idols', while Rudolph (103) emends it to עֻזֶּיךָ 'your refuges'. Rudolph is influenced by the exegesis which he imposes on the passage: v. 13aβ is a summary conclusion to vv. 9–13aα and 'refuges' is a reference to the false supports on which Israel had relied, armaments, sorceries, soothsaying and idolatry. Nor is Wolff's proposal a serious contribution to the lexicography of עָרֶיךָ. Its emendation of עָרֶיךָ to צָרֶיךָ is hardly necessary in view of 1 Sam. 28.16 and, in any case, the primary problem is the defective parallelism of אֲשֵׁירֶיךָ and עָרֶיךָ or צָרֶיךָ. צָרֶיךָ is exegetically obscure, while no such obscurity attaches to אֲשֵׁירֶיךָ and it is an odd way to repair this defect by emending אֲשֵׁירֶיךָ to אוֹיְבֶיךָ in order to produce synonymous parallelism with עָרֶיךָ. עֲצַבֶּיךָ should be adopted (cf. Sellin, צִירֶיךָ 'your images').

Smith (115) declares that 5.9–12 is a promise that Yahweh's help will be all-sufficient, though he acknowledges that it has a 'negative tone' (so Hillers, 72): it is a statement that Yahweh will destroy every source of human confidence and all supposed manifestations of divine help. Smith, unlike Weiser (277) does not relate the promise in vv. 9–13 to the background of the advent of the Messianic Age which is described in chapters 4 and 5. He notices that some scholars assign 5.9–13 to Micah and he acknowledges that it may be a Micah oracle, though he concludes (116) that it is probably late.

Weiser (276) holds that a convincing objection cannot be raised to the authorship of Micah for 5.9–13, but a firm dating is not possible. Hillers (72), similarly, contents himself with the statement that 'it is congruent with the times of Hezekiah and the situation of Micah and the villagers in Judah' who nourish a Messianic hope and look for the onset of a new age of which a purging of the nation will be the prelude. Hillers (74) is not so sympathetic as Rudolph (105) to the suggestion of Willis (1969: 353–368) that 5.9–13 have a direct connection with the reform of Hezekiah. Thus both Weiser and Hillers interpret 5.9–13 against a background of Messianic hope, but they are aware of the paradox of conferring the title of 'promise' on a passage whose emphasis is explicitly and exclusively destructive. Weiser (276) describes it as a catalogue of Israel's sins, a series of threats and words of reproach—a

judgement (276, *Gericht*). He combines judgement and threat with
promise by affirming that vv. 9–13 are not ultimately a threat of
destruction but a promise which gives life, a direct contribution of
Yahweh to the well-being of his people. He will set aside everything
which obstructs his complete sovereignty and mars a pure and untroubled relation between God and people. So his criticism is directed
against reliance on all additional helps, whether on the flesh or the
spirit, whether on human power or allegedly divine powers. Hillers (72)
conjectures that the introductory formula in v. 9aα (והיה ביום ההוא) is a
throw-back to והיה in vv. 4, 6 and 7 and a clue to the Messianic
background of 5.9–13.

Robinson (145), on the other hand, does not find such a background
for 5.9–13 and I have already suggested that Wellhausen (143), in
suggesting that 5.9–13 might be assigned to Micah, was assuming that
these verses contained an oracle of doom. Robinson gives 5.9–13 the
title 'The Punishment of Israel' (*Die Bestrafung Israels*), with the
comment 'a reproof directed against the sins of Israel, probably pre-
exilic'. Hence he concludes that the verses are polemical through and
through, that they are condemnatory not promissory and that they have
no benevolent aspect.

Rudolph (103–106) deals with the emphasis on destruction in
5.9–14 by subjecting the passage to two exegeses, a condemnatory one
which he assigns to Micah and a promissory one which is a redactional
reinterpretation of Micah's polemic: threat and condemnation are thus
set in a Messianic context. Rudolph (104) disposes of the address to the
enemy in 5.14 by vocalizing הגוים as הגֵּאים (= הגאואים) 'the proud': v. 14
is still an address to Israel. Without the opening formula (v. 9aα; cf.
Hillers, 72) 5.9–14 would be a threat. This would accord with the
attitude of Micah (cf. Wolff, 127) and there would be no question that
he is the author. Why does the passage stand here? The question is
answered by the introductory formula 'In that day' which has an
eschatological ring and the old words of Micah serve the compiler of
chapters 4 and 5. The fulfilment of Micah's threat is revealed as a
transparent consequence of a new situation of *Heil* and so it concludes a
series of oracles of weal effectively. It is a promise in the form of a
threat. Reliance (105) on armaments, fortifications, demons and idols
will not be features of the Messianic age, when Yahweh's protection of
his people will be all-sufficient.

What Micah delivered as a threat becomes a liberation. Yahweh and his 'man of peace' (5.4) will 'feed' (5.3) the people and there will no longer be any need to take precautions against enemy attacks (Rudolph, 106); no need of dark and mysterious powers which feed on anxiety. The future is an open book and sorcerers and soothsayers will have become redundant. Idols too will be things of the past, for Yahweh will exercise his sovereignty and the Messiah will be his only 'image'. Whoever is so arrogant (v. 14 emended) as to flaunt human pride in the presence of this fullness of divine grace will encounter Yahweh's anger and punishment: disobedience will not be tolerated.

Wolff (125–135) does not employ the Messianic context of chapters 4 and 5 in order to interpret 5.9–12. Instead he founds his exegesis of these verses on the assumption that they are part of a unit comprising 5.6–8, 9–12. The remnant's policy of self-help and its confidence that it will ravage the nations (v. 7) is followed by a prayer addressed to Yahweh (v. 8) asking him to exercise his power over these enemies and to root them out. Then there is an affirmation (vv. 9–12) that Israel will live in total dependence on Yahweh's help and that all other supports will be removed (134).

According to Wolff (134) the unit in 5.6–7, 9–12 is an 'undiluted promise' to Israel without a trace of accusation. The redaction (135) trumpets above all that Israel, which had previously been threatened and oppressed, would now dominate the nations. At a time when for long the remnant of Israel had not been 'like a lion' (5.7) among the nations, a prayer for Yahweh's help was necessary (v. 8). It corrected the impression given by v. 7 that the remnant of Jacob could with its own power dominate its enemies. This correction is reinforced in 5.9–12 and, secondarily, in vv. 13–14. It is made clear that Yahweh alone is their support and that victory is not in their own power. Without a word of reproof 5.9–12 represent that Israel, with its armaments, defences, sorcery, soothsaying and idolatry, is placing its reliance on human resources of security, when only Yahweh can guarantee it. According to the promise (5.9–12) Yahweh will destroy all these causes of anxiety, all efforts to be self-sufficient, and will liberate his people to put new trust in him.

The context in which Wolff sets the oracle contained in 5.9–12 is not an eschatological one. The background is not the advent of the Messianic age, but that of the fall of Jerusalem in 587 (134) or, less

precisely, that of the exilic period (127). The destructive blow of the
Babylonian conquest is the beginning of Yahweh's acts of purging
(5.9–12) which would set Israel free from the works of their own hands
(5.12). Perhaps prophets had already descried (134), in the fulfilment of
words of judgement (3.12), the beginning of such a liberation and had
interpreted punishment as a purification. Hence והיה ביום ההוא does
not exercise the major exegetical influence on Wolff which it has on
Rudolph and Hillers for whom it establishes that the context of the
oracle (5.9–13) is the advent of the Messianic age.

Interest should be focused on the paraphrase of Targ., different in
kind from that which it has hitherto attracted (cf. Wolff, 124). The
significance of the transformation of the second person suffixes into
עממיא 'nations' at vv. 9, 10, 12 and 13 is to drive home that Israel has
been undone by insidious, seductive and morale-sapping foreign
influences. This conclusion is reinforced by the presence of מקרבך
(MT) in v. 12 and v. 13 and by Targ.'s rendering of מידך (v. 11) which
is identical with what it gives for the occurrences of מקרבך (מבינך).
The influences which are to be eradicated have all insinuated themselves
into the heart of the community, but they have come from the outside
world and are alien to Israel. Hence קרוי עממיא (v. 10) for MT
ערי ארצך is not to be taken as 'cities of the nations': it does not utter a
threat against cities in foreign lands. Rather it is a polemic against cities
in Israel which have a foreign culture and have adopted alien customs.
Chapter 5.9–13 are directed against military equipment which has been
imported from abroad (סוסות עממיא, v. 9), against fortified cities,
sorcery, soothsaying and idolatry. It is a threat whose ingredients are
recognizably and typically prophetic. והיה ביום ההוא is a secondary
introductory formula which describes 5.9–13 correctly (נאם יהוה) as an
oracle, but which should not exercise any influence on exegesis. There is
nothing which precludes 5.9–13 from being a word spoken by Micah.

   9. It will come to pass in that day (it is Yahweh who speaks):
      I shall cut off your horses from your midst
      and I shall destroy your chariots.
  10. I shall cut off the cities of your land
      and I shall demolish your fortifications.
  11. I shall cut off sorceries from you
      and you will no longer have soothsayers.
  12. I shall cut off your images
      and your sacred pillars from your midst.

You will no longer worship what your hands have made.
13.   I shall pull up your sacred poles from your midst
      and I shall destroy your idols[1].
14.   I shall wreak vengeance with hot anger
      on the nations which disobey me.

[1]Reading עצביך (MT עריך).

CHAPTER 6

vv. 1–5 YAHWEH TAKES ISRAEL TO COURT

The unit is defined as 6.1–5 by Smith (119) and Robinson (144), as 6.1–8 by Weiser (277), Rudolph (106), Wolff (136f.) and Hillers (75). Smith supposes that 6.1–5 is of 'late origin' and Robinson dates it in the post-exilic period. Weiser, Rudolph and Hillers hold that 6.1–8 is an integral unit and Hillers (77) remarks that 6.1–5 is truncated without a final question and answer by Israel (following Ehrlich, 5, 286). He is more tentative than Weiser and Rudolph in claiming the piece for Micah and his conclusion (79) is that, while some of the vocabulary perhaps points to a late date, 6.1–8 may represent an early form of Deuteronomy from Hezekiah's reign. That he is hankering after the ascription of 6.1–8 to Micah is perhaps indicated by the significance which he attaches to a version (Levine, 1981, 195–205) of the Balaam myth dated c. 700 B.C. (78).

Weiser (278) describes 6.1–8 as the *apogée* of Micah's prophetic proclamation. The prophet finds for the essence of true religion a word which encompasses the breadth and depth of the biblical grasp of existence. Wolff (138) questions the original integrity of 6.1–8 and supposes that vv. 1–5 and vv. 6–8 became a unit (144) in the early Deuteronomic (seventh century B.C.) or the late Deuteronomistic period (fifth century B.C.). He picks out individual features which make the later date probable. He concludes (145) that 6.6–8 is a didactic piece which may have a pre-history reaching back to the early Deuteronomic period, but that its extant form is probably post-exilic. It is notable that neither Weiser, Rudolph, Wolff nor Hillers attaches weight to the circumstance that 6.1–5 and 6.1–8 are *Gattungen* which are far removed from each other, though they are aware of this. The one is a description of a legal process in which Yahweh and Israel are involved; the other, consisting of two questions and an answer, is addressed to an individual (אדם, v. 8) and is, perhaps, a tutorial device employed by a teacher. The affirmation that 6.1–8 is a coherent unit has some similarity to a shot-gun marriage.

Those who assert that Micah was the author of 6.1–8 land in serious

difficulties. This requires the assumption that the prophet who formulated the antithesis of cultic punctilliousness and true religion (even
allowing for the elements of hyperbole and parody in vv. 6–7; Wolff,
141) accepted, without the blink of an eye, that Yahweh compelled a
heathen diviner, domiciled at Pethor on the Euphrates (Num. 22.5),
who specialized in incantation for which he accepted fees (Num.
22.18), to utter a blessing, when he was hired to utter a curse. It is well-
nigh impossible to believe that Micah, whose moral sense was outraged
by the oppressive greed of landlords and its disastrous consequences for
small farmers, would have alluded with approval with such goings-on as
are attributed to Yahweh and Balaam. He would not have tolerated
such coercion of a wonder-worker, such a cheapening of Yahweh, such a
'magical, superstitious concept of religion' (Smith, 122).

Wolff does not escape from the problem by positing a secondary
combination of 6.2–5 and 6.6–8 and the formation of a Deuteronomist or Deuteronomistic didactic piece. Lescow (1972, 182–212)
similarly supposes that 6.1–8 is the consequence of a later compilation
of 6.1–5 and 6.6–8: 6.1–5 is a piece of cult-prophecy from the second
half of the fifth century B.C. (187) and 6.6–8 a prophetic sermon in the
form of a Torah from the first half of the fifth century B.C. (193). The
compilation of 6.1–5 and 6.6–8 is connected with an anti-Samaritan
tendency at the time of the schism. 6.1– 8 then assumes the form of a
lawsuit between Yahweh and Samaria and (ישראל = Samaria, v. 2)
sounds a polemical note (209).

First we should notice that 6.1, according to Wolff (139f.) is
redactional and that the lawsuit begins at 6.2. 6.1 is a continuation of
the polemic against the גוים which apppears in 5.14 and both display
the same redactional tendency. 5.14 is to be set apart from 5.9–13 and
6.1 is isolated in relation to 6.2–5. In 6.1 Yahweh summons a prophet
to indict the גוים for whom ההרים and הגבעות are ciphers. The
vocabulary of 6.1 (ריב; שמעו) shows that it was the intention of the
redactor to create the illusion of continuity with 6.2 (שמעו; cf. לא שמעו,
5.14). The weak link in Wolff's argument is his assumption that ההרים
and הגבעות in 6.1 are ciphers for the גוים and the other exegesis that
they are summoned as witnesses in connection with the lawsuit in
6.2–5 should be followed. It is difficult to believe that the mountains
and hills in v. 1 do not belong to the same context as the mountains
and foundations of the earth in v. 2. In 6.1 Yahweh addresses a prophet

(Micah, Rudolph, 109; Weiser, 278; perhaps Micah, Hillers, 79) and instructs him to summon the mountains and hills as witnesses in a lawsuit which the prophet is to conduct on behalf of Yahweh with Israel and which is set out in 6.2–5. The prophet is given two tasks, he has to find witnesses (or a jury) and he has to act as Yahweh's advocate, though he is supplied with his brief (Hillers, 77).

What has an account of a legal process (6.2–5) to do with the two questions and answer in 6.6–8, perhaps a tutorial ploy (Wolff, 140)? Let us consider Wolff's answer to this question. He is required to demonstrate that both 6.1–5 and 6.6–8 have Deuteronomic or Deuteronomistic characteristics. One of his arguments is that 6.6–8 is parasitic on 6.2–5. The questions in vv. 6–7 allude to the question by Yahweh in v. 3 and this complementary expression of dissatisfaction (vv. 6–7) is evidence that vv. 2–5 were combined with vv. 6–8 and that vv. 6–8 were generated by vv. 2–5. Hence 6.2–5 existed before 6.6–8 and this relation between the questions in 6.3 and 6.6–7 is maintained despite the circumstance that v. 3 was asked by Yahweh and addressed to Israel, while vv. 6–7 were asked by an anonymous person and addressed to an individual (everyman). Moreover, one is asked in the context of a legal process and the others, perhaps, in connection with a tutorial technique. Doubt arises whether the question in v. 3 and the questions in vv. 6–7 are meaningfully related: why a Deuteronomist or Deuteronomistic teacher should have united 6.2–5 and 6.6–8 in the late pre-exilic or post-exilic period.

The 'over-burdening' signified by ומה הלאתיך (v. 3) has been associated with the disappointed expectations or the straitened circumstances of the Israelite community following the deliverance from the Assyrians in 701 B.C. (Weiser, 278). Jerusalem had been spared, but the political conditions were depressed and Messianic hopes had not been fulfilled. Rudolph (110) fastens rather on disappointment with Yahweh's failure to respond favourably to the reform of Hezekiah (2 Kgs 18.4). Wolff (148) connects ומה הלאתיך with the perception of the people that Yahweh had made excessive cultic demands of them and this thought appears in the exegesis of Rashi who comments on ומה הלאתיך with בעבודתי, 'in my demands that you serve me in worship'. Further, 'I did not weary you with great demands and onerous sacrifices.' Wolff notices the use of נלאיתי at Isa. 1.14 in connection with sacrifices and cultic celebrations (vv. 13–14), where Yahweh declares that they weary him

beyond endurance. At Isa. 16.12 Moab is said to wear herself out (נלאה)
with cultic activity which is unavailing. Wolff supposes that a date in the
early Persian period would accord with a Yahwism which was characterized by such severe cultic demands. On this basis he produces another
reason for the integration of 6.2–5 with 6.6–8. In 6.6–8 Yahweh makes
it clear that the cultic sacrifices which the people complain are burden-
some, and with which he confesses that he is bored (Isa. 1.14), do not
number among his demands, 'Yahweh has told you what is good and
what it is that he requires of you: only to act justly and to love mercy and
to walk humbly with your God' (6.8).

For the reasons given above, and for others, Wolff argues that 6.2–8
is a carefully crafted and artistic composition. His argument is elaborate, but it lacks sharpness. His case for the Deuteronomist/Deuterono-
mistic characteristics in 6.2–5 rests largely on the recitation of the
Heilsgeschichte in vv. 4–5. There are special features in this, the mention
of Aaron and Miriam (v. 4) and the reference to Balak and Balaam (v.
5). The second is found in Numbers (22–24) not Deuteronomy and it
is not obvious that it would have been of interest to a Deuteronomistic
traditionist. Otherwise the recitation of the *Heilsgeschichte* is too general
an item with which to pinpoint a Deuteronomic/Deuteronomistic
connection and Robinson (145) has noted its presence in eighth
century prophetic literature, though he supposes that the mention of
Aaron and Miriam points to a post-exilic date for 6.4–5.

In his comparison of Mic. 6.6–8 with Deut. 10.12–22, Wolff (144)
shrugs off the circumstance that the passage in Deuteronomy is
addressed to Israel (v. 12) whereas the passage in Micah is addressed to
an individual. The Micah passages (6.1–5; 6.6–8) are different in kind
and no advantage is gained by joining them in a secondary alliance as
Wolff does. The most that can be done for Wolff's theory that 6.6–8
was generated by 6.2–5 in a Deuteronomic/Deuteronomistic redaction
is to admit that they display a common didactic interest. In the one case
this is developed by conjuring up a legal process between Yahweh and
Israel in which a puzzled Yahweh expresses bewilderment, feels badly
done by and affirms with an appeal to history his steadfastness and
benevolence. Another tutoral device is used in 6.6–8. The questions
bear on the distinction between offering sacrifices to Yahweh, asked
with exaggeration, and the practice of true religion.

For שמעו נא את אשר יהוה אמר (v. 1) Sept.[B] has ἀκούσατε δὴ λόγον.

κύριος Κύριος εἶπεν and Sept.ᴬ ἀκούσατε δὴ λόγον κυρίου. κύριος
εἶπεν. Ziegler (221) prefers Sept.ᴬ, but both Sept.ᴬ and Sept.ᴮ represent
דבר for אשר and Sept.ᴬ represents את דבר יהוה. Sept.ᴮ, with κύριος for
κυρίου is probably a lapse and λόγον should not be thought to have
text-critical significance: it does not reflect a different Hebrew text from
MT. MT does not present any difficulty and is followed by Vulg., Pesh.
and Targ. The word-order, יהוה אמר rather than אמר יהוה favours the
vocalization of MT (אָמַר) and NEB (REB) translates: 'Hear now what
the LORD is saying.' Sept. (εἶπεν), Vulg. (loquitur), Pesh. (ʾmr) and
Targ. (אמר) have preferred אָמַר; also Pesh. with a change of word-order
(ʾmr mry).

את² (v. 1) is rendered by Sept. as πρός 'to' or 'against', the latter
appearing in Vulg. (adversum) and Pesh. (ʾl). That Targ. עם for את
means 'against' and not 'with' = 'in the presence of' (Robinson, 144,
vor) is shown by the appearance of עם in Targ. at v. 2 for Hebrew עם,
where it refers to the lawsuit between Yahweh and Israel and must have
the force of 'against'. The sense 'to the mountains' (Sept. πρός) has
been achieved by emending את to אל (Wellhausen, 143; Duhm, 90;
Smith, 119; Hillers, 75?) and it is given by Wolff without the
emendation of את to אל. Rudolph (117) also refuses to countenance the
emendation of את to אל and he rejects 'with' for את on the ground that
the ריב is not with the mountains and that 'in the presence of' cannot
be had out of את = 'with'. 'In the presence of' is the translation which
he favours (also Weiser, vor) and it may be that he takes את as a mark of
a direct object: 'ריב the mountains', that is, state your case to the
mountains that they may weigh it as witnesses. Rashi and Kimchi notice
a reading in Targ (Speiser, 3,447) which explains הרים as אבהתא
'fathers' and גבעות as אמהות 'mothers'.

For והאתנים (v. 2) Sept. has καὶ αἱ φάραγγες, 'and the chasms' and
Pesh., similarly, uʾmwqʾ, 'and the depths' (cf. Targ. ועקריא 'and the
roots'). Vulg. fortia 'steadfast' translates האתנים as an adjective, 'and the
everlasting foundations of the earth'. This is nearer to the attested
occurrences of איתן in biblical Hebrew (BDB, 450f.) and Vulg. is closely
followed by NEB, 'you everlasting pillars that bear up the earth'. The
literal translation of the Hebrew is 'and the everlasting ones, the
foundations of the earth', with האתנים and מסדי ארץ in apposition, and
this is the construction shown by Sept. (καὶ αἱ φάραγγες θεμέλια τῆς
γῆς) and Targ. (ועקריא יסודי ארעא). Pesh. indicates a construct

relationship, 'and the depths of the foundations of the earth' (wᵉmwq̇ dšt̲syh dʾrᵃ'). Kimchi explains that האתנים are what support the הרים and that, as such, they are the foundations of the earth, that is, ארץ מסדי is in apposition to האתנים.

The text of MT has been suspected and והאתנים, which is retained by Rudolph (106), Wolff (136) and Hillers (75), is emended to והאזינו by Wellhausen (143), Duhm (90), Smith (119), Weiser (277) and Robinson (144). והאזינו, 'and give ear', is then in synonymous parallelism with ושמעו. Smith (119) remarks that the absence of ה in the case of הרים and its presence in האתנים makes the form of האתנים suspicious. The sense 'grievous', 'causing sorrow' is conveyed by Sept.'s rendering of הלאתיך (ἐλύπησά σε) at v. 3 and Vulg.'s molestus fui tibi is similar. Pesh. 'kryt lk, 'offended you', conveys a different nuance from 'overburdened you' or 'made too many demands on you' (Rudolph, 106; Wolff, 136). Hillers (75) 'troubled you' is more cautious and Targ. offers a paraphrase of v. 3: 'My people, what good have I offered to do to you which I have not done and what grievous evils have I multiplied for you.' Rashi comments, 'Pay attention and recognize the good which I have done to you' and on כי העליתיך (v. 4) he remarks 'For I heaped all this goodness on you and I did not weary you with great demands and onerous sacrifices.' Sept. has a plus, a double rendering of ומה הלאתיך (Smith, 119; Rudolph, 107; Wolff, 137) at v. 3, namely, ἢ τί παρηνώχλησά σοι, 'or with what have I harassed you'.

A textual point arises in connection with the mention of Aaron and Miriam along with Moses in v. 4. The question is whether עמי (v. 5, MT) should be emended to עמו and attached to v. 4. Verse 5 would begin with זכר and v. 4b would read 'and I sent before you Moses, Aaron and Miriam with him'. Moses would then have a principal role and Aaron and Miriam would be a supporting cast. All three would not receive equal mention as they do in MT. The emendation of עמי to עמו and its attachment to v. 4 is the proposal made by Weiser (277), Robinson (144) and Hillers (75). Rudolph (107) assumes rather that עמו has been missed out by a copyist at v. 4 because of its similarity to עמי (v. 5) and so his emendation consists of the addition of עמו to v. 4. MT should be retained with Wellhausen (26) and Wolff (136). Ibn Ezra's comment on Moses, Aaron and Miriam is, 'The Torah was given by Moses and Aaron was his mouth. Miriam taught it to women' (Exod. 15.20–21).

מן השטים עד גלגל (v. 5) has a defective grammatical connection with the rest of the verse in MT, Sept., Vulg. and Pesh. This is repaired by the paraphrase of Targ., 'Were not mighty deeds done for you from the plains of Shittim to Gilgal.' Ehrlich (5, 286) has filled out the verse by suggesting that זכר נא at the beginning of the verse is implicit before מן השטים עד גלגל and Smith supposes that זכר נא is superfluous where it stands and should be transposed to precede מן השטים עד גלגל. This converts the opening of v. 5 into two questions: 'What did Balak counsel?. And what did Balaam answer him?' זכר נא is not noticeably superfluous and Smith should not be followed. Weiser (277) has emended בן בעור to בעברך 'when you crossed' and assumed an implicit זכר נא and Robinson (144), with עברך instead of בעברך, makes a similar proposal. Both Weiser and Robinson judge that מלך מואב and בן בעור are secondary additions. NEB, 'Consider your journey from Shittim to Gilgal' is founded on the addition of בין עברך (Brockington, 256) and NEB retains both בן בעור and מלך מואב. Rudolph (108) and Wolff (138) suppose that בין עבור 'consider the crossing' is a near haplography of בן בעור. Wellhausen (143) and Duhm (90) have concluded that מן השטים עד גלגל is out of place in v. 5 and they are attracted by Ewald's suggestion that it is a marginal note indicating what part of the Torah should be consulted (Num. 22–24) for more information about Balak and Balaam, though Wellhausen asks whether such a marginal note would not be superfluous. Wolff (149) remarks that the author makes a short mention of the Balaam story without supplying any detail and so assumed that his readers would know it.

Neither Targ.'s paraphrase, the emendations proposed nor Ewald's explanation lends weight to the connection of the reference to שטים with Israel's apostasy at that place, though this is a feature of the exegesis of Rashi, Kimchi, Ibn Ezra and Ehrlich (5, 286). Rashi comments on מן השטים, 'For you sinned against me there. 'Know my righteous acts (צדקותי) that I may not withhold my goodness and help from you, until I have brought you to Gilgal and subdued before you all the land.' Kimchi too associates שטים with sin, punishment and its remission, Gilgal with the crossing of the Jordan dryshod and the arrival in the Promised Land. Ibn Ezra remarks that Gilgal marks 'the beginning of the land of Israel' and that from Shittim, where Israel committed a great sin, to Gilgal 'was only a short journey and the

crossing of the Jordan'. But Shittim is not a symbol of apostasy and
Gilgal a symbol of fulfilment in the phrase מן השטים עד גלגל. Rather
מן השטים עד גלגל is the final stage of the journey, the last lap (cf. Ibn
Ezra) of the long trek from Egypt (v. 4) to the Promised Land (Smith,
122; Weiser, 279; Robinson, 146; Rudolph, 110; Wolff, 149f.; Hillers,
78).

Sept.'s rendering of מן השטים, ἀπὸ τῶν σχοίνων 'from the reeds', is
mysterious. It has been suggested that σχοίνων is an error for σχίνων
'mastich trees' (Smith, 119; Rudolph, 108) and Rudolph has remarked
that Sept. does not appear to have recognized שטים as a place-name.
The weakness of the proposal that σχίνων is the original is that it does
not give any better sense than σχοίνων and Wolff's proposal (138) that
ἀπὸ τῶν σχοίνων is a reference to the Sea of Reeds deserves consideration. The Greek translator may have supposed that מן השטים עד גלגל
was a reference to the journey from beginning to end, from Egypt to the
Promised Land, and not just to its final stage. If so, he is reinforcing
Rudolph's point (110) that the mighty acts (צדקות) of Yahweh which
Israel are to discern are not only those of the final part of the journey
(מן השטים עד גלגל) but also those related in v. 4 and v. 5a. צדקות יהוה
(v. 5) occurs in the context of a speech by Yahweh and, to correct this
oddity, its emendation to צדקותי 'my saving acts' has been proposed: י
has been wrongly taken as an abbreviation for יהוה instead of a first
person suffix (Robinson, 144). This is dismissed by Wolff (138) and
Hillers (76) on the ground that the appearance of of יהוה in an oracle
conforms with Hebrew practice.

Yahweh announces (v. 2b) that he is to bring a legal action against his
people and he summons the mountains and the hills as witnesses or as a
jury to weigh up the case. Yahweh is then the plaintiff and Israel is the
defendant (Weiser, 279). Verses 3–5, however, have the form of an
apologia, with Yahweh engaging in self-justification and defending
himself against an accusation made by his people (v. 3) rather than
launching an accusation against them: he is on the defensive, not on the
attack. According to Weiser, the injured innocence, the pained self-
defence which reverberates in his question is in effect an accusation and
a declaration that his people are the guilty party. Even if this were
granted, the mild tones of the prosecutor in vv. 3–5 would be
remarkable. Again, if the question (v. 3) is ironical (Hillers, 77) or if the
recitation of what Yahweh has done is a jogging of the memory of his

people, one has to say that vv. 3–5 do not look like the opening submission of an accuser in a lawsuit and their eirenic and conciliatory character has been noticed by Smith (121), Rudolph (109) and Wolff (147). Yahweh's tone is that of a parent pleading with his child, not that of a prosecutor (Smith). He engages in self-defence and justifies his record rather than making an indictment (Rudolph). Verses 3–5 are spoken by Yahweh in self-defence and are marked more by warm appeal than by self-assertion. The basis of the legal process, as it is set out, is Yahweh's self-imposed responsibility for Israel. He speaks as one who is accused and who would make peace with his people (Wolff). Moreover, if צדקות יהוה (v. 5) means 'acts which justify Yahweh' (Wolff, 150) as well as 'saving acts' (*Heilsgeschichte*), the note of self-justification is present in the final words of the lawsuit. Nevertheless, Yahweh gently implies that the guilt is on the side of the people rather than on his. Whatever may be the nuance of the second question (v. 3; ומה הלאתיך) there is little doubt that 'What (evil) have I done to you?' is the correct sense of the first (Kimchi; Ibn Ezra). Rashi's elaborate paraphrase of מה עשיתי לך does not recommend itself ('Pay attention to recognize the good which I have done to you').

1. Hear what Yahweh has to say:
    Stand up and state the case to the mountains,
    Let the hills hear your voice.
2. Hear Yahweh's case, you mountains,
    You everlasting foundations of the earth;
    for Yahweh is taking his people to law
    And is to argue his case with Israel.
3. My people, what have I done to you?
    What excessive demands have I made on you?
    Bring forward your evidence against me.
4. For I brought you up from Egypt,
    I set you free from slavery
    and I sent before you Moses, Aaron and Miriam.
5. My people, remember what plots Balak, king of Moab, laid
    and how Balaam, son of Beor, answered him.
    (Remember) your journey[1] from Shittim to Gilgal,
    that you may discern Yahweh's saving acts.

[1]Inserting עברך.

vv. 6–8 YAHWEH'S REQUIREMENTS ARE JUSTICE, MERCY AND HUMILITY

Pesh. is corrupt at v. 7 (*brbwtʾ dḥylʾ dmwšḥʾ* 'with ten thousand of the power of heifers') and the Hebrew text before the translator was probably MT (*brbwtʾ dnḥlʾ dmšḥʾ*, 'with ten thousand rivers of oil'; so Rudolph, 108). Targ. with ברבוב נחלי דמשח is a translation of MT.

Vulg. in *multis millibus hircorum pinguium*, 'with many thousands of fat he-goats', is reading a different text from MT which apparently derives from Sept.ᵛ χιμάρων 'he goats' (Ziegler, 221). The Greek text which Ziegler prefers is that of Sept.ᴮ χειμάρρων 'torrents' (Swete, 35). If this preference is followed the text of Sept. is ἐν μυριάσι χειμάρρων πιόνων of which 'with ten thousand oily torrents' is the strict translation; 'with ten thousand torrents of oil' would be a freer rendering. The question is whether χιμάρων which agrees with Vulg. *hircorum* represents the original Greek text, 'with ten thousand fat he-goats'. The disadvantage of this assumption is that χειμάρρων equates with MT נחלי, while the Hebrew word for 'he-goat' has no resemblance to נחלי (תיש, Prov. 30.31; עתיד, Jer. 51.40). Whatever conclusion is reached about this it is probable that Vulg. *in multis millibus hircorum pinguium* is a survival of the Old Latin and that the Greek text translated was ἐν μυριάσι χιμάρων. The safer conclusion is that Sept. read MT (so Rudolph, 108; Wolff, 138; Hillers, 76) and offered χειμάρρων πιόνων as a rendering of נחלי שמן. In that case Vulg. is the product of a corrupt Greek text with χιμάρων for χειμάρρων.

The earlier English versions (KJV; RV; RSV) set out the syntax of v. 8 as follows: 'He hath shewed you, O Man, what is good; and what does the LORD require of thee, but to do justly and to love mercy and to walk humbly with thy God?' (KJV). This makes a question out of ומה . . . אלהיך and כי אם is rendered as 'but' (Sept. ἀλλ᾽ ἤ; Targ. אלהין). This is the syntax of Sept. and Targ. and is followed by Robinson (146) and Rudolph (107). NEB adopts a different syntax: 'God has told you what is good; and what is it that God asks of you? Only to act justly, to love loyalty, to walk wisely before your God.' The question consists of ומה . . . ממך and the answer is given by כי אם . . . אלהיך. כי אם in both NEB and REB is translated by 'only', but REB reproduces the syntax of Vulg. and Pesh. and both מה and ומה are dependent on הגיד: 'The Lord has told you mortals what is good and what it is that the Lord requires of you: only to act justly, to love loyalty and to walk humbly with your God.' Verse 8 is then a statement which does not contain a rhetorical question (Wellhausen, 26; Weiser, 278; Wolff, 137; Hillers, 75).

אדם is taken by Ehrlich (286) as the subject of הגיד, 'One has told you', but the vocative 'O man' is generally and correctly preferred (Wellhausen, 26; Weiser, 278; Robinson, 146; Rudolph, 107; Wolff, 137; Hillers, 75). Rudolph's rendering is *Man hat dir kundgetan, O Mensch* and so he confirms 'One has told you', but not at the cost of making אדם a subject instead of a vocative. 'It has been told you' has been offered as a better way of rendering הגיד לך אדם (Wellhausen, 26; Wolff, 137). Wolff (138) holds that the emendation of הגיד to הֻגַּד is not necessary to achieve this, though the emendation is made by Smith (124, 127) and Robinson (146). There are those who conclude that 'He = God is the subject of הגיד (Weiser, 276; Hillers, 75; KJV, RV, RSV) and this is made more explicit by NEB ('God') and REB ('The Lord'). The appearance of יהוה in the second stich is difficult to explain, if 'Yahweh' or 'God' is the subject of הגיד. MT should be retained and translated 'It has been told you, O man' or 'You have been told'.

Wellhausen (144) has remarked that a succinct summary (v. 8) is impaired by the obscurity of הנצע for which he offers the translation *demütig* (Weiser, *in Demüt*; KJV, 'humbly'; also Smith, 123). Smith (128) observes that הנצע is a Hiphil infinitive absolute used adverbially, but the difficulty is lexicographical, not grammatical. צנע appears in one other place (Prov. 11.2) in biblical Hebrew and the form צנועים is a passive participle for which the sense desiderated is 'modest' or 'modesty' (if צנועים is an abstract noun). The parallelism is antithetic and 'modest' (cf. Smith, 128) or 'modesty' is a better antithesis for זדון 'impudence', 'arrogance', than is 'sagacity' (NEB 'but wisdom goes with sagacity'). There have been second thoughts in REB, 'but wisdom goes hand in hand with modesty'. At Mic. 6.8 הצנע לכת has similarly been rendered by NEB 'to walk wisely' (Hyatt, 1952, 253–259; Stoebe, 1959, 180–194; Hillers, 76) for which REB has substituted 'to walk humbly'. The further evidence which requires examination appears in the Manual of Discipline and in the Hebrew text of Ben Sira. There are three occurrences of הצנע לכת in the Manual of Discipline (4.5; 5.4; 8.2) and four occurrences of צנע in Ben Sira (16.23; 31.22; 32.3; 42.8).

It is a reasonable hypothesis that והצנע לכת (Mic. 6.8) is the model of
והצנע לכת which occurs three times in the Manual of Discipline,
though, unlike Mic. 6.8, the occurrences all deal with relations between
men in society rather than relations between man and God. This hypothesis has to to be balanced against the circumstance that הצניע לכת is a
phrase which is current in modern Hebrew and which means 'to walk
humbly', 'to behave modestly' (Alcalay, 1963, 2197). Further, the
Hiphil of צנע has the sense 'to withdraw', 'to hide' in post-biblical
Hebrew and this is matched by the Aramaic Aphel, אצנע 'to withdraw',
'to hide', 'to guard' (Jastrow, 1903, 1292f.). 'To be circumspect'
(*bedachtsam*, Rudolph, 107) and 'to be vigilant' (*aufmerksam*, Wolff,
137) are proposals influenced by the nuance 'to be on one's guard'. The
evidence from post-biblical Hebrew and Aramaic, which is general,
suggests that הצנע at Mic. 6.8 could have the nuance 'privately' or 'self-
effacingly' and this would be a confirmation of the rightness of 'humbly'
or the like over against 'wisely'.

The first occurrence in the Manual of Discipline (4.5) is the word-
string והצנע לכת בערמת כול (Lohse, 1964, 12) which is rendered by
Gaster (1957, 64) as 'a modesty of behaviour coupled with general
prudence'. More literally, 'to walk modestly with sagacity in all things'.
It is probable that 'modesty' and 'sagacity' are complementary virtues
and that it is illegitimate to use בערמת כול in order to demonstrate that
הצנע means 'wisely'. The passage deals with relations between man
and man not between man and God. This is also the setting of
והצנע לכת בכל דרכיהם (5.4), where another phrase from Mic. 6.8
appears (אהבת חסד) along with צדקה ומשפט: 'Righteousness and
justice and love of mercy and a modest (wise) walk in all their ways
(Lohse, 1964, 16). This is close enough to Mic. 6.8 to be regarded as a
paraphrase of עשות משפט ואהבת חסד והצנע לכת. The final occurrence
(8.2) features man and his neighbour again, not man and God as in
Mic. 6.8: והנצע לכת איש את רעהו (Lohse, 1964, 28), 'and that each man
should behave modestly (wisely) in his relations with his neighbour'.

Neither 5.4 nor 8.2 furnish any contextual indications as to whether
הצנע לכת is modest (self-effacing) behaviour or wise behaviour, so they
do not take the lexicographical argument any further. 4.5, on the other
hand, could be used to support either 'modestly' or 'wisely' and I have
already suggested that the former inference is more solid than the latter.
If the correct translation of 4.5 were 'to walk wisely with sagacity in all

things', והצנע לכת and ערמה would be synonymous and בערמת כול
supplementary, even superfluous. The sense of the word-string is akin
to 'be harmless as doves and wise as serpents' (Mt. 10.16).

The most interesting of the four occurrences of צנע in the Hebrew
text of Ben Sira is מלל שב כי הוא לך והצנע שכל ואל תמנע שיר (32.3;
Levi, 1963, 33): 'Speak, O old man, for it is appropriate that you
should and with modest discrimination do not withhold a song.' The
verse could equally well be rendered 'and with wise discrimination do
not withhold a song'. This is a case where 'wise' perhaps has the edge
over 'modest', though it is not decisive and 'with modesty and
discrimination' might be the correct translation. ובצנע אחוה דעי (16.23;
Levi, 26) can be rendered either 'and with modesty I shall declare my
knowledge' or 'and with wisdom I shall declare my knowledge'. צנוע
(cf. Prov. 11.2) is the form in the other two occurrences and the choice
is between 'modest', 'wise', 'circumspect' or 'wary'. בכל מעשיך היה צנוע
(31.22; Levi, 32) is followed by 'and no injury will overtake you'. The
translation of צנוע might be either 'modest', 'wise' or 'wary'. There is
the same degree of indeterminacy in ואיש צנוע לפני כל חי (42.8; Levi,
53), 'and (you are to be) modest (wise, wary) in the presence of all other
men'. Wolff's rendering of הצנע 'watchful', is tilted towards agreement
with 'wise' (Hyatt, Stoebe) and he finds more support for this in the
four occurrences of Ben Sira than I have suggested (156).

The conclusion of this discussion is that 'humbly' is probably the
right sense for הצנע at Mic. 6.8, though 'humbly', because of its
association with humbug (Uriah Heep), should be avoided. A mini-
mum alteration would be 'walk in humility with God', but 'modestly',
'self-effacingly', 'in privacy' may be nearer to the nuance of הצנע לכת.

Some modern commentators divide up Mic. 6.8 between ethics and
piety (Smith, 127; Weiser, 281; Robinson, 147; Rudolph, 113; Wolff,
156). The moral demands are that justice should be done, that there
should be a love of mercy (KJV) and compassion (חסד), kindness
(RSV) or loyalty (NEB, REB) and that these public manifestations of
goodness should be nourished by the inwardness of a spirituality and by
the privacy of communion with God. Wolff tempers this sharp division
into ethics and piety with the remark that the third demand is not
separate from the first two. The third demand is complementary to the
first and second and the three in indissoluble unity add up to the good
life. The threefold division is reinforced by Herz's philological account

of הצנע לכת (1935, 188), where the emphasis is laid on 'purity' (of heart) and this is taken up by Robinson (146), *in Reinheit*. The final demand of v. 8 is for purity of heart or holiness without which no man can see God. Robinson overworks this philology correlating justice with Amos, mercy (חסד) with Hosea and holiness with Isaiah.

This division between ethics and piety more or less accords with the comment of Ibn Ezra: 'He (God) does not seek rams nor your children, but only that you do justice, that you do not deceive your friend by speech or fraud and that you are merciful to him with all your might; that you walk with God humbly (הצנע) in all your ways, with integrity of heart and not with a stiff neck.'

Rashi notices Targ. but takes a different line from it and from Ibn Ezra. 'To walk modestly with your God' does not mark a transition from ethics to piety, from public life to the secret place of the Most High; it is not a shift from relations between man and man in community to a relation between man and God. On the contrary 'walking modestly with your God' is a description of doing justice and extending mercy to one's neighbour. It is our conduct and dispositions in the world, the attitudes which we strike with our fellow-men, which are the acid test of the nature of our relation with God. He comments: 'A man who has put his friend to shame comes to be reconciled to him and says, "I shall not be reconciled to you until such and such a person who insulted me in public comes (and makes an apology to me in public)." God takes no delight in this and would have him make up his difference with his friend in private.'

Kimchi's comment lacks the sharpness of Rashi's and is difficult to disentangle. On the one hand he appears to underline the unique character of the relation between man and God who is יחיד 'The One', the incomparable, and is to be loved with the heart and the mind. He glosses הצנע with צניעות 'modesty' or 'privacy'. His point may be to contrast the privacy of walking with God as opposed to the public character of doing justice and performing acts of charity (חסד). There is, however, something of Rashi's emphasis in his exegesis: 'And what matters are there which do not need to be done with צנעה? The Torah says that הצנע לכת concerns matters which have to be done to Tom, Dick or Harry.' 'To walk in private' and perhaps 'to walk in private with God' belong to ethics and Kimchi is apparently issuing a warning against a selective justice and a selective charity; against justice which is

done or charity which is extended in the full light of day as opposed to
the unseen constancy of just conduct and acts of charity which are
carried out irrespective of who benefits from them.

According to Rudolph (111) Mic. 6.1–8 is a coherent unit and
describes the progress of a law-suit between Yahweh, represented by
Micah, and Israel. 6.6–8 is then a continuation of 6.1–5 and the whole
is set in the time of Micah. Verses 6–7 are spoken as a response to
6.1–5 by an individual (v. 7b) who has heard Micah's submissions on
behalf of Yahweh and who decides to make a contribution to the legal
process, to offer a rejoinder to vv. 1–5 which states Yahweh's case. The
questions which are raised in vv. 6–7 are those which are in the heads of
others who have been listening to Yahweh's self-defence as expounded
by Micah and betray the circumstance that the individual concerned
had been influenced by Hezekiah's reform of the cult (2 Kgs 18.4) and
had belonged to the circle of reformers associated with it.

The questions asked in vv. 6–7 amount to 'What remains for us to
do?' and their contents reveal a mind which is imprisoned in cultic
thought. Micah supplies the answer to the questions (v. 8) and he
corrects them. They are misdirected. Yahweh asks his worshippers for the
giving of themselves, for obedience to His will, not for the giving of their
possessions, not for the offering of sacrifices. The intention is not to
debunk the cult, but to establish an order of priorities (113). An ascend-
ing order of the quality or quantity of cultic offerings is not a substitute
for ethical or social commitments which make demands on the whole
man and are more difficult to fulfil than acts which demonstrate cultic
devoutness. The line which Rudolph draws between establishing an
order of priorities and adopting an anti-cultic attitude is a very fine one.

Rudolph's argument as a whole is strangely unreal and unconvincing.
He establishes the coherence of vv. 6–8, but he does not make a
satisfactory connection between vv. 6–8 and vv. 1–5 and his reconstruction leans heavily on the assumption that Micah is the speaker in vv. 1–5
(for Yahweh) and in v. 8. Why should an individual who has heard the
basis of Yahweh's self-defence (vv. 1–5), the *Heilsgeschichte*, ask such
elaborate questions about cultic sacrifices? The situation is like that
where a question is asked after a lecture which has no bearing on the
contents of the lecture. The questions in vv. 6–7 bear no relation to the
statement of Yahweh's case in vv. 1–5. This is explained by Rudolph as a
consequence of the questioner not having taken it in, because of his

one-track cultic mind. The argument is hard to swallow and a more
reasonable conclusion is that vv. 6–8 are separate from vv. 1–5 and that
they are not part of the legal process outlined in these verses. Hence vv.
1–5 contain only part of a legal suit, Yahweh's self-defence, and the
contribution to the ריב made by Israel does not appear.

If 6.1–8 is not in the first place a coherent unit (Wolff), how is this
unity achieved? Wolff's answer to the question assumes that 6.6–8 has
the form of a priestly instruction pressed into didactic service by a
Deuteronomistic author whose sympathies were akin to those of the
canonical prophets and who had an anti-cultic tendency (144). The
extant form of the compilation of 6.1–5 and 6.6–8 is probably post-
exilic, but it may have a pre-history reaching back to the early
Deuteronomic period. The foundation of the compilation is a wrong
exegesis of ומה הלאתיך (v. 3) which was mistakenly taken as a reference
to excessive cultic demands made by Yahweh and which triggered the
questions in vv. 6 and 7. Hence the didactic ploy is to make a point
(Yahweh will have mercy and not sacrifice) by coining questions which
are founded on a wrong exegesis of ומה הלאתיך. This gives the teacher
an opportunity to supply an answer which affirms that Yahweh does not
demand elaborate sacrifices, but the steadfastness of the whole man, his
ethical integrity and his social commitment (156). This is a narrow
explanation of how 6.1–5 and 6.6–8 came to be compiled. It is more
an elucidation of 6.6–7 than a demonstration of why 6.1–5 and 6.6–8
are intertwined and it does not reduce the distance between the setting
of the two passages, the one a law-suit and the other a didactic device. It
is an explanation of why 6.1–5 and 6.6.8 are adjacent rather than an
account of the manner in which they were compiled.

6.   With what shall I appear before Yahweh?
     How shall I worship God Most High?
     Shall I appear before him with whole-offerings,
     with calves of a year old?
7.   Will a thousand rams be acceptable to Yahweh,
     Or ten thousand rivers of oil?
     Shall I give my first-born son for my transgression,
     the fruit of my body for my own sin?
8.   You have been told what is good
     and what it is that Yahweh asks of you:
     only to do what is just, to love mercy
     and to walk modestly with your God.

vv. 9–16 YAHWEH THREATENS THE CITY

Sept. and Vulg. reproduce the syntax of MT, whereas Pesh. and Targ. connect יקרא with ותושיה יראה שמך (v. 9). Pesh. renders 'The voice of the Lord concerning the city, proclaiming teaching to those who fear his name.' יקרא is rendered as *mkrz*, ותושיה as *ywlpn'* and יראה is derived from ירא. MT שמך appears as *šmw* (שמו). Targ., 'The voice of the prophets of Yahweh concerning the city; they cry out and teach those who hear thy name.' 'The prophets of Yahweh' replaces 'Yahweh', יקרא is represented by a plural participle and is supplemented by another plural participle, ומלפיא 'and teach' for תושיה. Again יראה is represented as דחלין (יראי), 'those who fear', while שמך of MT is reproduced. Vulg. shows תושיה as *salus* 'safety' and derives יראה from ירא, 'and to whose who fear your name (*timentibus nomen tuum* = ליראי שמך) will be prosperity'. Sept. renders ותושיה as καὶ σώσει, 'and he will save those who fear his name' (φοβουμένους τὸ ὄνομα αὐτοῦ). Ibn Ezra explains ותושיה as ואיש תושיה and יראה as יראי, 'And men of wisdom are fearers of your name'. Sept., like Pesh., represents MT שמך as שמו. The versions all derive יראה from ירא. NEB with יראי שמו (Brockington, 256) attempts to fit תושיה into v. 9 ('Hark, the LORD, the fear of whose name brings success'), whereas REB makes תושיה יראי שמו into a parenthesis (the fear of his name brings success). Most scholars have identified it as a secondary fragment or gloss (Wellhausen, 26; Smith, 130; Weiser, 282; Robinson, 146; Rudolph, 114; Wolff, 159; Hillers, 80). Wolff translates, 'It is wisdom to fear your name' and vocalizes יראה (MT) as יִרְאָה, an infinitive construct of ירא (also Smith, 130; Ps. 86.11).

The closing words of v. 9 are obscure: שמעו מטה ומי יעדה, 'Hear, O tribe. and who has appointed it'. Rudolph (114) inserts מה before מטה (ממטה—haplography of מ) and translates 'Hear <of what kind> the rod is and who has appointed it'. He notices that מטה is masculine and assigns a 'neutral' sense to the feminine suffix of יעדה. *šbṭ* (Pesh.) has the same ambiguity as MT, but Sept. (φύλη) and Vulg. (*tribus*) render מטה as 'tribe'. Targ.'s extended paraphrase of מטה is also an indication that it has been taken as 'tribe': 'Hear, king, rulers and the remaining people of the land.' ומי יעדה is a minus in Targ., Vulg.'s rendering of it agrees with MT, while Pesh., does not represent the suffix and renders יעדה as *nshd* 'witness' (a verb) which may be derived from עוד (יעיד)

'to witness'. Sept., on the other hand, would seem to have derived יְעָדָהּ from עדה 'to adorn', though the sense of κοσμήσει might be 'order', 'arrange', in which case it would not be far removed from 'appoint' and would represent the vocalization of MT (יְעָדָהּ) *ex* יעד.

An emendation which has generally been accepted (Wellhausen, 145; Smith, 130; Weiser, 282; Robinson, 146; Wolff, 159; Hillers, 80), and for which the support of Sept. has been claimed, is שמעו מטה ומועד העיר, 'Hear, O tribe, and assembly of the city.' If it is thought that this emendation explains why MT has שמעו and not שְׁמַע, it should be noticed that Sept. (ἄκουε), Pesh. (šmʿ) and Targ. (שמעו) represent שמע. Rudolph, who does not adopt this emendation, argues that the two occurrences of עיר in a single verse is stylistically bad, but a more serious question about its text-critical basis in Sept. should be raised. It is held that עוד (v. 10) is a remnant of מועד which supplies the ד, the ו and the ע and πόλιν (Sept.) is then produced as evidence that the Greek translator read a Hebrew text which included עיר. It is doubtful whether πόλιν has such text-critical significance and, if מועד העיר is adopted, it should be admitted that the emendation has a larger element of conjecture than the account given allows. It is more probable that the Greek translator read a Hebrew text which was the same as MT (ומי יעדה) and that he was puzzled by the feminine suffix, since מטה required a masculine suffix. So he referred the feminine singular suffix to עיר (v. 9aα) and substituted πόλιν for the suffix. If there never was a Hebrew text which read מועד העיר, the *raison d'être* of the emendation has all but disappeared and it becomes no more than a complicated conjecture. In these circumstances ממטה for מטה (a haplography of מ; ממטה = מה מטה, Rudolph) is a simpler repair of MT which deserves consideration: 'Hear <what is the nature> of the tribe and who has appointed it.' The feminine suffix remains unexplained.

האש (v. 10) could be vocalized as הָאָשׁ, defective for הָאִישׁ 'the man', but it is vocalized as הָאֵשׁ 'the fire' by Sept. (πῦρ), Vulg. (*ignis*), Pesh. (nwr) and Ehrlich (287). It is elucidated by Targ. (דאית) as הֲיֵשׁ and also by Rashi, Kimchi, Ibn Ezra, KJV and Hillers (80; cf. 2 Sam. 14.19). The pointing of ה (הַ) lends weight to the conclusion that it is an interrogative particle. The sense requires that בית should be taken as בבית and 'in the house' appears in Pesh. (bbyth dʿwlʾ), Wellhausen (26) and RSV. The emendation of בית to בבית is proposed by Hillers (81;

cf. Ehrlich, 287—בית an accusative of location). A different resolution of האשׁ is its emendation to האשׁה 'Can I forget?' or האשׂא 'Can I forgive?' Wellhausen (145), Smith (130), Weiser (282), Robinson (146), NEB (Brockington, 256), Rudolph (114) and Wolff (159) prefer האשׁה; REB ('forgive') prefers האשׂא. בית is emended to בת in order to restore the parallelism of v. 10: 'Can I forget (forgive) the false measure ... the accursed, short bushel?' בת is a measure of liquids איפה of dry commod-ities. This emendation is accepted by NEB (Brockington, 256) after Duhm (1911, 90), REB, Rudolph (115), Wolff (160) and אצרות רשׁע is deleted as an addition. According to Rudolph it is a consequence of the corruption of בת to בית and the uncertainty about what it was that made the house of the godless so wicked. אצרות רשׁע supplies the answer to the query. Hence the insertion of אצרות רשׁע is associated with the alteration of בת רשׁע to בית רשׁע (NEB [Brockington, 256], REB; Wolff, 160). Wellhausen (26), Weiser (282), Robinson (146) and Hillers (80) retain MT (בית רשׁע אצרות רשׁע).

MT האזכה (v. 11) 'Can I be innocent?' gives poor sense (Yahweh is the speaker) and it has been repaired in different ways. Targ. substitutes היזכון for האזכה, 'Can they be declared innocent?' Sept. (δικαιωθήσεται) and Pesh. (nzddqwn; Ithpael) represent האזכה as a third person passive, the one singular and the other plural. Vulg. *Numquid iustificabo* would appear to have vocalized האזכה as הַאֲזַכֶּה (Piel) and this is the emendation which is commonly adopted, 'Can I justify?' or 'Can I declare innocent?' (Weiser, 282; Robinson, 148; Rudolph, 116; Wolff, 160; Hillers, 81; Smith, 130—האזכהו). Ehrlich (287) proposes התזכה 'Can you be innocent?' כיס אבני מרמה 'a bag of false weights' is translated literally by Sept., Vulg. and Targ., while Targ. renders אבני מרמה as מתקלין רברבין ודעדקין, 'weights which are diverse (?) and in smithereens', which might be understood as 'weights which are not standard and from which pieces have been chipped off.' Rudolph (116) has supposed that Targ. is an allusion to Deut. 25.13, 'You must not have unequal weights in your bag, one over-weight and the other under-weight.' Kimchi also refers to Deut. 25.13 and comments that v. 11 is directed against those who keep weights of different value and diverging from the norm in the same bag: 'When he buys, he takes too much weight and when he sells, he gives under-weight.' Kimchi continues: 'You are not to have in your bag weights of different value.'

In order to supply an antecedent for אשר (v. 12) the verse-order 9, 12, 10, 11 is adopted (Smith, 129; Weiser, 282; Robinson, 146; Hillers, 80). Wellhausen (145) and Ehrlich (287) find the antecedent in v. 9, but do not propose an alteration of the verse-order. Weiser reinforces the order 9, 12, 10, 11 by introducing an exegetical consideration: v. 12 states the indictment in general terms and it is made more specific in v. 10 and v. 11. A counter-argument supporting the order of MT (Wolff, 168f.) is that v. 10 and v. 11 deal with particular iniquities and that v. 12 is an enlarging and generalizing of the indictment: wealth is used to abet lawlessness with violence (חמס) and lies are its currency. The antecedent of אשר is then מועד העיר (if MT is emended) or the feminine suffix of יעדה, if MT is retained (Rudolph, 114). Sept., with ἐξ᾽ ὧν for אשר, and Vulg., with in quibus, connect v. 12 with v. 11. Pesh. represents אשר by ו and Targ. by ד. ולשונם רמיה בפיהם, 'and they speak with deceitful tongues', is deleted as an addition from Ps. 120.2f. (Weiser, 282; Robinson, 146; Wolff, 160) and MT is retained by Wellhausen (26), Rudolph (116) and Hillers (80)—also by NEB and REB. Sept. ὑψώθητι for רמיה, 'their tongues will be exalted (with pride) in their mouths', is either a derivation of רמיה from רום (Wolff, 160) or a misreading of רמיה as רמה ex רום (Rudolph, 116).

MT החליתי הכותך (v. 13) is rendered by REB as 'But now I shall inflict severe punishment on you' and Rashi's comment is 'I shall injure you, so that you are incurably sick'. Kimchi and Ibn Ezra attach the sense 'oppress' to החליתי and Ibn Ezra paraphrases v. 13, 'I shall oppress you at a time when you will be chastised and reduced to ruin.' Sept. (ἄρξομαι), Vulg. (coepi) and Pesh. ('śr̂) represent החלותי 'begin' and this is the emendation adopted by Wellhausen (145), Smith (131), Ehrlich (288), Weiser (282), Robinson (146), Rudolph (116) and Wolff (160). It appears in RSV, while KJV, NEB, REB and Hillers (80) retain MT. Ehrlich (288) emends השמם to השמד 'destroy'.

The versions render וישחך בקרבך (v. 14) variously. Sept. σκοτάσει ἐν σοί, 'it will be dark in you' is perhaps accounted for by a metathesis of ש and ח (יחשך, so Rudolph, 116; Wolff, 161) and Vulg. humiliatio tua, 'your abjectness', appears in Kimchi, 'submission will be in you'. Pesh. represents וישחך בקרבך by wbrî thwh bgwy, 'and dysentery (diarrhoea) will be within you' and Targ. by 'and you will have belly-ache'. So Wolff (161), but וישחך בקרבך is deleted by him as an addition along with ואשר ... אתן). Wellhausen (26, 145) and Hillers

(81) also translate יֶשַׁח as 'belly-ache', 'colic'. Rashi comments similarly, 'The food which you eat will mix with a curse in the bowels.' Kimchi and Ibn Ezra suppose that the sense of וְיֶשְׁחֲךָ בְּקִרְבֶּךָ is 'and your pride will be overturned' and Kimchi elucidates this as a reference to submission to an enemy and exile.

BDB (445) does not offer any philology for יֶשַׁח, but remarks that the sense 'hunger' is conjectured from the context ('You will eat and not be satisfied'). In that case וְיֶשְׁחֲךָ בְּקִרְבֶּךָ means 'and you will have pangs of hunger' or the like. This guess at the sense of יֶשַׁח is dismissed by Pope (1964, 270); it is given credence by Wolff (161) who, however, does not adopt it. It is accepted by Rudolph (116) with dubious philological support: Arabic *wḫš* becomes *wšḫ* by metathesis. It is not clear why Rudolph prefers *wḫš* to Arabic *wsḫ* and the consequence is that he has to postulate a metathesis and ends up with an imperfect equation: Arabic *wḫš* should produce Hebrew יֶשַׁח. Smith (133) makes a different guess at the meaning of וְיֶשְׁחֲךָ and supposes that it is a synonym of חֶטְאָךְ, 'your transgressions' and 'your sins'.

Another proposal is that יֶשַׁח is a reference to 'blockage of the bowels' or 'constipation'. יֶשַׁח 'excrement' is given by KB³ (426) and this agrees with Ehrman (1959, 156) and G. R. Driver (*JSS*, 1965, 114). Ehrman translates וְיֶשְׁחֲךָ בְּקִרְבֶּךָ as 'and your wastes will be locked up within you' and Driver glosses יֶשַׁח as *faeces*. The Arabic form is *wasḫu* 'dirt', 'filth', 'excrement'. Driver remarks that Pesh. ʾbrî 'dysentery' 'approximately suggests 'constipation'. It certainly points to trouble in the same area, but it is a different kind of affliction. NEB (REB) 'Your food shall be heavy on your stomach' is a polite rendering of 'You will be constipated'. This conjecture does not lack coherence because 'constipation' appears as a consequence of וְלֹא תִשְׂבָּע which is not necessarily to be followed by a reference to 'hunger'. The sense of וְלֹא תִשְׂבָּע may not be adequately given by 'and your appetite is not satisfied' and its nuance may be the feeling of well-being induced by a good meal. In that case it is the absence of this which is the point of וְיֶשְׁחֲךָ בְּקִרְבֶּךָ (NEB, 'Your food shall lie heavy on your stomach').

An appeal to the same Arabic word (*wasḫu* 'dirt', 'filth') is developed in a different way by Ehrlich (288). טִפָּה סְרוּחָה 'putrid drop' refers to semen at Pirqe Aboth 3.1 and Ehrlich suggests that a similar comtemptuous allusion is present in יֶשְׁחֲךָ 'your filth' = 'your semen' at Mic. 6.14. In this he is followed by Pope (1964, 270). The conjecture

requires the emendation of בקרבך to בקרבה and of ותסג to תסג (= תשׂג
ex נשׂג), 'Your semen reaches her'. Ehrlich (288) comments: תסג is third
person feminine agreeing with the suffix of בקרבה. The Israelite wife
will take up the semen and become pregnant, but she will not bear a
child' (ולא תפליט). This explanation of ותסג ולא תפליט appears in Ibn
Janah (A. Neubauer, 1875, 462). ותסג is derived from נשׂג and *tdrk*
'overtake' is glossed as *t'lq* 'be pregnant'. ולא תפליט is a reference to a
miscarriage. If the verse is about pregnancy and miscarriage, the person
referred to is presumably a woman and in that circumstance the third
person feminine is appropriate and the second person masculine
inappropriate, but the suffixes of וישׂחך בצרבך are masculine. A
reconciliation can be effected only by assuming an address to a male and
by supplying 'your wife' as the subject of תסג and חפליט (twice). The
other way out of the difficulty is to introduce the wife earlier in the verse
by emending בקרבך to בקרבה (Ehrlich). A male is then referred to.
The emendation of וישׂחך to ויש כח is proposed by Weiser (282) and
Robinson (148). If this is accompanied by the emendation of ותסג
to תסגר, it produces a result similar to that of Ehrlich, provided that
תסגר, תפליט and תפלט are parsed as third feminine singular: 'And
though you have procreative power, your wife's womb will be shut and
she will not bear a child. Any child that she bears I shall give to the
sword.'

ותסג is derived from סוג by Sept. (καὶ ἐκνεύσει 'remove') and from
נשׂג (נסג) by Vulg. (*et apprehendes*), Pesh (*wtdrk*), Targ. (ותדביק),
Kimchi, Ibn Ezra, Ehrlich (288) and Hillers (81). Wellhausen (26)
leaves a blank in his translation on the ground that ותסג is obscure
(145). It is thought to be a Hiphil of סוג 'remove' by Smith (131),
Rudolph (117) and Wolff (161). The elucidation of תפליט as 'save'
goes in tandem with the derivation of ותסג from סוג. תפליט 'save' is
represented by Sept. (διασωθῇς), Vulg. (*salvabis*), Pesh. (*tpṣ*) and Targ.
(תשׁיזיב), Wellhausen (26), Weiser (282), Robinson (148, Rudolph
(114) and Wolff (159). Rashi comments, 'Your enemies will lead your
sons and daughters captive and you will not save them.'

There is a like correspondence between ותסג or תסג (Ehrlich) *ex* נשׂג
and תפליט 'give birth' (cf. Job. 21.10, used of a cow calving; Ehrlich,
288). NEB, 'You will come to labour, but not bring forth.' Kimchi
comments, 'The woman will become pregnant and not bear a child. It
will die in her womb.' The Hiphil of נסג (= נשׂג) is given the sense

'become pregnant' (so Ibn Janah; cf. Ibn Ezra, 'become pregnant, but not
bear a child). Vulg. Pesh., Targ. and Hillers (80) are exceptions to this
trend, since they derive תסג from נשג and attach the sense 'save' to הפליט:
'You shall overtake something, but not carry it off' (Hillers).

The change from second person masculine to third person feminine
which is assumed by the 'will be pregnant and give birth' interpretation
is very difficult and the best that can be done is to accept the remove/
save sequence. Rudolph (117) inserts טף 'infant' after הפליט and has
Frauen und Kinder in his translation: 'When you evacuate wives and
children, you will not make them secure.' The presence of 'wives and'
and the word-order (טף inserted after הפליט and not after ותסג) makes
this a free translation. We should be content with 'Though you remove
(them from harm's way), you will not save (them) and those whom you
save I shall give to the sword.'

Of תירוש (v. 15) Köhler (1928, 219) remarks that it has a recognizably
Canaanite etymology and Brown (1969, 169) notices that it is attested in
Phoenician, while יין is not attested. The conclusion which both draw is
that יין and תירוש are synonyms, the one of Hebrew origin and the other
Canaanite; that תירוש is not unfermented wine and that where יין and
תירוש occur in the same verse (Mic. 6.15; Hos. 4.11), they are doublets.
Hence (Köhler, 1928, 219; KB³, 421; Rudolph, 117) ותירוש should be
emended to ותירש, second person singular Qal imperfect *ex* II ירש 'to
tread (grapes)'. This improves the balance of the first and second stichs of
v. 15b: תדרך זית ולא תסוך שמן matches ותירש ולא תשתה יין, 'You will
press the olives, but not anoint yourself with oil; you will tread grapes,
but not drink the wine' (RSV, NEB, REB). Sept. represents only one
occurrence of 'wine' (καὶ οἶνον καὶ οὐ μὴ πίητε); Vulg. represents both
תירוש (*mustum*) and יין (*vinum*) as do KJV, Wellhausen (27), Smith
(131), Weiser (282), Robinson (148), Wolff (159) and Hillers (80).
Wellhausen, Weiser, Wolff and Hillers acknowledge the need of a
second verb in their translations, but they do not identify it with
תירש (תירוש). Pesh. supplies a second verb which might represent ותירש,
though it is the same verb as is used for תדרך (*tᵉṣwr* 'to trample', 'to
crush'). Pesh. has a different word-order from MT in respect of יין (ḥmrʾ):
wtᵉṣwr ḥmrʾ wlʾ tšt. Targ., with two different verbs (ותעצר; תבדיר), and
with the word-order of MT, supports the emendation of תירוש to ותירש,
'You will press the olives but not anoint yourself with oil; you will tread
the grapes (ענבין) but not drink the wine.'

At v. 16 Sept. (ἐφύλαξας), Vulg. (*custodisti*) and Pesh. (*'l dntrt*) represent ותשמר which is adopted by Wellhausen (27, 145), Ehrlich (288; third feminine singular), Smith (131), Weiser (282), Wolff (161), NEB (Brockington, 256), REB and Hillers (81) who follows Ehrlich. Rudolph (117) emends וישתמר (MT) to ותשמרו with Targ. (על דנטרתון). Wolff's explanation of the corruption of וישתמר to ותשמר assumes a metathesis of שׁ and ת and does not account for the absence of י. Rudolph (117) proposes that ותשמרו has been corrupted to ישתמר and has become a gloss on v. 16a, 'one should be on one's guard against the Samaritans'. Wolff (also Robinson, 148) supposes that v. 16 is a secondary addition (see further below).

ותלכו (second person plural) is reproduced by Sept. (ἐπορεύθητε), Pesh. (*whlktwn*) and Targ. (והליכתון). Vulg. *et ambulasti* represents ותלך and is followed by Wellhausen (145), Weiser (282), Robinson (148) and Ehrlich (288: third person feminine—also Hillers, 81). Rudolph (114) and Wolff (159) retain MT which is supported by Sept., Pesh. and Targ. In respect of אתך and וישביה Sept. Vulg. and Targ. represent MT, whereas Pesh. represents תי אתה (*yhbth*). This is an easier emendation of MT than the change of וישביה to וישביך, though Wellhausen (27; cf. 145) has shown *deine Bewohner* in his translation. וישביך is preferred by Weiser (282), Robinson (148), Wolff (161), NEB and REB. Smith (131) and Rudolph (117) retain MT. Ehrlich (288; Hillers, 81) emends אתך to אתה, ותלכו to ותלך, תשאו to תשא and takes all the verbs in v. 16 as feminine singular: 'She (Jerusalem) has kept the the statutes of Omri and all the practices of the house of Ahab. She has adopted their policies, so that I shall give her over to ruin and her citizens will be objects of horror and she shall bear the scorn of the nations (עמים = Sept. λαῶν; MT עמי). Vulg. (*populi mei*), Pesh. (*d'my*), Targ. (עמי) and Hillers (81) follow MT. Wellhausen (145), Smith (131), Ehrlich (288), Robinson (148), Rudolph (117), Wolff (161), NEB (Brockington, 256) and REB adopt עמים.

וישתמר should be emended to ותשמרו (Targ.), אתך to אתה and all traces of grammatical incongruence are removed: 'You kept the statutes of Omri and all the practices of the house of Ahab. You adopted their policies, so that I shall give it (Jerusalem) over to ruin and its citizens will be objects of horror. You will bear the scorn of nations.' Smith (135) deletes ותלכו במעצותם and וחרפת עמי תשאו as expansions. תשאו (MT) is represented by Sept. (λήψεσθε), Vulg. (*portabitis*), Pesh.

(*tqblwn*), Targ. (תקבלון), Wellhausen (27), Weiser (282), Rudolph (117), Wolff (161). Robinson (148) emends תשאו to תשא. Rudolph and Wolff should be followed in leaving the verbs in v. 16 (MT) unchanged (apart from וישתמר). Rudolph's emendation of וישתמר to ותשמרו (Targ.) should be preferred to ותשמר, because it has the effect of disposing entirely of the grammatical incongruence and making all the verbs second person plural. The only other emendation which is needed is the change of אתך to אתה.

There is general agreement that 6.9–16 does not continue 6.1–8 (Weiser, 282; Wolff, 161; Hillers, 81). Rudolph (118) raises the question of the intention of the redactor who joined 6.1–8 with 6.9–16. Why did he associate these disparate verses? The answer is that the presence of שמעו at v. 2 and v. 9 exerted an influence and, more intrinsically, the distance between the requirements of Yahweh at v. 8 and the behaviour described in vv. 11–12 were deliberately underlined. The second part of the argument has weight only if it is assumed that the first unit in the chapter is 6.1–8 and not 6.1–5 (as I have maintained; also Smith, 129; Robinson, 146).

A question arises whether the scope of the final section of the chapter is 6.9–16 (Smith, 129f.; Weiser, 284; Rudolph, 119f.) or 6.9–15 (Robinson, 148; Wolff, 162f.). This may be taken together with the evidence which has been adduced for the secondary character of parts of other verses in 6.9–15 (vv. 9, 12, 14). The relation of these pieces to v. 16 is the particular interest of Wolff (163f.) who classes them with v. 16 as indications of the secondary editing of 6.9–15. He thus connects his discussion with a consideration of the authorship of 6.9–16 which he denies to Micah, though he admits the presence in these verses of old Micaianic material, the rhetorical questions (vv. 10–11) and the 'futility curses' (vv. 14–15). The historical setting of 6.9–16 is, however, not in the eighth century B.C. Chapter 6.9–16, without the secondary editing, reflects conditions prevailing around the time of the fall of Jerusalem (587 B.C.) and editorial additions were made c. 550 which show Deuteronomistic traits (9aβ, 12aα, 12b, 13aα, 14bβ, 16).

Verse 9aβ is a parenthesis (161f.) which takes up the previous mention of the divine name (יהוה) and which supplies a ground for attentiveness to the קול יהוה. It features wisdom vocabulary (תושיה) which is a mark of lateness, 'It is wisdom to fear thy name' (159). 9aα (161f.) may be a literary embellishment, establishing that Yahweh is the one who makes the summons (יקרא) and that Jerusalem is the city addressed (העיר). On the naming of Jerusalem as העיר Wolff (163) remarks that from the time of Jeremiah and Ezekiel it was the title used particularly of Jerusalem (Jer. 6.6; 8.16; 17.24f.; Ezek. 4.3; 5.2; 7.15). Verse 12b is an addition of the same kind as v. 9aβ: it is an elaboration which paints the lily and its vocabulary is that of the wisdom literature. Verse 14bβ (Wolff, 163) disturbs the series of futility curses in vv. 14–15 and its vocabulary (נתן לחרב) is Deuteronomistic (Jer. 15.9). These stereotypes are also a feature of v. 16 (163): לשמה ולשרקה (Jer. 19.8; 25.9); לשמה לרקרה (25.18); Ezek. 36.15, וחרפת עמים לא תשאי (cf. Mic. 6.16β). אשר (v. 12aα) with the force of יען אשר or יען and continued by וגם אני (v. 13) appears in Jer. 13.25b–26 (cf. Ezek. 16.43, יען אשר; Ezek. 20.24–25, יען). As a method of connecting indictment and punishment it points to a date around 600 B.C. (164). This is not only an indication of late lexicography (אשר = 'because') and style, since אשר is not then a relative particle, so that there is no case for proposing that the verse-order of MT should be altered, that אשר is too distant from its antecedent in v. 9. Wolff (161; cf. Smith, 131–136) remarks that the *Grundtext* of 6.9–15 consists of indictment (vv. 10–12*) and threat (vv. 13–15*); that the recurrence of indictment at v. 16 after the transition to threat at vv. 13–15 is evidence of the secondary status of v. 16 (163).

Robinson (148) remarks that the indictment and threat of 6.9–15 might well be traced to a pre-exilic prophet and that the content does not preclude Micah from being the author. His conclusion, however, is that this similarity to pre-exilic prophecy is to be accounted for by the circumstance that the author was a late imitator of Amos and that this is evident from the vocabulary (cf. Wolff, above). He describes v. 16 as a fragment added by a collector. Smith (129f.) who is more non-committal on authorship, holds that 6.9–16 could be assigned to any period of Israelite history subsequent to the reign of Ahab, either to the time of Micah or to the last days of pre-exilic Judah. The tradition which claims the passage for Micah (so Smith) cannot be proved wrong and the question remains open.

Weiser (282) holds that the text of 6.9–16 is not well preserved and that it has been secondarily expanded, but that Micah could well be the author. The reference to the decrees of Omri and the practices of Ahab (v. 16) suggest a historical setting in the reign of Ahab (742–725 B.C.)

or that of Manasseh (696–642 B.C.). This conclusion stems from
Weiser's persuasion (284) that Omri and Ahab are condemned both for
their idolatry and their persecution of the prophets and that v. 16 is
directed by Micah against those in Jerusalem who are godless and are
tempted by the power which their wealth confers on them to employ
dishonest trading practices and to engage in lawless and violent
infringements of justice. Rudolph (119f.) connects the reference in v.
16 not with the idolatrous practices of Omri and Ahab but with their
persecution of the prophets, especially the judicial murder of Naboth by
Ahab. He admits that v. 16 may originally have been separate from vv.
9–15 and may have been incorporated in vv. 9–16 by Micah. Before
that incorporation v. 16 gave voice to the behaviour of Samaritan kings,
both religious and social, while Micah had in mind particularly the
nefarious policies of Ahab and his murder of Naboth.

Rudolph (120) robustly defends the integrity of 6.9–16 and assigns it
to Micah, though he acknowledges that the moment of history which it
reflects cannot be precisely determined. He repulses Robinson's statement that the author was a late imitator of Amos and asserts that it has
no foundation. The connections with Amos are to be explained by the
similarities of the social misery which they confronted and he is not
impressed by the evidences of the lateness of language which are alleged.
Wolff (171f.) associates v. 16 with the other Deuteronomistic additions
of vv. 9–15. The wickedness of Omri and his idolatry are mentioned in
1 Kgs 16.23–28 and it is recorded in 2 Kgs 8.26 (2 Chr. 22.2) that he
was the grandfather of Athaliah (Ahab's daughter) who became notori-
ous in Jerusalem (2 Kgs 11.1–3) as Joram's queen (2 Kgs 8.18). His
appearance in v. 16 may be connected with the circumstance that he
was founder of Samaria which acquires prominence in the Deuteronomistic historical literature, in connection with the scandalous behaviour
of Manasseh as the wicked city which presages the fall of Jerusalem (2
Kgs 21.13). Ahab appears frequently in the same literature. At 2 Kgs
21.3 the idolatry of Manasseh is compared with that of Ahab and the
main line of thought which engages the Deuteronomists in v. 16 is that
Jerusalem is imitating the wickedness of Samaria and will suffer the
same destruction. The name of Ahab perhaps receives a particular
mention with reference to the Naboth narrative.

The content of the threat element of 6.9–15 is stated by scholars in
different ways. Smith (133) holds that the chastisement (הכותך) of v. 13

is administered by a hostile invader and that the laying waste (השמם)
which ensues is a consequence of the ravages of war. With Weiser (282)
and Robinson there is a special relation between their discernment of
conditions of war and the emendations which they adopt at v. 14 (with
a change of verse-order): ויש כח בקרבך ותסר ולא תפליט, is thought to
refer to a counter-attack which peters out (ותסר) and does not have a
victorious outcome (ולא תפליט). There are reinforcements, stocks of
arms, which can be brought into play (ויש כח בקרבך), but the attack
which is launched will turn into a retreat (ותסר) and the noose will
tighten.

Wolff (164) supposes that the threat of the imminent fall of
Jerusalem, conveyed by a Deuteronomistic formula (אשר ... וגם אני), is
the background of vv.12–13 and that הכותך is a reference to this dismal
prospect. השמם (v. 13), however, refers to the trail of wreckage left
behind by an invading army and 'chastisement' includes both failures of
harvests and the destruction caused by military operations (169).
Rudolph (119) is influenced by the mention of the 'sword' (v. 14) and
holds that v. 14a (eating and not being nourished), 15a (sowing and not
reaping) and 15b (pressing olives and not having the use of the oil;
treading grapes and not drinking the wine), along with 14b (the
impossibility of ensuring the safety of wife and children), are not the
results of disorders of nature but are envisaged as the consequences of
war.

Rudolph's reliance on the mention of the sword (v. 14) in establishing the link between the assertions of futility (vv. 14–15) and war needs
further investigation. It is not clear why Weiser (13, 14b, 15, 14a; 282)
and Robinson (13, 14b, 14a, 15; 148) alter the verse-order of MT, but
it is presumably because they suppose that it improves the coherence of
the series of the 'futility-clauses'. Wolff's opinion (161, 162f.) that this
end is achieved by deleting ואשר ... אתן (v. 14) has more point. It
disturbs the formal solidity of the other 'futility-clauses' and has the
appearance of a secondary elaboration of ולא תפליט. The series then has
five items, located in vv. 14–15: (a) eating but not being satisfied (b)
removing but not saving (c) sowing but not reaping (d) pressing olives
but not having the use of the oil (e) treading grapes but not drinking the
wine. The conclusion of Rudolph that (b), (c), (d), and (e) are the
consequences of dislocations caused by military operations is seriously
weakened if אשר ... אתן is deleted from v. 14. Wolff's correlation of

threat with punishment, his demonstration that the punishment matches the crime, is overdone and is too nice to be convincing (173). Its neatness is excessive, and the formulations of futility have a proverbial character, an openness of reference, which makes it inappropriate to link them precisely to the crimes committed in the way that he does. They do not have this degree of exactness and do not aim to be specific. They outline activity which encounters unexpected frustrations, plans which go wrong, results which are not obtained, disasters which are round the corner and, in general, they prescribe as a punishment a state of affairs which reduces all human effort to futility, which introduces privations and misery.

9. The voice of Yahweh calls out to the city:
    [It brings success to fear[1] your name][2]
    Hear what is the nature[3] of the tribe
        and who has ordered it.
10. Shall I continue to forgive[4] the falsified measure[5], the accursed short
        bushel[6]?
11. Shall I declare the innocence[7] of those who use untrue scales
    and have a bag of misleading weights?
12. Because[8] the wealthy men in the city are full of violence
    and its inhabitants utter lies,
    [and have deceitful tongues in their mouths][2]

13. I shall begin[9] to chastise you
    and lay you waste for your sins.
14. You will eat but not feel well fed;
    [you will suffer from constipation][2]
    You will remove (from danger) but not save.
    [And those whom you save I shall give to the sword][2]
15. You will sow but not reap; You will press olives but not be anointed
        with oil;
    You will tread[10] (grapes) but not drink the wine.

[1]Reading יִרְאָה.
[2]Secondary additions to the text.
[3]Reading מה מטה = ממטה.
[4]Reading הַאִשָּׂא.
[5]Reading בת רשע.
[6]Deleting אצרות רשע.
[7]Reading אֲזַכֶּה.
[8]יען אשר = אשר.
[9]Reading הַחִלּוֹתִי.
[10]Reading וְתִירָשׁ.

16. [You observe[11] the decrees of Omri
and all the practices of the house of Ahab.
You have conformed to their policies,
so that I shall give Jerusalem[12] over to ruin;
its citizens will be objects of horror
and will endure the jeers of the nations[13]][2]

[11]Reading ותשמרו.
[12]Reading אֹתָה.
[13]Reading עמים.

CHAPTER 7

vv. 1–7 MORAL AND SOCIAL COLLAPSE

Sept. ὡς συνάγων (v. 1) vocalizes כאספי as כְּאֹסֵף 'a gatherer' and אספי has been explained as a Qal participle with *yodh compaginis* (Hillers, 83; cf Rudolph, 121; Wolff, 174) or it has been emended to כאסף (Robinson, 148). Vulg., which renders כאספי as *qui colligit*, follows Sept. συνάγων, while Pesh. *lwṭ* 'gleanings' vocalizes כאספי as כְּאָסְפֵּי (MT), 'like gatherings' (also Rashi) and takes אספי and עללת (*buʾi*) as synonyms (so Ehrlich, 289; Smith, 139; Wolff, 174). Weiser (284), Robinson (148) and Hillers (83), on the other hand, emend כעללת to כעולל in order to effect the match 'gatherer' and 'gleaner'. 'Like gatherings of the harvest, like gleanings (Sept. ἐπιφυλλίδα, small grapes left for the gleaners) of the vintage' should be adopted (Pesh., Wolff) and 'gatherings' has the nuance of 'left-overs'. קיץ is thought by Sept. to refer to the grain harvest (καλάμην ἐν ἀμήτῳ, 'as one gathering a stalk at harvest-time'). Pesh. reproduces קיץ and like Sept. renders בציר with 'vintage' (ἐν τρυγήτῳ; *dqṭp*). Vulg. telescopes MT, 'for I am as one who collects in autumn clusters of grapes'. Targ. interprets the imagery: The prophet says, 'Woe is me for I was as at the end of the time of good men, the period when men of integrity perished from the land!'. Rashi comments, 'Woe is me for I have been appointed a prophet in this time, an unrighteous generation!' Ibn Ezra explains כאספי קיץ as 'like the left-overs of the harvest which the poor gather from the fruit that remains.' Ibn Ezra, like Targ. and Rashi, concludes that the imagery is a משל and Kimchi similarly comments, 'The prophet laments the godlessness and wickedness of the people ... There remains to me a word which is like the gleanings of the harvest, like what is left after the fruits have been gathered in or like what remains after the vintage is over.' Hence Ibn Ezra and Kimchi think in terms of the fruit harvest, vines and figs (Rashi) rather than the grain-harvest and the fruit harvest (Sept.). The exegesis of modern scholars tends to agree with this (Wellhausen, 27; Ehrlich, 289; Smith, 139; Robinson, 149; Rudolph, 120f.; Wolff, 174; Hillers, 83). Wolff (178) supposes that קיץ refers to the harvesting of the 'most important summer fruit'—the fig.

The gleanings from the vines and the figs yield nothing, not a grape nor a fig is to be had, nothing to relieve hunger when the desire to eat is strong. בכורה אותה נפשי is elucidated grammatically by equating נפשי with 'I' and assuming a relative clause with an implicit אשר (Rudolph, 121; Wolff, 175). אין is carried over from the first part of the verse, 'not an early fig which I would dearly love' (Wellhausen, 27; Weiser, 284; Robinson, 148; Rudolph, 121; Wolff, 174). Kimchi comments, 'I cannot find a single cluster of grapes on the vines to eat which has not been plucked, as if to say, there is not a single good or upright man from whose deeds I may learn.' On בכורה אותה נפשי he remarks, 'If there are no longer any good and upright men, I desire that one would arise now from this generation who would learn the ways of the good and upright. He is to be likened to an early fig.'

Vulg. comes nearest among the versions to a satisfactory rendering of בכורה אותה נפשי, but it does not parse אותה נפשי as a relative clause: *Praecoquas ficus desidaverit anima mea*, 'I have a great desire to taste baked figs.' Alone among the versions it translates בכורה as 'fig' Pesh. *wlbkrî rgt npšy*, 'and I desire to eat first-fruits'. Targ. interprets the משל, 'There are no men who are concerned with doing good deeds to good men.' חמידת נפשי is then stranded, 'my soul desires'. The most troublesome of the versions is Sept. which makes בכורה a continuation of οὐχ ... τοῦ φαγεῖν and represents it by τὰ πρωτόγονα, 'the first-born', presumably 'the first-fruits', though this sense does not appear in Liddell and Scott, 1949, 1545). 'There is no cluster (of grapes) to eat the first-fruits' makes poor sense and this is followed by οἴμοι ψυχή 'Alas! O soul'. ψυχή is a rendering of נפשי and οἴμοι has been accounted for (Rudolph, 121) as a rendering of אוי (MT אותה).

Verse 2–4a is an interpretation of the metaphorical language of v. 1 (Weiser, 285; Robinson, 149; Rudolph, 124; Wolff, 179; Hillers, 85). The scavenging of the last remnants of the harvest which yields little or nothing is a משל for the demise of the good and upright man, for the disappearance of integrity and honesty. A new generation, malevolent and vicious, has replaced them, who lay ambushes for their fellows and for whom human life is cheap. If violence serves their ends, they do not hesitate to employ it and their relationsip with others is that of hunters to the hunted: they set traps for men as they would for animals. Sept.[B] translates חסיד as εὐσέβης 'pious' and Ziegler (223) prefers εὐλάβης which has the same sense and is attested by Sept.[AQ]. Rudolph (121) supposes that εὐσέβης is avoided because of its associations with Hellenistic thought. δικάζονται may arise from a misreading of יארבו as יריבו (Hillers, 83f.) or it may be an interpretation of 'laying a bloody ambush' and 'hunting a prey' in terms of a fierce thirst for litigation (Rudolph, 122; Wolff, 175).

Vulg., Pesh. and Targ. represent יארבו and לדמים is a minus in Pesh., where יארבו is rendered by km'n kmnyn 'lay ambushes'. יצודו חרם is rendered by Sept. as ἐκθλίβουσιν ἐκθλιβῇ 'they oppress mercilessly' which is probably an exegesis of יצודו חרם. Rudolph (122) and Wolff (175) limit the element of interpretation to חרם = ἐκθλιβῇ and suppose that ἐκθλίβουσιν is a misreading of יצודו as יצורו. Vulg. (ad mortem venatur), Pesh. (l'bdn'), Targ. (לגמירא) have taken חרם as 'ban', 'destruction', rather than 'net' and have not preserved the figure of the hunter and the net. It is the end of the ambush which they describe, 'death and destruction' rather than the hunting of men as if they were animals (Wolff, 179). חרם is translated as 'net' by Rashi, Kimchi, Ibn Ezra, Wellhausen (27), Smith (139) and Hillers (83). It is deleted by Robinson (148) on metrical grounds (cf. Hillers, 84). Wolff (174) zu Tode follows Vulg., Pesh. and Targ. in identifying חרם with 'destruction' Kimchi comments, 'Each man hunts his brother to slay him as a fowler traps birds with his net.' The hunting metaphor should be maintained, the ambush and the trap, and חרם should be translated 'net'. NEB, 'All lie in wait to do murder, each man drives his own kinsman like a hunter into the net.'

Sept. ἐπὶ τὸ κακόν represents MT על הרע (v. 3) and translates הרע as a noun. τὰς χεῖρας αὐτῶν represents כפיהם (MT כפים) and ἑτοιμάζουσιν represents היטיבו (MT להיטיב). Sept. 'Concerning evil they prepare their hands' makes better sense than MT and has influenced the emendations which have been proposed. Vulg. manuum suarum also represents כפיהם and dicunt bonum is perhaps a rendering of היטיבו, 'they call good'. Malum manuum suarum does not show על and the sense of the line is poor, 'They speak good of their evil hands'. Pesh. wydyhwn mtybn lbyšt wl' mṭ'byn, 'and they make their hands more skilful to do evil, not to do good'. על הרע is rendered as lbyšt, כפים as כפיהם (also Sept. and Vulg.) and MT is filled out with wl' mṭ'byn. Targ.'s free translation has a similar sense to Pesh., 'To do evil with their hands is not good'. On על הרע להיטיב Kimchi comments: 'They devote their knowledge to the evil which is at their disposal so as to improve and reinforce it. The

reference is to taking bribes in order to pervert justice.' Wellhausen (146)
remarks that MT is corrupt and he adopts the Hebrew text represented
by Sept., על הרע כפיהם היטיבו (see his translation, 27). Ehrlich (289)
urges that MT can stand and that the meaning is akin to that of
John 3.19, 'men loved darkness rather than light because their deeds
were evil'. They varnish evil so that it has a beneficent appearance.
Smith (139) follows Wellhausen closely, but he emends על הרע
to להרע (infinitive construct Hiphil of רעע), 'They have prepared
their hands to do evil' (also Robinson, 148; Wolff, 175; Hillers, 84).
Rudolph (122) vocalizes חרם (v. 2) as חֹרֵם, or emends it to הַחֹרֵם 'the
notables', and attaches it to v. 3. על הרע is an accidental contraction of
עלהֲרֵעַ לְהָרַע and כפים is to be emended to פנים. The first part of v. 3
then reads, 'The nobles turn to do evil against their fellows'. להיטיב has
adverbial force, 'exquisitely', 'elegantly': the rulers know how to make
their demands elegantly. The conclusion is that על הרע should be
retained with MT (so Sept.) and Sept. should be followed in respect of
כפיהם and היטיבו.

Sept. represents והשפט בשלום (v. 3) with καὶ ὁ κριτὴς εἰρηνικοὺς
λόγους ἐλάλησεν. ἐλάλησεν indicates that דבר is vocalized as דִּבֶּר (MT
דֹּבֵר), והגדול is a minus and בשלום is mistranslated as 'peaceful words'.
The insertion of λόγους is connected with the attachment of דבר to the
word-string והשפט בשלום דבר and the absence of והגדול. Vulg. renders
בשלום as in reddendo est, 'delivers judgements'—a free translation. Et
magnus locutus est desiderium animae suae is a literal translation of
והגדול דבר הות נפשו with הוא a minus. Pesh. šʾl dhb, 'he asks for gold' is a
supplementation of MT שאל and the proposal has been made that שחד
should be inserted in the Hebrew text (Hillers, 84). Rudolph's analysis
(122) of dhb, the particle d and the imperative of yhb 'give' is wrong.
והשפט בשלום is rendered by Pesh, as wdynʾ ʾmr šhwd. šhwd is the equivalent of שחד and it renders שלום. Hence it is unlikely that dhb has text-
critical significance and that שחד appeared in a Hebrew text after שאל
(Hillers). dhb is an insertion by Peshitta to fill out the sense and to
provide a match for בשלום. Some scholars have detected a haplography
of שפט in MT (Weiser, 284; Rudolph, 122; Hillers, 84) and it might be
supposed that ʾmr (Pesh.) represents שֹׁפֵט 'judges'. Wolff (175), on the
other hand, conjectures that שאל and בשלום do double duty, the former
is the predicate of both השר and והשפט and the latter the object of השׁר
and והשפט.

Targ. renders והשפט בשלום as ודינא אמר עבד לי דאשלים לך, 'And the judge says, "Do something for me that I may requite you"'. Rashi comments, 'The judge also asks for a reward when he gives his verdict and threatens that he will find a person guilty who does not pay up'. All the versions derive דבר in the word-string דבר הות נפשו from דבר 'say', 'speak' (Sept. ἐλάλησεν; Vulg. *locutus est*; Pesh. *mmll*; Targ. ממלל). A derivation from II דבר 'lead', 'govern' has been proposed by G.R. Driver ((1937, 71; Syriac *dbr*). The translation in NEB, 'harps on his desires', is founded on I דבר. The sense 'decide' (Wellhausen, 27; Weiser, 284; KB³, 201; Wolff, 174) is founded on I דבר (cf. Hillers, 83 'pronounces'). Rudolph (121, 122) 'govern' is better suited to II דבר. הוא appears in Sept. as ἐστιν and is a minus in Vulg. and Pesh. Targ. has expanded MT, 'Woe to them because they destroy it': הוי may be a corruption of הוא. Wolff (174)shows הוא as an emphatic subject of דבר and Wellhausen (27, 146) indicates a break in the Hebrew text between הוא and ויעבתוה which he emends to ויעותוה 'and they pervert it', noting that the suffix lacks a reference. Hillers (184) mentions the proposal that משפט should replace the suffix, ויעבתו משפט 'and they twist justice' or 'and they pervert justice'. Whether or not the emendation is adopted this is presumably the sense of 'so they twist it' (Hillers, 83) or 'and they pervert it' (Wellhausen, 27; Wolff, 174). Rudolph (121, 122) emends הוא ויעבתוה to יחדיו יעבתוה 'together they twist it'. ויעבתוה is attached to v. 4 in Sept. and Pesh: καὶ ἐξελοῦμαι τὰ ἀγαθὰ αὐτῶν, 'And I shall remove their goods' is to be compared with Pesh. *wslyw ṭbthwn* 'And they have rejected their goodness'. In neither is ויעבתוה correctly represented.

Kimchi explains ויעבתוה as a reference to three strands of a rope (עבת) which symbolize a triple strenghtening of evil by the corruption of justice practised by the שר, the שפט and the גדול (Rudolph, 125). At v. 4 Sept. diverges considerably from MT. For כחדק ... מצפיך it has ὡς σὴς ἐκτρώγων καὶ βαδίζων ἐπὶ κανόνος ἐν ἡμέρᾳ σκοπιᾶς. ἐπὶ κανόνος can be roughly correlated with ישר and σκοπιᾶς with מצפיך, but otherwise the rendering is far removed from MT: 'like a moth which devours undeviatingly on a day of look-out'. The remainder of the verse is also aberrant. αἱ ἐκδικήσεις σου ἥκασιν, 'your punishments have come', is related to פקדתך באה and νῦν ἔσονται κλαυθμοὶ αὐτῶν, 'now their weeping will come to pass' is a mistranslation of עתה תהיה מבוכתם, 'now their confusion will come to pass'. οὐαὶ οὐαί, 'Alas! Alas!' is a plus. Pesh.

also has a mention of the ravages inflicted by the moth and, in this regard is probably dependent on Sept.: 'And they have rejected their goodness like a piece of cloth which a moth eats through' (*'yk 'wrq't d'kl ss'*). It then diverges from Sept., 'The day of your ignomiy and your redemption will come. Then will be their house of weeping'. *rwqyky* 'your ignomiy' is a mistranslation of מצפיך and פקדתך is represented by *wpwrqnyk* and is parsed as if it were ויום פקדתך (a second *nomen rectum*). פקדתך 'visitation' is taken as 'redemption' rather than 'judgement'. *bkyhwn* reproduces Sept. κλαυθμοὶ αὐτῶν.

Vulg. follows MT closely in v. 4a, 'The best of them is like a thorn and the most upright like a hedge', but it represents כמסוכה (*quasi spina de sepe*) rather than ממסוכה (MT). This emendation is preferred by Smith (139) and Weiser (295). Ehrlich (289) explains ממסוכה (MT) as comparative in force, 'more than a hedge' = 'worse than a hedge' (cf. Ibn Ezra, 'more prickly than a hedge of thorns'; also Kimchi). ישרם and מסוכה (a redivision of consonants) are favoured by Rudolph (122), Wolff (175) and Hillers (84): ישרם matches טובם and the repetition of כ is not required. Even the good and upright are forbidding and obstructionist. They draw blood like a briar or they present a barrier like a prickly hedge. They are formidable, not approachable (Wolff, 180f.). Vulg. vocalizes מצפיך (4b) as מְצַפֶּיךָ 'your watchtower' (*speculationis tuae*) and renders פקדתך as *visitatio tua*. It assumes the same construction as Pesh.: יום is a construct both of מְצַפֶּיךָ and פקדתך, 'the day of your look-out (MT 'your seers') and of your visitation will come'. *vastitas eorum* (Vulg.) may be a misreading of מבוכתם as מבוקתם (Rudolph, 123). Wellhausen (27) retains MT in respect of יום ... באה and assumes that יום does double duty as a *nomen regens*, 'the day of your watchers, the day of your punishment, will come'. Smith (140) deletes מצפיך (also REB) as a gloss and emends פקדתך to פקדתם (also Weiser, 285). Wolff (175) deletes פקדתך as a secondary interpretation of מצפיך 'your seers'. Rudolph (123) adopts Robinson's proposal (148) that מצפיך should be emended to מצפון and he makes the further conjecture that יום should be emended to הוי. Finally he changes פקדתך to פקדתם: 'Woe from the north will come their punishment'. Hillers (84) proposes יום מצפה ... בא: מצפה is an abstract noun 'expectation', 'dread': 'the expected time of punishment has come'.

The most significant of these emendations for exegesis is the alteration of פקדתך to פקדתם (Smith, Weiser, Robinson, Rudolph).

This, however, requires the deletion of מצפיך as a gloss (Smith, Weiser) or its emendation to מצפון (Robinson, Rudolph). It removes the puzzling alternation of second person singular (פקדתך; מצפיך) and third person plural (מבוכתם). Since there is no direct address in vv. 1–4, its appearance at v. 4b is an inconcinnity which should be removed (REB, 'The day of their punishment has come; now confusion seizes them'). Targ, paraphrases MT: 'Their goodness is as difficult as a thorn to extract from the hand and their uprightness is like a prickly hedge. The day for which you hope will be an evil one for the virtuous; a time of punishment will come. Now will be your confusion.' מצפיך is represented by סבורך 'in which you hope' and ישרם is indicated, though it is unlikely to have been read in the Hebrew text. Rashi is close to Targ. and comments, 'They have a goodness which is difficult to remove from the hand just as a thorn is difficult to extract'. Kimchi is similar, 'Their goodness is like a thorn which injures those who touch it'. Ibn Ezra interprets מצפיך like Targ.: 'The day for which you are looking will be followed swiftly by your day of reckoning. Confusion will overtake statesmen, judges and notables.'

Sept. represents באלוף (v. 5) as ἐπὶ ἡγουμένοις 'leaders'. The plural is an indication that the translator supposes באלוף is a collective as he does with ברע (ἐν φίλοις). It is more important to notice that he does not render אלוף as 'friend' and so destroys the synonymous parallelism of רע and אלוף. This is also a feature of Vulg. (amico/in duce, while Pesh. (lrḥmykwn/'l qrybykwn) and Targ. (בקריב/ברחים) preserve the synonymous parallelism. Kimchi, following Sept. and Vulg. (אלוף = גדול), comments 'that is, his kinsman who is a notable'. Wellhausen (27), Weiser (285), Robinson (148), Rudolph (121, 122) and Wolff (174) translate אלוף as 'friend'. Sept. transforms משכבת חיקך 'from her who lies on your breast', that is, 'from your wife', to ἀπὸ τῆς συνκοίτου σου 'from her who shares your bed', while Vulg. ab ea quae dormit in sinu tuo is a more literal translation of MT. Pesh. renders the Hebrew simply as wmn 'nttk 'and from your wife'; Targ. has מאיתת קימך 'from your established wife'.

Sept. translates שמר פתחי פיך, 'Guard the openings of your mouth' freely: φύλαξαι τοῦ ἀναθέσθαι τι αὐτῇ, 'Be on your guard when you tell her anything'. פתחי פיך is rendered by Vulg. as claustra oris tui 'door of your mouth', but the assumption that 'doors of your mouth' or 'gates of your mouth' are a reference to the lips is probably correct.

Wellhausen (27), Weiser (285), Rudolph (121, 123) and Wolff (174) translate 'the gate of the mouth' on the ground that the mouth has only one opening, but the reference may be to the lips (cf. Robinson, 148, 'the gates of your mouth' and Hillers, 83, 'the doors of your mouth'). The sense is 'be tight-lipped'. Pesh. and Targ. have the paraphrase 'words of your mouth' (*mly pwmk*; מילי פומך).

Verse 6 describes the overturning of established respect for ranks of seniority in the domestic ordering of society (Kimchi), in the solidarity of the household and the safe haven of the home. The home is no longer a place where loyalty and mutual regard can be taken for granted, no longer a shelter and a resting place from which enemies are shut out. Hillers (83, 84) places too great limitations on the scope of איבי איש אנשי ביתו with his translation 'A man's own slaves are his enemies' (also Rudolph, 126; Wolff, 182). The verse deals with unnatural kinds of insubordination: a son despising his father, a daughter rebelling against her mother, a daughter-in-law at loggerheads with her mother-in-law. The final expression of this malaise is not the enmity between the master of a household and his slaves, which would not be unheard of, but bad blood between the members of a family.

Verse 7 is not an integral component of vv. 1–7 (*pace* Weiser, 286; Hillers, 85) and is best accounted for as the secondary riposte of a man of faith (so Robinson) to the gloom and doom of vv. 1–6, its picture of decadence, malevolence and domestic disorder. Verse 7 is a 'nevertheless', an affirmation of hope in Yahweh in the face of the unpropitious signs of the times: the speaker will keep a look-out for Yahweh and nourish his hope in God, his saviour, to answer his prayer (Targ., 'my God will accept my prayer'). Weiser describes it as a concluding expression of prophetic faith by Micah and Rudolph (126) as an apt affirmation of faith by Micah to conclude the unit vv. 5–7. Wolff (183) similarly holds that v. 7 is a prophetic 'nevertheless' which resolutely confronts the conditions described in vv. 1–6 with a declaration of hope in Yahweh. This he prefers to the alternative conjecture that v. 7 is a redactional link between vv. 1–6 and vv. 8ff. (176f.). It is, however, not Micah who utters the lament in vv. 1–6 and the robust 'nevertheless' in v. 7, but a prophet who was a contemporary of Trito-Isaiah (so Wolff, 177f.) in a period which was marked by a depressing instability. Hillers (85) argues that ואני connects v. 7 with vv. 1–6 (also Wolff, 176), whereas Smith (145) urges that ואני is evidence that v. 7 is not continuous with vv. 1–6: the antithesis established by ואני is inappropriate as a continuation of vv. 1–6. Wolff (184) comments on the solitariness of the prophet in a historical setting where he sees no light at the end of the tunnel and does not expect any amelioration from a continuation of history. The present time displays the signs of the end, the situation is eschatological, and he looks for a new age. He does not foresee how the great change is to be effected and does not describe the process, but his hope is placed in the intervention of God, his saviour.

Ehrlich (289) has an explanation which preserves the integrity of vv. 1–7. The hope expressed in v. 7 is not that of the prophet but of the people. Hence v. 7 is a different kind of 'notwithstanding'. Despite the state of affairs described in vv. 1–6, the moral chaos, the corruption of public life and the topsiturviness of domestic relations for which they have been responsible, the expectations of the people in Yahweh are high. The prophet is exposing their impudence and laying bare the absurdity of their pious postures. But there is nothing in the text to indicate that the prophet is citing in v. 7 words spoken by the malefactors of vv. 1–6 with such an ironic intention and v. 7 is more naturally taken as a secondary riposte by someone whose hope in Yahweh has survived the dark picture painted in vv. 1–6.

Weiser (285f.) is untroubled by the circumstance that v. 4b issues a threat of judgment, or describes the onset of judgement, whereas vv. 5–6 resume the theme of general decadence and inhumane behaviour, v. 5 by issuing a warning against putting trust in a friend or revealing confidences to a wife, v. 6 by describing the despising of a father by his son, the conflict of mother and daughter, mother-in-law and daughter-in-law and a household where enmity has replaced affection. His explanation of the interruption caused by v. 4b is that vv. 5–6 are an elaboration of v. 4b, that the punishment inflicted takes the form of the falling apart of relations of trust between man and man in the community and the replacement of peace and tranquillity in the house by disregard and bad blood. God allows human sins and self-seeking greed to bring the community to the ground. Thus Weiser reconciles vv. 3–4 with vv. 5–6.

Wolff (183) has something of Weiser's attitude, but he eases the problem by making v. 4b secondary. He notices that vv. 2–6 contain lament after lament but no threat of judgement, and remarks that the moral decay in the community and the collapse of the integrity of the household are themselves the judgement. He acknowledges (176) that the coherence of vv. 1–4a and vv. 5–6 is a problem , that the admonishment of v. 5 is a departure from the lamenting of vv. 1–4a and v. 6. He appeals to the combination of admonishment and indictment in Jer. 9.1–5 and 12.6, and adds that vv. 1–4a and vv. 5–6 are closely bound together both form-critically and in content. He identifies v. 4b as an exegetical refinement of v. 4a of which פקדתך is a secondary item. יום מצפיך 'the day of your seers' is a reference to the old prophets, and what they predicted, the evil day, has now come to pass: 'The day of your seers has come, now will be their confusion', that is, chaos will reign in the community. The suffix of the secondary פקדתך refers to Yahweh: what the prophets foretold was the day of his judgement. Rudolph (122f.) emends מצפיך to מצפוך, פקדתך to פקדתם and יום to הוי. Verse 4b becomes an exclamation of woe occasioned by the prospect of an imminent invasion from the enemy of the north.

Robinson and Rudolph supposes that 7.1–4 and 7.5–6 are separate units. Robinson (149) assigns vv. 1–4 to the late post-exilic period because of חסיד—a late usage (Ps. 12.2). Verses 5–6 are not continuous with vv. 4; they are a parallel passage which deal with different aspects of the disintegration of the community. They could manifest themselves at different periods and so cannot be dated. Rudolph (123f.) notices that v. 4b (an intimation of judgment) is followed by admonition (v. 5) and further lament (v. 6). Rudolph (124) holds that v. 5 gives advice for the future (אל תבסחו; אל תאמנו) and so he disjoins vv. 1–4 from vv. 5–7. Both pieces are from Micah but they were joined by a redactor who took vv. 5–6 as a new proof of the situation which is the subject of lament in vv. 1–4.

> 1. Woe is me! I am like the gatherings of the harvest,
>   like the gleanings of the vintage.
>   There are no grapes to eat,
>   no early figs which I desire so passionately.
> 2. Men of integrity have vanished from the land,
>   not a single upright man is left.
>   All lie in wait to shed blood,
>   each hunts his brother with a net.
> 3. They have made their hands[1] expert[2] at wrongdoing:

[1]Reading כפיהם.
[2]Reading היטיבו.

the statesman asks (for money), the judge for a bribe
and the great man governs[3] capriciously.
All three twist their offices.

4. Their goodness[4] is like a briar, their uprightness (like) a hedge[5].
   The day[6] of their judgement[7] has come to pass;
   now their confusion is here.

5. Do not rely on a companion;
   do not trust in a friend.
   From her who lies on your breast
   keep your lips tight.

6. For a son disparages his father,
   a daughter rises against her mother,
   a daughter-in-law against her mother-in-law.
   A man's enemies are those of his household.

7. But I shall watch for Yahweh,
   I shall hope in God, my saviour.
   My God will hear me.

vv. 8–10 AN EXULTING ENEMY WILL BE CONFOUNDED

7.8–20 have been described as a 'liturgy' or a piece which has liturgical
origins (Weiser, Rudolph, Wolff, Hillers) and a consideration of what is
involved in postulating a unity of this kind has been left to the end of
the chapter. Smith (144) and Robinson (150) suppose that the unit is
vv. 8–10 and Robinson remarks that to posit the continuation of vv.
8–10 with vv. 11–13 is akin to forcing a square peg into a round hole.
Wolff (199), who does not argue for the coherence of 7.8–10, 14–20,
has described vv. 11–13 as exegetical additions to vv. 8–10. vv. 11–13
are oracular in form (Weiser, 287; Rudolph, 131; Hillers, 89) and
contrast with vv. 8–10, 14–17, 18–20, where the utterances are those
of the cultic congregation, perhaps speaking for Zion or Jerusalem
(Robinson, 150; Rudolph, 131), the 'I' in vv. 8–10 being communal.
Rudolph is not deterred by the presence of an oracle in vv. 11–13 from
affirming that vv. 7–20 contain a coherent liturgy (131) and Hillers

---

[3]Deriving דבר II *ex* דבר.
[4]Reading טובָם.
[5]Reading ישרם מסוכה.
[6]Deleting מצפיך 'your seers' as a gloss. יום מצפיך 'the day which your seers predicted'.
[7]Reading פקדתם.

assumes this, without making a case for it. Weiser supposes that the function of the prophetic promise is to reinforce the hope which is expressed by the cultic community.

What is the identity of איבתי (v. 8) 'my enemy' to whom the advice is given that she should not exult? איבתי is a feminine singular participle with a first person singular suffix. Targ. identifies the enemy with רומי 'Rome' and Rashi with Babylon (also Wellhausen, 146; Weiser, 288; Wolff, 195), while Kimchi and Ibn Ezra associate 'my enemy' with the גוים 'nations' (cf. Smith, 145; Rudolph, 132; איבתי has a collective sense) among whom Israel was still dispersed at the time they wrote. Ibn Ezra: 'He will bring me from among the nations into the light.' Rudolph (131f.), however, makes the alternative proposals that the setting of 7.8–10 is the Persian period and that Persia is the world-power who is the enemy; or that neighbouring states are the enemy, for example the enemies of Nehemiah. Kimchi does not suppose that the reference is to the Babylonian exile which lies in the past but to a scattering of Jews among the nations which was still a feature of his own time: 'For the exile of Israel under its enemy's sovereignty has been long drawn out, more than a thousand years. It was reckoned that the hope of Israel had perished and her enemy rejoiced at her distress.' קמתי is a prophetic perfect which descries the future as if the outcome were so certain that it could be expressed as having already happened. Hence the גולה in which Israel sits in darkness is not the Babylonian גולה and the redemption for which the prophet looks still lies in the future.

The punctuation of MT is correct. קמתי is linked with נפלתי just as אשב בחשך is linked with יהוה אור לי. They are antithetic parallels and, for the most part, this is how they have been taken (Sept; Pesh.?; Targ.; Ibn Ezra; Kimchi; Wellhausen, 27; Smith, 144; Weiser, 286; Robinson, 150; Rudolph, 127; Wolff, 186; Hillers, 87; NEB; REB). Vulg.: *Ne laeteris, inimica mea, super me, quia concidi; consurgam cum sedero in tenebris*, 'Do not rejoice, my enemy, over me, because I have fallen. I shall arise (again) after I have sat in darkness.' It is unlikely that Sept. (ὅτι 'because'?) is showing the same punctuation as Vulg. (*pace* Wolff, 187). וקמתי is translated literally by Sept. as καὶ ἀναστήσομαι and is unmistakeably joined to כי נפלתי. ὅτι can be rendered as 'that' rather than as 'because': 'Do not rejoice, my enemy, that I have fallen, for (literally 'and') I shall rise again.' Both occurrences of כי should be construed as concessives, 'Do not exult, O my enemy, over me; though

I have fallen, I shall rise again; though I (now) sit in darkness, Yahweh is (or 'will be') my light.'

There is exegetical significance in the choice between 'is' (Vulg. *est*; Wellhausen, 27 *ist*; Weiser, 286; Robinson, 150; Rudolph, 127; Wolff, 186; NEB; REB) and 'will be'. Pesh. (*mry' mnhr ly*) and Targ. (יוי ינהר עלי) could be either 'is' or 'will be'. Sept. φωτιεῖ μοι 'will give me light', Smith (144) and Hillers (87) support 'will be'. If 'is my light' is preferred, the parallelism of v. 8b is not precisely that of v. 8a: v. 8a is a contrast between defeat followed by exile (dispersion) and deliverance, while v. 8b opposes sitting in darkness, that is, suffering the ills of subjection, to the consolation of the light of Yahweh's presence. This is the exegesis of Rudolph (132) founded on 'is my light'. For Wolff (196) it is an affirmation not only that Yahweh is a light in the present darkness but that he is a future redeemer. If 'will be my light' is preferred, both v. 8a and v. 8b are setting the descent into exile against the resurgence in the time of deliverance. יוציאני לאור (v. 9) is a reference to the future and Yahweh is the subject: 'He will lead me into the light, I shall feast my eyes (cf. Wolff, 198) on his righteousness' (or 'his salvation', cf. Wolff, 197, 198). This might be an indication that יהוה אור לי (v. 8) also refers to future deliverance rather than present consolation; in that case, 'Yahweh will be my light' is the correct translation and the parallelism of v. 8a and v. 8b is exact. This is the preferable conclusion.

כי חטאתי לו (v. 9) is a parenthesis (Smith, 144, 146; Rudolph, 127; Wolff, 186) and עד אשר ... משפטי continues זעף יהוה אשא, I shall endure the anger of Yahweh, (for I have sinned against him) until he takes up my case and gives judgement for me.' ועשה משפטי, if it appeared in isolation, might have the sense 'and decides my sentence', but in conjunction with יריב ריבי it almost certainly refers to a favourable outcome, 'a just verdict on my behalf' (Wellhausen, 27; Weiser, 286; Robinson, 150; Rudolph, 127; Wolff, 186; Hillers, 87), rather than 'my sentence'. No further light is thrown on this by the renderings of משפטי which appear in Sept. (τὸ κρίμα μου) and Vulg. (*iudicium meum*) 'my judgement' and Pesh. *tb'ty* may have this sense, though it could mean 'my punishment' and *wn'bd tb'ty* would be rendered 'and he will exact my punishment'. The objection to this conclusion is that 'and he will exact my punishment' will not serve as a continuation of 'he will take up my case'. Targ., which has ויתפרע עולבני for ועשה משפטי is the most perplexing of the versions. ועשה is represented by a passive, ויתפרע 'and will be repaid', while משפטי is given as עולבני 'my humiliation'. The sense turns on the interpretation of 'my humiliation'. Is it the humiliation heaped on me by the enemy? In that case 'my humiliation will be repaid' is 'revenge'. Or is it the humiliation which I will suffer as a punishment for my sins against Yahweh? It is then more or less equivalent to the Scots legal phrase 'to thole one's assize', that is, to serve one's sentence. The objection raised in respect of Pesh. that this is not an appropriate continuation of יריב ריבי is again valid and Targ. should be explained as a paraphrase of MT. Kimchi comments, 'I shall carry my burden, until he becomes my advocate against the nations which have abused me, for he will avenge me of them (ועשה משפטי).'

When the enemy sees that Yahweh has brought Israel out of the darkness of exile and subjection into the light of freedom (v. 10), shame and consternation will cover her. The taunt which she uttered was 'Where is Yahweh, your God?' and for Israel the reversal of fortune will be sweet. Ehrlich (290) holds that there is no need to emend איו to איה, the normal form of 'where', while Wellhausen (146) and Wolff (188) make this proposal. Wolff's elaborate explanation of how the corruption from איה to איו came about is too contrived to be convincing and it involves the deletion of יהוה: איה was written erroneously as איהיה, the second יה was misread as an abbreviation of יהוה and איה was emended to איו so as to avoid a repetition of יה.

Sept., Vulg., Pesh. and Targ. render תראינה ב as 'observe' (Sept. ἐπόψονται; Vulg. videbunt in; Pesh. nḥzyn b; Targ. יהזיין ב) and they do not attach to ראה ב the nuance 'look on with satisfaction', 'gloat'. Ibn Ezra gives both senses: 'I shall see when he illumines my heart' (v. 8). 'Then I shall discern (אראה ב, v. 9) that God is righteous concerning all that has come upon me.' But (v. 10), 'I shall gloat at his righteousness (בצדקתו = בה) in that he avenges me for the wrongs of my enemies.' Kimchi also takes the sense of ראה ב in v. 10 as 'gloat', 'ראה ברצוני or ראה בחפצי'—look with pleasure. This has been followed by most modern commentators (Wellhausen, 27; Rudolph, 127; Wolff, 186). Smith (144), Weiser (286) and Hillers (87) prefer 'look on them' (cf. Targ 'look on her downfall'—במפלתה). Robinson (150) deletes עיני תראנה בה. Smith's exegetical comment (147) that the gaze is one of gloating falls short of a lexicographical recognition that ראה ב means 'look with pleasure'.

The enemy will become like streets which have been trampled into mud (v. 10). Pesh. (*'yk syn' dšwq'*) and Targ. (כסין שוקין) have in mind market-places whose surfaces have been churned up. Wolff (198) notices that למרמס is used in connection with the trampling into mud of arable fields or vineyards by cattle or wild beasts who have transgressed into them (Isa. 5.5; 7.25). Robinson (150), following Smith (147) deletes כטיט חוצות which has been taken as an addition from Ps. 18.43 (cf. Isa. 10.6, כחמר חוצות; Hillers, 88). Smith describes it as an editorial expansion which he deletes for metrical reasons.

There is general agreement that the date of 7.8–10 is post-587 (Wellhausen, 146; Smith, 145; Weiser, 287; Rudolph, 131, Wolff, 193). Hence it is not the work of Micah and it does not have an eighth century B.C. setting (*contra* Hillers, 89, 90). Judgement is no longer threatened by the doom prophets as impending. Rather it has come and is accepted as Yahweh's punishment for the sins of his people (v. 9a). Judah has fallen, Jerusalem has been laid waste and its people have gone into exile, but they will rise again and Yahweh will be their redeemer. This note of hope is connected by Wellhausen (146) with the age of Deutero-Isaiah at the end of the exilic period and with the mood reflected in Isa.40ff. Weiser (287) favours the early post-exilic period and Wolff (194) the exilic period or early post-exilic period. Since Weiser treats 7.8–20 as a unity, he may, like Rudolph (131), be leaning on vv. 12 and 14 to establish the early post-exilic date of vv. 8–10. According to Rudolph, the place where vv. 8–10 were spoken is shown by vv. 12 and 14 to be Jerusalem; the speakers are those who were in exile and have returned to that city. Wolff (193f.) halts between two opinions, because he is impressed by the evidence supplied by Lamentations that the date is exilic and also by the evidence of Trito-Isaiah that it is early post-exilic. The passages referring to vv. 8–10 which he cites are these: Lam. 1.21; 3.31–33; 4.21; 5.17; Isa. 59.9, 11b, 12a, 14; 64.4b, 8.

8.   Do not exult over me. O my enemy[1],
        for as I have fallen so I shall rise[2].
        Though I sit in darkness,
        Yahweh will be[3] my light.

[1]Above, pp. 218.
[2]Above, pp. 128f.
[3]Above, p. 219.

9. I shall endure the anger of Yahweh
(for I have sinned against him)[4],
until he fights my case
and wins me justice[5].
10. My enemy will see it
and shame will cover her.
She who says to me, 'Where is the Lord, your God'?
My eyes will feast on her;
now she will be like streets trampled into mud.

vv. 11–13 A PROPHETIC ORACLE

According to Rashi the oracle consists of vv. 12–13 and v. 11 is spoken by 'the enemy' of v. 8 and v. 10. Thus Rashi supposes that there is a continuity between vv. 8–10 and vv. 11–13. Although vv. 8–10 and vv. 11–13 are formally different, the one is an affirmation of confidence in Yahweh and vv. 12–13 is an oracle, in virtue of the link between v. 11 and vv. 8 and 10, vv. 11–13 are not a new beginning. Rashi holds that in v. 11 the enemy is deriding Israel's expectations voiced in vv. 8–10: 'As for the rebuilding of your walls, that time (חק?) is distant and will never come to pass.'

Kimchi's method of linking vv. 11–13 with vv. 8–10 is different. Verses 11–13 are spoken by the prophet and v. 11 is a riposte to the enemies who are laying plans for a future invasion of Israel. They propose to fence Israel in, to build walls around her, but the prophet predicts that Israel will fend off the threat and will defeat the invaders, so that her boundaries will be extended (ירחק חק) and the territories of the גוים will be laid waste. Rashi also makes vv. 12–13 a prophecy of weal spoken by the prophet.

Another exegesis which links vv. 11–13 with vv. 8–10 is that of Ehrlich (290). Verses 11–13 are spoken by the prophet, but they are an oracle of doom and the land (הארץ) which is to be laid waste is that of Israel (v. 13). V. 11 is a pouring of cold water on the hopes entertained by the people in vv. 8–10: the day when the walls (of Jerusalem) will be rebuilt lies in the distant future (deleting חק as a dittography).

On the assumption that vv. 11–13 are a prophetic oracle there are

[4]Above, p. 219.
[5]Above, pp. 219f.

those who render v. 11 so as to create continuity with vv. 8–10 by establishing a connection between the time of dominance alluded to in vv. 9–10 and the rebuilding of the walls of Jerusalem and the extension of borders to which v. 11 refers. There are others who translate v. 11 in such a way that vv. 11–13 are made to refer to a different future day from that of vv. 9–10, so that the oracle is a new departure and there is no continuity between vv. 8–10 and vv. 11–13. The translations which produce these different results are as follows: the rendering which attaches vv. 11–13 to vv. 8–10 is 'That will be a day for rebuilding your walls, a day when your boundaries will be extended' or the like (Wellhausen, 27; Weiser, 287; Hillers, 87; RSV, NEB, REB). The rendering which detaches vv. 11–13 from vv. 8–10 is 'There will come a day when your walls will be rebuilt, on that day your boundaries will be extended' or the like (Smith, 148; Rudolph, 127; Wolff, 186; KJV, 'In the days that thy walls are to be built' etc.). Robinson's translation (150) aligns him with the first group (*Ein Tag ist dies*), but his exegesis makes it clear (151) that his intention is to set out vv. 11–12 as discontinuous with vv. 8–10: they are a fragment of an apocalyptic portrayal of the triumph of Zion at the end of time.

At v. 11 יום לבנות גדריך is rendered by Sept. as ἡμέρας ἀλοιφῆς πλίνθου and יום ההוא and יום הוא (MT, v. 12) are both translated ἡ ἡμέρα ἐκείνη. The punctuation is different from MT and יום הוא is part of v. 11 rather than the beginning of v. 12. Robinson (151) has remarked on the deviation of Sept. (vv. 11–12) from MT and supposes it to be evidence that Sept. was interpolated in the course of transmission. ἡμέρας is perhaps a lapse for ἡμέρα and ἀλοιφῆς πλίνθου is derived from the vocalization of לבנות as לְבֵנוֹת (usually לְבֵנִים, *BDB*, 527) 'bricks'. ἀλοιφῆς πλίνθου is a reference to the process of making bricks and ἐξάλειψίς σου is an elaboration which apparently refers to the scraping or pointing of bricks in connection with their use in building walls. Rudolph (128) has supposed that it may rest on a metathesis of ר and ד (גרדיך instead of גדריך; *BDB*, 173, גרד 'scrape'). ἀποτρίψεται is probably a free translation of ירחק (Rudolph, 128) in place of the normal ἀπώσεται: 'Your regime (νόμιμά σου: חקך, MT חק) will fade into the distance' is interpreted as 'Your regime will be rubbed out' or 'Your regime will be effaced'. Vulg. also takes חק as 'law' rather than 'boundary' ('On that day the law (*lex*) will be distant') and Pesh., which does not represent חק, renders ירחק as *dištqlyn*, 'that day on which you will be removed (?)'. νόμμά σου 'your regime' (Sept.) perhaps refers to the regime imposed on Israel by the גוים who ruled it. This is the sense of the paraphrase of Targ., 'At that time the community of Israel will be rebuilt; at that time the decrees of the nations will become null and void (יבטלן). KJV follows Targ., 'In that day shall the decree be far removed.' Rudolph (128) asks why, if this is the sense, the Hebrew text does not read חק הגוים. Modern scholars have tended to follow Kimchi and have preferred 'On that day your boundaries will be extended' (Smith, 148; Weiser, 287; Robinson, 150; Wolff, 187; Hillers, 87), though Rudolph queries whether חק 'limit' can be used of an extension of boundaries.

Among the versions only Vulg. represents ועדיך יבוא (v. 12) faithfully (*et usque ad te veniet*). Sept. has read a Hebrew text which had ועריך or it has misread ועדיך as ועריך (καὶ αἱ πόλεις σου). Targ. has paraphrased ועדיך יבוא as יתכנש גלותא, 'the exiles will be regathered'. Pesh represents ועדיך as *dzbnky* 'your time' (= עתיך?). Sept. εἴξουσιν 'they will yield' (ἥξουσιν?) for יבוא (MT יבוא) may be accounted for by postulating a metathesis of א and ו, whether in MT or in the Hebrew text which the Greek translator read (Wolff, 188). Wolff assumes יבאו in his translation, but remarks that יבוא can stand with the sense 'one will come'. Vulg. (*veniet*) and Pesh. (*n't*) represent MT. Rudolph's elucidation of εἰς ὁμαλισμὸν καὶ διαμερισμὸν 'Ασσυρίων (v. 12) is so complicated that it increases confusion rather than throwing light on the Greek text. His final remark that it is a mystery how the Greek translator contrived to make such a meal out of למני אשור 'from Assyria' will suffice (Vulg. *de Assur*; Pesh. *mn 'twr*; Targ. דמן אתור). For MT וערי מצור the versions have all given 'and fortified cities' (Sept. καὶ αἱ πόλεις σου αἱ ὀχυραί; Vulg. *et usque ad civitates munitas*; Pesh. *wmn mdynt 'synt*; Targ. וקרוי תקפא). *usque ad* is a plus in Vulg., 'from Assyria to the fortified cities' and, according to Rashi, this is the sense of the Hebrew. Another explanation of Vulg. *et usque ad civitates munitas* is that *civitates munitas* is derived from מצור (cf. v. 12b) and MT וערי is read as ועדי. ולמני מצור is rendered by Sept. as ἀπὸ Τύρου = למני צור 'from Tyre' and *wmn ṣwr* also appears in Pesh. Vulg. supposes that מצור[2] is an equivalent of ערי מצור, 'and from the fortified cities to the river'. Similarly Targ. renders מצור[2] as וקרוי צירא, 'and cities to withstand siege'. Hence the versions do not recognize מצור as another form of מצרים nor do Rashi and Kimchi.

Modern scholars, for the most part, follow Targ. and conclude that v. 12 is a reference to the ingathering of the Jewish diaspora (Wellhausen, 27f.; Smith, 150; Weiser, 287; Rudolph, 127; Wolff, 186f.) and that הארץ (v. 13) is to be identified with the lands of the גוים ('the earth')— Wellhausen, Smith, Rudolph, Wolff, Hillers, 87, 91). Robinson (151), however, supposes that a streaming of the Gentile world to Zion is depicted at v. 12 and, in that case, it is covering the same ground as Isa. 2.2–4/Mic. 4.1–3. He separates v. 13 from vv. 11–12 as a solitary fragment and holds that ארץ (v. 13) may refer either to 'the land of Israel' or to 'the earth'. The redactor who combined vv. 11–12 and v. 13 took it as a reference to the Gentile world. Hillers (91) leaves the question open: the reference is either to the return of dispersed Jews or to the homage paid to Jerusalem by גוים making a pilgrimage.

Since Targ. produces the sense of the return of the diaspora from its reading of MT, it cannot be asserted that the discernment of this follows from the emendation of ועדי (v. 12) to ועדי or ועד (Wellhausen, 147; Smith, 149; Ehrlich, 290; Weiser, 287; Robinson, 150; Rudolph, 127, 129; Wolff, 184, 188; Hillers, 87, 88) and the identification of מצור as another form of מצרים, but it is evident that MT ערי, a misreading of עדי, in conjunction with מצור led all the versions astray (including Targ.), produced the translation 'fortified cities' and encouraged the opinion that the subsequent מצור was an equivalent of ערי מצור. This was the case also with Rashi and Kimchi. Hence the 'from ... to' pattern is not grasped in למני אשור וערי מצור and its significance is blurred in ולמני מצור ועד נהר when מצור is taken as shorthand for ערי מצור. It is not appreciated that the same outreach of the diaspora is being given in reverse order, 'from Assyria to Egypt' and 'from Egypt to the Euphrates'.

In connection with his preference for צור 'Tyre' (Sept. and Pesh.) over מצור Rudolph (129) suggests that this repetition of the boundaries of the diaspora in reverse is heavy-handed, but there is more of effective literary invention in it than he allows. His hypothesis that a north–south indication of the extent of the Jewish dispersion (Assyria to Egypt) is followed by a west–east one (Tyre to The Euphrates) is ingenious, but it does not provide an adequate reason for emending the Hebrew text (also Robinson, 151). 'From Assyria to Egypt' and 'from Egypt to the Euphrates is a kind of parallelism, neither synonymous nor antithetic, which should be retained. It is almost synonymous, because of the degree of repetition in it. The small change which is made underlines the vastness of the dispersion.

A comparison between Rashi and Kimchi, on the one hand, and Ehrlich (290) on the other is instructive. That Rashi and Kimchi interpret vv. 11–13 (Rashi vv. 12–13) as a prophecy of weal is evident in their identification of הארץ (v. 13) as the lands of the גוים. The conclusion is then that the גוים will suffer retribution and that their territories will be laid waste. However, both, in their comment on v. 12, declare that, although it portrays a hostile invasion of Israel by Gentile nations, it assumes that this attack will be successfully repulsed and that Israel will experience תשועה 'salvation'. Verse 13 is the culmination of a prophecy of weal contained, according to Kimchi in vv. 11–13 and, according to Rashi, in vv. 12–13, since the latter holds that the words in v. 11 are those of enemy pouring cold water on the expectations voiced in vv. 8–10.

Ehrlich nicely illustrates that the exegetical significance of the emendation of ערי to עדי, which he adopts, should not be over-estimated. Ehrlich also equates מצור with מצרים and yet he interprets vv. 11–13 as a prophecy of doom in which the prophet counters the optimism of vv. 8–10 with a more sombre prediction of the shape of the future. The day when the walls of Jerusalem will be rebuilt lies in the distant future (deleting חק). Enemies, in the meantime, will come against (עדיך is emended to עליך) Israel from the ends of the earth, from Assyria to Egypt and from Egypt to the Euphrates, and the land will be laid waste (v. 13, הארץ = Israel).

The grammar or lack of grammar in וים מים והר ההר (v. 12) is treated variously by the versions. Vulg. assumes that the 'from … to' scheme of the earlier part of the verse is being retained by the cryptic Hebrew: *Et ad mare de mari; et ad montem de monte*, 'and to sea from sea and to mountain from mountain'. Pesh. supposes that there is a reference to a particular mountain, Mount Hor (Num. 34.7f.) and reproduces the 'from … to' pattern for וים מים: *wmn ymʾ wdmʾ lymʾ wdmʾ lhwr ṭwrʾ*. Targ. וימא מערבאה וטורא טורא leaves the impression of not having given much thought to the Hebrew and contrasts with the perphrastic method which it sometimes employs. It identifies only one ים, the Mediterranean, and Rashi similarly comments on ים מים, 'הים האחרון (the Mediterranean Sea) which is in the west'. But ים מים is evidently a reference to two seas and the sense 'from one sea to another' has generally been adopted (Wellhausen, 27; Weiser, 287; Robinson, 150; Rudolph, 127; Wolff, 186; Hillers, 87). Rudolph (133; also Robinson, 151) supposes that the two seas are the Mediterranean and the Persian Gulf and that a west–east orientation comparable with 'from Tyre to the Euphrates' is indicated. והר ההר is even more problematical than ים מים and Wellhausen (147) has emended ההר to מהר in order to squeeze out the sense 'from mountain to mountain' (followed by Wolff, 188). Hillers (88) emends MT to ומן ים עד ים ומהר עד הר and recovers the 'from . . . to' pattern unambiguously. Rudolph (133; so Robinson, 151; cf. Wolff, 200) discerns here a north–south orientation ('from the Armenian highlands to Mount Sinai') corresponding with 'from Egypt to Assyria'.

I have left Sept. to the last, because its textual criticism is complicated and there are two translations of וים מים והר ההר. Sept.^{WQ} has one, Sept.^{B} has another and Sept.^{A} has both. Sept.^{WQ} renders וים מים והר ההר as καὶ ἡμέρα ὕδατος καὶ θορυβοῦ and this is the text which Ziegler adopts (226). καὶ ἡμέρα ὕδατος is founded on a different vocalization of וים מים from that of MT, namely, וְיֹם מַיִם, but how καὶ θορυβοῦ is derived from והר ההר is a mystery which Rudolph (129) tries too laboriously to elucidate. Sept^{B} has a rendering which agrees with Hillers' emendation of MT: καὶ ἀπὸ θαλάσσης ἕως θαλάσσης καὶ ἀπὸ ὄρους ἕως τοῦ ὄρους. Sept.^{A} adds to this καὶ ἡμέρα ὕδατος καὶ θορυβοῦ which, despite the obscurity of καὶ θορυβοῦ, would seem to be a second translation of וים מים והר ההר. The integrity of וים מים והר ההר has not, so far as I am aware, been challenged. I suggest that it may be a secondary addition made by someone in order to go one better than 'Assyria to Egypt' and 'Egypt to the Euphrates'. In that case it is a kind of vague 'overkill' or obscure hyperbole, a striving after comprehensiveness, in defining the outreach of the Jewish dispersion (cf. Smith, 150).

Weiser (288) remarks that the confidence in Yahweh voiced by the community in vv. 9–10 is confirmed by a promise from the mouth of a prophet (vv. 11–13). This prophetic oracle answers the expression of hope in three respects: it proclaims the coming of a 'day' when the walls of Jerusalem will be rebuilt and the boundaries of the land of Israel extended (v. 11); when the dispersed of Israel will return home from the ends of the earth (v. 12); when Yahweh's punishment will be administered to the גוים and their lands laid waste (v. 13; also Smith.149).

Rudolph (132f.) similarly comments that the oracle in vv. 11–13 contains the Divine answer to the hymn of confidence uttered by the community in vv. 8–10. He makes the point that the normal order of the liturgy was for a lament, a prayer or a voicing of confidence in Yahweh to be followed by an oracle. This is a contribution to his contention that vv. 8–20 is a unity and that the sequence of its parts is that of a liturgy. Rudolph (128f.) by deleting חק and emending ירחק to ידחקחק expunges the reference to the extension of the boundaries of the land and replaces it by the information that the 'day' is near. It 'presses on', that is, it approaches with haste. Wolff (198f.) contends that the oracle in vv. 11–13 is not an answer to vv. 8–10. Rather it is a secondary epexegesis of vv. 9–10, a commentary which expands on these verses and supplies concrete detail. It specifies a 'day' when the walls of Jerusalem will be rebuilt, when Israel's boundaries will be extended, the Jewish diaspora ingathered and the lands of the גוים devastated.

It was noted (above, 4f.) that Targ. already has the diaspora exegesis on the basis of MT and that the emendation of ערי to עדי, and the identification of מצור with מצרים, are consequently not essential for its discernment. Conversely, that the adoption of עדי and the equation of מצור with מצרים do not lead inevitably to the diaspora exegesis is shown by the interpretations of v. 12 which appear in Robinson and Eissfeldt. Robinson (151) supposes that v. 12 is not a reference to the dispersed of Israel but an account of the streaming of the גוים to Jerusalem in the manner of Isa. 2.2–4 and Mic. 4.1–3. Eissfeldt (1968, 68f.) postulates a close connection between v. 11 and v. 12 in connection with which he cites Isa. 49.17 and 60.10. Those who come to Samaria (Samaria not Jerusalem is the city) are גוים who are to help with the rebuilding of its walls, not Jews who have been dispersed. Neither of these elucidations of v. 12 should be preferred to the exegesis which identifies the verse as an account of the homecoming of Jews who had been dispersed to the ends of the earth. The *terminus a quo* of vv. 11–13 is the fall of Jerusalem and the demolition of its walls by the Chaldaeans (2 Kgs 25.10); the *terminus ad quem* is the rebuilding of the walls by Nehemiah. It is certainly post-exilic.

11.   A day will come when your walls will be rebuilt;
       on that day[1] your borders will be extended.

[1]Reading ביום ההוא.

12.   On that day they will come[2] to you
      from Assyria and as far as Egypt,
      from Egypt and as far as the Euphrates;
      from sea to sea and from mountain to mountain[3].
13.   The earth will be laid waste,
      because of (the evil of) its inhabitants,
      because of the consequences of what they have done.

vv. 14–17 A PRAYER FOR ISRAEL AND AGAINST THE NATIONS

שֹׁכְנִי (v. 14) is rendered as a plural by Sept. (κατασκηνοῦντας), Vulg. (*habitantes*), Pesh. (*nšrwn*) and Targ. (ישרון). This produces grammatical unevenness and, on the assumption that שֹׁכְנִי agrees with עַמְּך, it has been taken as singular שֹׁכֵן with *hireq compaginis* (Rudolph, 129; Wolff, 188; Hillers, 88; cf. GK90m). Yahweh's flock, Israel dwells solitary on poor land in the midst of rich pastures to which it has no access (Wellhausen, 147; Smith, 153; Rudolph, 134) כַּרְמֶל is not a place-name, though Sept., Vulg., Pesh. and Targ. suppose that it is and this has been reasserted by Eissfeldt (1968, 165ff.) in connection with his contention that the provenance of the passage is North Israelite, but Kimchi defined כַּרְמֶל as a place with fields, vineyards and fruit trees, and most modern commentators settle for 'fertile land' (Wellhausen, 28; Smith, 151; Weiser, 287; Robinson, 150; Rudolph, 127, 129; Wolff, 187; Hillers, 87). 'Dwelling solitary in the wild' has been interpreted by Kimchi as a reference to exile and he has associated life in the יַעַר with the enjoyment of an unusual security (cf. Rashi). Yahweh will bring Israel out of exile and will pasture them with a crook as a shepherd pastures his flock. Kimchi continues: 'He says that they will dwell in safety in the יַעַר which is a place of wild beasts (Wolff, 201) in which they will not be afraid.' They will enjoy the same sense of security as those who live in fertile country. They will graze Bashan and Gilead which are on the other side of the Jordan and are regions noted for fat cattle (cf. Rudolph, 134). Thus v. 14 is largely explained as Divine promise rather than as a prayer to Yahweh and יִרְעוּ is construed as 'they will graze' rather than 'let them graze'.

---

[2]Reading יבאו.
[3]Above, pp. 226f.

This trend can be detected in Sept. and Vulg. in which v. 14 is a mixture of prayer (v. 14a) and promise (v. 14b). ירעו is rendered by νεμήσονται/*pascentur*, 'They will graze Bashan and Gilead as in the days of old.' Pesh. may be taken as a prayer, since *nrʿwn* is an equivalent of MT ירעו which is almost certainly a jussive and this makes v. 14b part of a prayer (so Wellhausen, 28; Smith, 151; Weiser, 287; Robinson, 150; Rudolph, 127; Wolff, 187; Hillers, 87; KJV, RSV, NEB, REB). Targ.'s paraphrase is perhaps best read as a rambling prayer: 'Feed your people with your Memra, the rod of your inheritance for ever, who are about to be renewed. May they dwell in Carmel, may they be fed in the region of Bashan and Gilead.'

Verse 15, according to MT is not a continuation of the prayer in v. 14 but is an oracular utterance. Only Yahweh could have affirmed 'As in the days of your coming out of Egypt I shall show them miracles'. ארץ is not represented by Sept. which reads ὄψεσθε 'you will see' for MT אראנו 'I shall show him (them)'. The masculine singular suffix refers to עמך. Vulg. *Ostendam ei* reproduces MT and translates the suffix of אראנו as a singular. In rendering כימי צאתך as *ʾyk ywmʾ dnpkw bh* 'as on the day in which they came out' Pesh. deviates from MT. Targ. with כיום מפקכון represents 'as on the day (I) brought you out of Egypt'. אראנו (MT) is reproduced by Pesh. (*ḥwʾ ʾnwn*) and Targ. (אחזינון), the suffixes being shown as third plural. If the text of MT is retained at v. 15, so that there is a transition from prayer (v. 14) to oracle (the view of Kimchi, Ibn Ezra, KJV, RSV, Hillers, 87), there may be an advantage in making the transition from prayer to promise at v. 14b which is then also to be regarded as oracular (note the continuity suggested by the double occurrence of כימי (vv. 14b, 15).

The continuance of the prayer in v. 15 is saved by the emendation of אראנו 'I shall show them' to הראנו 'Show us' and this is the procedure adopted by most modern scholars (Wellhausen, 147; Smith, 152; Ehrlich, 291; Weiser, 287; Robinson, 150, הראה; Rudolph, 130; Wolff, 189; Hillers, 88; NEB, Brockington, 257; REB). The intention of Sept. ὄψεσθε (v. 15) after νεμήσονται (v. 14b) may be to discourage the conclusion that v. 15 is 'word of Yahweh' and to reduce it to the level of the promise in v. 14b.

Verse 16 can be taken as a prayer or a promise. 'Let the nations see and be so undone that all their strength ebbs away. Let them put their hands on their mouths and let their ears be stopped.' Or: 'The nations will see and be so undone that all their strength will ebb away. They will put their hands on their mouths and their ears will be stopped.' מן in מכל גבורתם is privative, literally, 'let the nations be so undone that they are deprived of all their strength'. Wolff (187) translates, 'Let the nations be put to shame in spite of their strength'. The prayer or the promise in v. 16b is that the גוים may be or will be reduced to speechlessness and that 'deafness' may or will overwhelm them—an inability to take in the scale of the experience which has overtaken them. Wolff (203) suggests that their 'deafness' is connected with the thunder which accompanies Yahweh's theophany (cf. Job 26.14).

According to the punctuation of MT (*athnach* at ממסגרתיהם) v. 17b. is to be translated, 'Let them come out of their strongholds shaking; to Yahweh, our God let them shudder and let them fear you.' Or, if it is a promise, 'They will come out of their strongholds shaking; to Yahweh, our God they will shudder and they will fear you.' This is difficult. 'To Yahweh, our God, let them shudder' (or 'they will shudder') makes poor sense and it is improbable that ממך is a reference to Israel, though Sept., Vulg. and Targ. suppose that it is. אל is rendered by Sept. as ἐπὶ, by Pesh. as *wmn* and by Targ. as ומן קדם. ממך is a minus in Pesh.: the Syriac translator may have balked at introducing a reference to Israel at the end of the verse. אל is a minus in Vulg. which renders 'They will fear the Lord, our God' (*Dominum deum nostrum formidabunt*). Ehrlich (291) proposes that אל be deleted and construes יהוה אלהינו as a vocative, 'Let them shudder, O Yahweh, our God, and let them fear because of you' or 'They will shudder, O Yahweh, our God, and they will fear because of you'—ממך refers to Yahweh. NEB, more or less follows Ehrlich, 'Let them come trembling and fearful from their strongholds, let them fear thee, O Lord, our God', though Brockington (257) does not record the deletion of אל. KJV ('They shall be afraid of the Lord, our God, and shall fear because of thee') and RSV ('They shall turn in dread to the Lord, our God, and shall fear because of thee' assume that ממך refers to Israel and, more recently, Hillers (87), with the *athnach* on אלהינו, has followed them: 'They will come quaking out of their dens to Yahweh, our God, they will be terrified and afraid of you.'

With the same punctuation as Hillers, Wellhausen (28) has avoided the reference to Israel by substituting ממנו 'from him' (Yahweh) for ממך 'from you'. He does not indicate this change of text (147). Rudolph

(128) also adopts this punctuation, but emends אל to אליך (haplogra-phy, the copyist's eye jumped from the *yodh* of אליך to the *yodh* of יהוה) and refers ממך to Yahweh: 'May they come out of their strongholds shaking, to you Yahweh, our God; may they tremble and fear you.' REB, with the *athnach* on אלהינו, follows Pesh. (minus ממך) and translates 'Let them come trembling from their strongholds to the Lord, our God; let them approach with awe and fear.'

These complications are avoided by retaining the punctuation of MT and deleting אל יהוה אלהינו as an ill-conceived secondary addition (Smith, 152; Weiser, 287; Robinson, 150; Wolff, 187, 189): 'Let them tremble and be afraid of you' (Yahweh) or 'They will tremble and be afraid of you'. Even in this simplified form of the text, 'They will tremble and be afraid of you' is no more compatible with an oracular utterance ('word of God') than is MT, and v. 17, with or without אל יהוה אלהינו, destroys the hypothesis that vv. 15–17 or vv. 14b–17 are oracular. Moreover ממך points to prayer rather than promise. It suggests that Yahweh is being addressed in petitions rather than that a promise is being made in v. 17. Hence vv. 14–17, with הראנו for אראנו at v. 15, should be interpreted as prayer (Smith, 151; Weiser, 287; Robinson, 150; Rudolph, 127f.; Wolff, 187) and vv. 14b–17 (Sept.) or vv. 14b, 16–17 (Vulg.) or vv. 16–17 (Wellhausen, 28; Hillers, 87; KJV, REB) are not promise. In Pesh., which renders אראנו (MT) at v. 15, v. 14, 16, 17 can be construed as prayer.

The shepherd/sheep metaphor is maintained to the end of v. 14 (Rudolph, 134) and so it is the sheep who graze (שכני) in the יער, in scrub which affords meagre pasture on which they eke out a bare subsistence. כרמל, in the context of the metaphor, is the rich pasture, where the sheep enjoy plenty, and Bashan and Gilead are areas in Trans-Jordan which provide ideal conditions for the rearing of sheep and cattle (Wolff, 201f.). The interpretation of the metaphor focuses on the period after 587 B.C. and into the post-exilic period (cf. Smith, 152) when the Judaeans were cabined, cribbed and confined in a strip of inferior land in and about Jerusalem (2 Kgs 25.12) and did not have access to the more fertile parts of the country which they had once possessed. Their prayer is that they may be given more room to live and they may prosper on better land.

The interpretation of vv. 16–17 (Weiser, 287; Robinson, 152; Rudolph, 134f.; Wolff, 203f.) has leaned too much towards the conversion of the גוים and the universalism of the prayer in vv. 16–17. This tendency is present in the exegesis of Rudolph and Wolff, but it is tempered by some of the details of their exegesis. Wolff comments on ירגזו ממסגרתיהם (v. 17) that what it describes is a capitulation rather than a setting free and that the expression 'licking the dust' (v. 17) is used of defeated enemies (Ps. 72.9; Isa. 49.23). Wolff's treatment of the verbs in v. 17 associates the first two with uncontrollable terror at the exhibition of Yahweh's power: the nations capitulate, shaking with terror (ירגזו) and shuddering with fear (יפחדו). They have to reverse their former opinion that Yahweh is innocuous (cf. Smith, 154), that he is an absent God (v. 10) and only ויראו ממך can be taken to mean 'fear of God', a reverence for him and a confession that Yahweh is God indeed. It is their defeat by Yahweh which is described in vv. 16–17 rather than their conversion (Smith, 154 'complete humiliation and demoralization'; Hillers, 91: 'reduced to creeping impotence').

Rudolph (135) acknowledges that there is an element of triumphalism in vv. 16–17, but not so much as to obliterate the universalist vision that the גוים will embrace Yahwism. The prayer, however, is not so much concerned with the conversion of the heathen as it is with the victory of Yahweh and Israel over them, with their discovery that the power in which they boasted is insignificant when matched against Yahweh's omnipotence, with the vengeance which is called down on Israel's enemies (Smith, 152).

14.   Pasture your people with your crook,
        the flock which belongs to you,
        which dwells[1] apart in the scrub,
        in the midst of fertile land.
        May they graze Bashan and Gilead as in the days of old.
15.   As in the days when you came out of Egypt,
        show us[2] miracles.
16.   Let the nations see and be so undone
        that all their strength drains away[3].
        Let them put their hands to their mouths,
        let their ears be stopped.
17.   Let them lick the dust like snakes,
        like reptiles which crawl on the ground.

[1]שכני, above, p. 229.
[2]Reading הראנו, above, p. 230.
[3]Above, p. 231.

Let them come out of their strongholds shuddering[4];
let them be in fear and terror because of you.

vv. 18–20 A HYMNIC AFFIRMATION OF YAHWEH'S FAITHFULNESS AND MERCY

At v. 18 the question מי אל כמוך is changed by Pesh. (*lyt 'lh' 'kwtk*, 'There is no God like you') and Targ. (לית בר מנך את הוא אלהא, 'There is no God apart from you') into an affirmation. In vv. 18–19 the incomparability of God is focused on his readiness to forgive sin and subdue it, to show mercy again to Israel and to cast the sins of his people into the depths of the sea (Rudolph, 135; Wolff, 204f.). Wolff (207) supposes that the final item is an allusion to the engulfing of Pharaoh's army and its chariots in the Red Sea at the exodus from Egypt (Exod.15.4).

נשא is rendered by Sept. (ἐξαίρων), Vulg. (*aufers*), Pesh. (*šbq*) and Targ. (שביק) as 'take away' and עון as 'sins' (ἀνομίας; *iniquitatem*; '*wl*'; לעויין). Thus the versions take the sense of עון as 'sins' or 'sin' and they are followed by KJV, RSV, Hillers, 87 ('iniquity'), Wolff, 187 (*Vergehen*). Other recent commentators (Wellhausen, 28; Weiser, 287; Robinson, 152; Rudolph, 128) and translators (NEB, REB) have translated עון as 'guilt', but עון 'sin' (so Wolff, 205) is a better match for פשע 'transgression' than is עון 'guilt' (Sept. ἀνομίας/ἀσεβείας; Vulg. *iniquitatem*/*peccatum*; Pesh. '*wl*'/*ḥṭy*'; Targ. חובין/עויין.

ועבר על (v. 18a) 'pass by' does not have the sense of turning a blind eye to transgression. 'Overlooking transgression' (Sept. ὑπερβαίνων) or passing it by (Vulg. *transis*; Pesh. *m 'br*; Targ. מעבר על) is not indicative of an attitude of indifference to sin but of the will to forgive it. לשארית נחלתו is deleted (Smith, 155; Weiser, 287) as a gloss whose intention is to limit Yahweh's forgiveness and long-suffering to the Israelites and to exclude the גוים from its operation.

Verse 18a is a direct address to Yahweh in the second person (כמוך), 'Who is a God like you, taking away sin and passing by transgression'. An additional consideration in assessing the status of לשארית נחלתו is that the continuation of direct address requires נחלתך for נחלתו which

[4]Deleting אל יהוה אלהינו, above, p. 232.

is represented by Vulg. (*haereditatis tuae*). Sept. Pesh. and Targ. follow MT. NEB, REB ('thy own people') makes the same adjustment as Vulg. without recording a change of text (Brockington, 257). The grammatical concord of v. 18a requires נחלתך and this is another reason for concluding that לשארית נחלתו is secondary. The matter, however, is complicated by the third person verbs in v. 18b (חפץ; יחזיק) and v. 19a (יכבש; ירחמנו; ישוב), since they cause a further incongruence with the emended v. 18a (מי ... פשע).

Smith (155) deals with these difficulties by deleting v. 18b and v. 19a and by resuming v. 18a (without לשארית נחלתו) with the second person verbs in v. 19b (ותשליך) and v. 20 (נשבעת; תתן). Another proposal tolerates the third person suffix in v. 18a and the third person verbs in v. 18b and 19a (Rudolph, 128; Wolff, 187; Hillers, 87). Robinson (152) tolerates נחלתו (v. 18a) and the third person verbs at v. 18b, but emends תכבש to יכבש and תרחם to ירחמנו, תשוב to ישוב at v. 19a. He retains MT ותשליך (v. 19b) as does Wolff (189) and Hillers (89). Weiser (287) deletes לשארית נחלתו at v. 18a and reads the third person verbs at v. 18b and 19a. ותשליך (v. 19b) is emended to והשליך by Ehrlich (291) and Rudolph (130). והשליך is assumed in the translations of Well-hausen (28) and Weiser (287). Sept.[A] represents the third person (ἀποῤῥίψει) as does Vulg. (*proiiciet*), Pesh. (*nšd'*) and Targ. (ירמי). MT ותשליך is followed by Robinson (152). Wolff (189), Hillers (89), KJV and RSV. The emendation of חטאותם (v. 19b) to חטאותנו, which is generally accepted (Wellhausen, 147; Weiser, 287; Robinson, 152; Rudolph, 130; Brockington, 257; Wolff, 189; Hillers, 89), is supported by Sept., Vulg., and Pesh. Targ. has כל חטאי ישראל 'all the sins of Israel'.

Some loose ends remain. ישוב (v. 19) has an auxiliary function in relation to ירחמנו with the adverbial sense 'again' or 'again and again': 'He will show us mercy again'. תתן (v. 20) is either 'You will give' or 'May you give' (Hillers, 87) and so the reference is not to the patriarchs Abraham and Jacob, but to future generations of Israelites (so Wolff, 207) who are 'sons of Jacob' (Gen. 35.22b–25) and 'the seed of Abra-ham' (Isa. 41.8) or 'sons of Abraham' (Mt. 3.9; Lk. 3.8). Rudolph's paraphrase (135) of v. 20b (which you swore to our fathers, Abraham and Jacob, in the days of old) makes no contribution to the elucidation of v. 20a. He comments, 'Abraham never stands for the Israelite people in the Old Testament and so he is here (v. 20a) the forefather as also is

Jacob'. But how can Abraham and Jacob in v. 20a be references to the historical patriarchs in assocation with תתן which has a future sense?

More important, and more complex, is the lexicography and philology of כבס/כבש (v. 19) in biblical Hebrew. Gordon (1978, 355), with reference to Akkadian *kabasa*, has proposed that יכבש has the sense 'forgive', but the main trend of its use in Akkadian is towards the meaning 'tread' (Von Soden, 415), agreeing with Aramaic כבש and Syriac *kbš*. In biblical Hebrew this is developed towards 'tread down', 'subdue', 'bring into bondage', 'force a woman' (*BDB*, 461), though the figure of sin being trampled on like a defeated enemy (Wolff, 207) does not occur elsewhere in biblical Hebrew (Smith, 155). It may, however, be that a different figure is employed, stamping out sin as one would stamp out a fire (Von Soden, 415). Arabic *kabasa* has the sense 'squeeze' or 'knead' and this may be connected with a further semantic development of *kbs/kbš*, namely, 'to wash by trampling on clothes with the feet' (Hebrew כובס; Ugaritic *kbs*, 'a fuller', one who treads on or beats cloth to cleanse it (Aistleitner, 1967, 145, no. 1281). The conclusion is that biblical Hebrew כבס/כבש is one and the same root and that its developed sense 'wash by treading on' has been assigned to כבס. Hence the proposal to emend יכבש to יכבס 'wash away' at v. 19 (Robinson, 152; Rudolph, 130; KB³, 438) should not be adopted. The versions attach a variety of meanings to יכבש and none of them points to יכבס as the original Hebrew text (Targ. יכבוש = MT; Sept. καταδύσει 'sink'; Vulg. *deponet* 'set aside'; Pesh. *niknwš* 'collect').

The translation technique of NEB and REB is to ignore the major inconcinnities of vv. 18–20 and to set out the passage in the second person as a direct address to Yahweh. Hillers, though his translation has a different pattern (87), holds that where the second person gives way to the third person an address to Yahweh is still 'implied' (89). His device is to display vv. 18b and 19a as a further elaboration of 'Who is a God like to you?' and to treat the third person verbs as a continuation of the participles (נשא; ועבר) in v. 18a. Thus, 'who will not hold on to his anger for ever, for he delights in clemency; who will have pity on us again and tread down our iniquities.' Rudolph (128) shows v. 18b in his translation as a continuation of the participles of v. 18a, 'who does not hold on to his anger for ever', and so as an elaboration of מי אל כמוך, but he renders v. 19 with future indicative verbs and he holds (135, n. 19) that the change from participles to finite verbs and from third person to second person does not constitute a grammatical problem. The appearance of the third person in v. 19a (he passes over its appearance in v. 18b) is connected by Wolff (206) with a transition from hymnic celebration to credal affirmation (first person plural suffixes) and he does not balk at another change of person in v. 19b (ותשליך), where he follows MT as does Hillers.

18. Who is a God like you,
    taking away iniquity and passing by transgression?[1]
    He will not hold on to his anger for ever,
    for he is a God who takes pleasure in kindness.
19. He will show us mercy again;[2]
    he will stamp out[3] our iniquities
    and cast[4] all our sins[5] into the depths of the sea.
20. You will show faithfulness to Jacob,[6]
    loving kindness to Abraham,[6]
    as you swore to our fathers in days gone by.

A POST-EXILIC LITURGY (7.8–20)

Rudolph (127) describes vv. 8–20 as a 'post-exilic liturgy' and, following Gunkel (1924, 145–178) he explains the order of the verses as corresponding to the movement of a liturgical performance. Verses 8–20 display an integrated liturgical structure and are a unity, with every part in its appropriate place ((131). Verses 14–17 come after the prophetic oracle (the divine voice, vv. 11–13), because the impressiveness of liturgical recitation is enhanced by recapitulation and reinforcement: the effectiveness of the movement of the liturgy requires that the same way should be travelled twice (134).

Gunkel (175) remarks that the variations produced by vv. 14–17 modify vv. 8–10 and expand the area which is involved. In vv. 8–10 Edom is the enemy which will be covered in shame, while in vv. 16–17 it is the גוים, the world outside Israel, which will be demoralized and scurry from its strongholds to surrender to Yahweh. In a similar way

---

[1]Delete לשארית נחלתו, above, pp. 234f.
[2]Above, p. 235.
[3]Above, p. 236.
[4]Reading והשליך, above, p. 235.
[5]Reading חסאותנו, above, p. 235.
[6]Above, pp. 235f.

Gunkel (175f.) explains the position of the oracle (vv. 11–13) in relation to the hymn (vv. 18–20). Not even the oracle, the note of divine authority, achieves the transition from hope to final assurance and so the divine voice does not preclude a further resort to petition (vv. 14–17). Only in the jubilant celebration of God's incomparability in the hymn is ultimate certainty of *Heil* reached and expressed.

Wolff (186) entitles vv. 8–20 'The Response of the Congregation' and, though he holds that it has a liturgical function, he does not regard it as a 'liturgy' in the same sense as Gunkel and Rudolph do. They suppose that it has the character of dialogue, that there is the response of the congregation (vv. 8–10; 14–17; 18–20) and the oracle delivered by a prophet (vv. 11–13). Hence Wolff's description of vv. 8–20 as 'The Response of the Congregation' has exegetical significance. Wolff holds (191) that vv. 11–13 are secondary: vv. 11–12 are a 'יום commentary' and v. 13 is triggered by it. This has the effect of removing the oracle from vv. 8–20 and, in Wolff's view, what is left is not an integrated liturgy but three independent psalms (vv. 8–10; 14–17; 18–20). He is unimpressed by the vigour and style of Gunkel's exposition and the order in which the verses appear inclines him to the view that vv. 8–10, 14–17 and 18–20 are separate psalms whose discontinuity cannot be overcome. He holds firmly to the opinion that, if vv. 11–13 are an oracle (as Gunkel and Rudolph suppose), they should come after and not precede vv. 14–17 and that vv. 8–10, a song of confidence, should come after, not precede vv. 11–13 (190).

Gunkel (171) classifies both vv. 8–10 and vv. 14–17 as 'Laments, a personified Zion being the speaker in vv. 8–10 and the Israelite community in vv. 14–17. Wolff's impression of the separateness of the pieces is emphasized by his categories: Song of Confidence (vv. 8–10), Petition (vv. 14– 17 and Hymn (vv. 18–20). Rudolph's description of the passages coincides with that of Wolff, but he has Oracle (vv. 11–13) in addition. Between a song of confidence, a petition and a hymn Wolff does not detect the complex movement of a liturgical recitation towards a climax for which Gunkel argues at length and with which Rudolph concurs.

Wolff accepts that the *Sitz im Leben* of vv. 8–20 is a public cultic event. The redaction of the book of Micah accommodated it for use in public laments when on certain days the fall of the city and the destruction of the temple were remembered by readings from the

prophetic books to which the congregation responded (xxxiv). Wolff
(xxxv) suggests that vv. 8–10 may have been the response to chapters
1–3 and that vv. 14–17 may have been similarly employed in relation
to chapters 4–5, but his final judgement is that the three psalms with
which the book concludes constitute a congregational response which
was made at the end of the reading of the whole book (xxxv). This is a
better account of the liturgical function of vv. 8–20 than that offered by
Gunkel and Rudolph.

Gunkel's exposition of vv. 8–20 betrays an interest in the passage
both as literature and as liturgical performance. He emphasises the
artistry and literary skills of the person who constructed the liturgy: he
was a *Künstler*. This appears so prominently (173, 175) that one is
tempted to conclude that Gunkel is presenting vv. 8–20 as a literary
imitation of a liturgy (a proposition which Rudolph, 136, rejects), as a
piece of writing which derives its inspiration from a liturgy recited in
the cult and which substitutes literary finesse for cultic impressiveness.
This, however, is not so and, according to Gunkel, vv. 8–20 were
written for public liturgical performance, for one of Jerusalem's
Trauertage (176) by a *frommen Künstler* (173). The writer has in mind a
special kind of recitation and performance and creates with con-
summate skill a work of art which will be liturgically effective and
impressive as an act of public worship. Gunkel's *Künstler* has first hand
experience of these cultic events as a member of the congregation. He is
fashioning a liturgy out of his experience of participating in them. He is
a 'pious artist' rather than a man who is appropriating liturgical forms
for literary ends.

INDEX OF AUTHORS

INDEX OF SUBJECTS